The Life & Letters of

Emma
Hamilton

The Life & Letters of

THE STORY OF ADMIRAL NELSON AND
THE MOST FAMOUS WOMAN OF THE GEORGIAN AGE

Hugh Tours

Frontline Books

THE LIFE AND LETTERS OF EMMA HAMILTON
The Story of Admiral Nelson and the Most Famous Woman of the Georgian Age

First published by Victor Gollancz, London, 1963.
This edition published in Great Britain in 2020 by Frontline Books,
an imprint of Pen & Sword Books Ltd, Yorkshire - Philadelphia

Copyright © Hugh Tours
ISBN: 978-1-52677-043-1

Typeset in 10.5/12.5 Palatino by Dave Cassan
Printed and bound by TJ International Ltd, Padstow, Cornwall

Pen & Sword Books Ltd incorporates the imprints of Pen & Sword Archaeology,
Air World Books, Atlas, Aviation, Battleground, Discovery, Family History,
History, Maritime, Military, Naval, Politics, Social History, Transport, True Crime,
Claymore Press, Frontline Books, Praetorian Press, Seaforth Publishing and
White Owl

For a complete list of Pen & Sword titles please contact:

PEN & SWORD BOOKS LTD
47 Church Street, Barnsley, South Yorkshire, S70 2AS, UK.
E-mail: enquiries@pen-and-sword.co.uk
Website: www.pen-and-sword.co.uk

Or

PEN AND SWORD BOOKS,
1950 Lawrence Roadd, Havertown, PA 19083, USA
E-mail: Uspen-and-sword@casematepublishers.com
Website: www.penandswordbooks.com

Contents

Foreword

By careful and, it is hoped, fair marshalling of the facts and by quoting as many as possible of Emma's letters in full, an attempt has been made to provide a true picture of the events in a life which has been sometimes over-glamourised, sometimes unnecessarily maligned.

Many books have been written about the mistress of one of the most famous characters in English history, but this phase of Emma's life represents only a period of some seven years. Among the comparatively few complete studies of her life, of which Walter Sichel's biography is certainly the most comprehensive, there is an undeniable lack of balance. By correlating the information to be gained from the many books and manuscripts, and by disregarding sources open to suspicion, I have done my best to present a more comprehensive and detailed account than has previously been available between the covers of one book. Where letters are not dated, the date in brackets is the estimated date given in the private edition, by Alfred Morrison, of the Hamilton-Nelson papers.

Hugh Tours

Acknowledgements

I am, in the first place, greatly indebted to Mrs Horatia Durant, Lord Nelson and Lord Warwick for their permission to use the letters of Emma Hamilton, the first Lord Nelson and the Hon. Charles Greville respectively.

I have received kindness and help at every stage of my researches. Mr J. Munday and Mr G.P.B. Naish of the National Maritime Museum, Greenwich, gave me encouragement from the very start and I am most grateful to them as I am to Mr A.C. Jones, Assistant Librarian of the Paddington Library, who so generously offered me the results of his investigations into the history of the Hon. Charles Greville's house in Paddington. I am also very indebted to Mr K.E. Kissack, Curator of the Monmouth Museum, for his assistance.

Many librarians gave me the benefit of their time and knowledge and I would like to thank Mr G.O. Randle of the Bank of England, Mr F.N. McDonald of Paddington, Miss E.M. Jowett of Merton and Morden, Miss A.A. Gough of the Home Office and Mr R.A. Riches of the Bar Library.

1 also appreciate very much the trouble taken on my behalf by Mr A.W. Brayley, Miss Antonia Bunch, Mr James Comyn, Q.C., Mr J.A. Comer, Miss S. Fisher, Mr J.T. Hayes (London Museum), Mr P. Hayes (County Records Office, Hawarden), the Rev. T. Hunter, Mr L.C. Johnson (British Transport Historical Records), Mr J.F. Kerslake (National Portrait Gallery), Mrs E. Foster Mann, Mr G.J. de C. Mead, Mr W.M. Schwab (Jewish Historical Society of England), Mr N.C. Selway, Mr A. Slinger, Mr and Mrs W. Tagg, Mrs P.D. Thomassin, Capt. and Mrs N. Garnons Williams, and Mrs G.L. Worlock.

Chapter 1

Childhood

THE STORY OF the child christened Emy Lyon, who was to become, in turn, Amy Lyon, Emly or Emily Hart, Emma Hart and finally Lady Hamilton, begins almost on the Sands o' Dee on the Wirral Peninsula near the villages of Ness and Denhall in the year 1765. She was born on 26th April and christened on the 12th of May at Neston parish church. Her father, Henry Lyon, was a blacksmith, referred to in two separate documents as "of Ness" and "of Denhall", who had married Mary Kidd in the same church on 11th June the previous year. Romance was all too soon marred by tragedy, for, less than two months after his daughter's birth, Henry Lyon died and his widow returned with Amy to her mother's cottage in Hawarden across the Dee. Many mothers might have given way to despair, for Mary Lyon's parents were extremely poor and the future must have seemed gloomy indeed. Old Mrs Kidd, however, was a thoroughly sensible, kind-hearted woman, generous, as will be seen later, to her last penny and a tower of strength in a crisis. The Kidd menfolk, mostly either labourers or sailors, seem by comparison a feckless lot. Amy's grandfather minded sheep on the Saltney Marshes, which does not suggest great enterprise, while his brother, William, who was the subject of a letter to Lady Hamilton in 1807, is reported to have expressed the opinion that he was not brought up to work and in the words of the writer, "the less pockit-money he has the better, for it wou'd onely be spent in the ale house, and then he gets abusive". The women were made of sterner stuff. Mrs Kidd had some sort of horse and cart with which she made a living by acting as carrier between Hawarden and Chester. Mary Lyon was able to cook and sew, and soon found employment locally. For some time, it appears, she went as sewing-woman to Stanstead Park, the home of Lord Halifax, who, as the story goes, made some contribution towards the early education of his employee's bright-looking child.

1

Amy's early years cannot have been unhappy. Her home, a white-washed and thatched "crock" cottage close to the "Fox and Grapes", was certainly a poor one, but it had an atmosphere of love and kindness created by her mother and her grandmother even if victuals and clothing were in short supply. Not far away were the walls and gates of Broad Lane Hall, now known as Hawarden Castle and owned by the Gladstone family, but then the house of Sir John Glynne. The coming and going of smart equipages were enough to fire the imagination, and open wide the eyes, of Mrs Lyon's little girl.

On the opposite side of the main road to Broad Lane Hall and quite near to the Kidds' cottage was the house of a notable local benefactor of both charity and skill, Dr Honoratus Leigh Thomas, who, according to the *Chester Courant*, made a speciality of inoculation for smallpox, with the help of a colleague named Sutton. The Thomas family was a very happy one, for the doctor's wife, Maria, whose brother was Alderman John Boydell, later to become Lord Mayor of London, was as kind-hearted as her husband. As Amy, or "Emly" as she was soon to call herself, reached her teens, the doctor and his wife were either asked or decided between themselves, to train the pretty, elfin-faced little girl as a nursemaid for their children. In a letter written in her early adult life, Emma refers to herself as "wild and thoughtless when a little girl" and Mrs Thomas must have had to use considerable tact and forbearance in teaching her small helper to make herself useful. That she did so is evident from the fact that throughout her life Emma was on the friendliest terms with her original employer. According to Sichel, one of the Thomas daughters, inheriting artistic enthusiasm, perhaps from her uncle, anticipated Romney, Reynolds, Gainsborough, Lawrence and many other less famous artists in making a sketch of the little nursemaid.

By the time that Emily, as it would now seem reasonable to call her, was fourteen, her mother obtained a situation in London. It is not clear, neither is it very important, whether she travelled to the capital and then sent for her daughter or whether she and Emily set off together, but towards the end of 1779 mother and daughter were in Town. The nature of Mrs Lyon's occupation remains a mystery, but it seems that, at this juncture, she started to call herself "Mrs Cadogan". It is possible that she married a Mr Doggin, for in a will which Emma made in 1808 she refers to "my dear mother, Mary Doggin or Cadogan". The attachment, if there was one, was short-lived as there are no further references to Doggin – either Mr or Mrs. There is no question that "Cadogan" is a social-sounding improvement on "Doggin" and its selection may have been due to Mary Lyon's invention with the idea of improving her status (she had learned to write since signing her original marriage certificate by mark), or she may have adopted the surname on being addressed by someone who had misheard her correct name. There would appear to have been some collusion between mother and daughter in the matter of names at this stage because, for an equally unexplained reason, Emily commenced to call herself Emily "Hart".

Emily's first employment in London was with Dr Budd, a surgeon of some standing, who lived in Chatham Place, Blackfriars, where she had the position of under-nursemaid. It was here that she struck up an acquaintance with another member of the household staff, Jane, who was destined to play leading roles on the Drury Lane stage after she had married the actor, William Powell the Younger, and whom Emily was to meet again when she had become Lady Hamilton.

For the next eighteen months or so Emily's movements become lost in a haze of romantic invention, scandal-mongering and malicious gossip. Many years later, the Prince Regent is reputed to have said that he remembered seeing her selling fruit and wearing pattens on her feet, but little credence can be given to such a man who deceived himself into believing that he was at the battle of Waterloo and even appealed to Wellington to confirm the fact – a request to which the Duke replied drily, "I have heard your Majesty say so before." It seems likely that Emily spent a short time as lady's maid to Mrs Kelly, a demi-mondaine known to her acquaintances as "The Abbess of Arlington Street". There is a strong suggestion that she was in the service of the family of Thomas Linley the Elder, manager of Drury Lane Theatre and father-in-law of Sheridan. The story goes that she nursed his young son who was a lieutenant in the Navy and on his death was so overcome with grief that she left the Linleys.

There is a clue in a letter she wrote to Romney after her marriage to Sir William Hamilton that suggests she had met the painter during this "lost" period of her life in London. "You have seen and discoursed with me in my poorer days," she wrote, "you have known me in my poverty and prosperity, and I had no occasion to have lived *for years* in poverty and distress if I had not felt something of virtue in my mind. Oh, my dear friend, for a time I own through distress my virtue was vanquished, but my sense of virtue was not overcome."

Tradition, more than evidence, points to Captain "Jack" Willet-Payne, who subsequently became a Rear-Admiral and an equerry to the Prince Regent, as being the first "vanquisher of her virtue". Romance has woven a tale that she exchanged her honour for the release of a cousin from the hands of the Press Gang. Whether this is true or not, two things are certain; firstly that, throughout her life, Emma's character was such that she would always have been ready to sacrifice herself for her friends or relatives, and secondly that even if it was not Captain Willet-Payne, it is extremely doubtful that she kept her virtue.

No information is forthcoming as to what Mrs Cadogan was doing during this period when her Emily's fortunes were at their lowest ebb. She could not help knowing that her teenage daughter was doing little more than roaming the town, but Emily's morals never seem to have weighed very heavily on her conscience. A few years later she was contentedly acting as housekeeper for the man who was living with her daughter. She may have tried to remonstrate and found her efforts to be useless, but it would not seem that she lost touch completely. When, a year or two later, Emily was about to have her first illegitimate child, she knew very well where her mother was, as her PS. in her letter to Greville "Dont tell my mother what distress I am in" shows quite clearly. It also suggests that she credited her mother with a softer heart than she, perhaps, had.

Chapter 2

The Temple of Health

N 1780 there was much talk among those seeking amusement in London
about the "Temple of Aesculapius", or, if one preferred a simpler name,
the "Temple of Health". This establishment was to be found in Royal
Terrace, Adelphi, facing the river, and had been opened by a certain Dr
James Graham. The price of admittance was five shillings, a sum which
in those days would have excluded all but the most inquisitive of the
general riff-raff who loitered around the entrance to gaze at the visitors
alighting from their carriages. Persons of the highest rank were seen to
enter the portals which were guarded by two gigantic footmen dressed
in splendid liveries, wearing gold-laced cocked hats and holding long
silver-mounted staffs. Ladies accompanying their menfolk took the
precaution of being veiled.

   The so-called doctor, whose father according to various authorities
was either a sadler or a soldier, had been born in Edinburgh and had
studied medicine at the University there although it is doubtful if he
qualified. He had been to America and to France and had made a study
of the discoveries of Benjamin Franklin. James Graham was a quack,
possibly even a madman, but among the confusion of his weird ideas
there was a trace of sense, and his theories of electrical treatment were
not altogether unsound. He carried his enthusiasm for mud baths to the
point of eccentricity by being on occasion buried in the nude up to the
neck. To add to the advertising value of this stunt, he was accompanied
by a young lady who permitted herself to be similarly planted in the soil,
the two of them with their heads beautifully coiffured looking, as a
spectator was heard to say, like two fine cabbages. Crazy as he may have
been in some directions, there was something to be said for his ideas of
open windows and fresh air as there also was for his opinion, hardly
universal at the time, that "a bath, a bason or rather a bideau are certainly
the most useful, the most healthful conveniences in any house".

Dr Graham was nothing if not a showman. He is said to have spent at least £10,000 on the house, the fittings and the decorations. The entrance hall was festooned with crutches no longer required by their owners and in the upper rooms were to be seen electrical machines and strange chemical apparatus. Music, statuary, paintings, stained-glass windows and even perfumes added to the attractions. In the "great Apollo apartment" he gave lectures on such subjects as:

The Causes, Nature and Effects of Love and Beauty at the different Periods of Human Life in Persons and Personages, Male, Female and Demi-Charactère… .

or

The Generation, Increase and Improvement of the Human Species interspersed with Precepts for the Preservation and Exaltation of Personal Beauty and Loveliness.

or

For prolonging Human Life, Healthily and Happily to the very longest possible Period of Human Existence.

In order to hold the attention of his audiences during these long, verbose and repetitive orations, the doctor arranged for tableaux to be staged, showing lightly draped young ladies posing as goddesses of Health, Beauty, Wisdom, etc., accompanied by their attendants. The sensual innuendoes which liberally bespattered the lectures were as thinly veiled as the young goddesses themselves.

Horace Walpole, who visited the "Temple" was of the opinion that Graham's was "the most impudent puppet-show of imposition I ever saw, and the mountebank himself the dullest of his profession, except that he makes the spectators pay a crown apiece".

In 1779 he had been, for a time, in Aix-la-Chapelle and had received testimonials regarding his treatments from many of the aristocracy, including Georgiana, Duchess of Devonshire – facts which his listeners were not allowed to forget. *The pièce de résistance* of his show was what he called the "Celestial Bed". This weird and over-ornate contraption was mounted on insulating glass pillars. His ludicrous description of the affair runs to great length and includes such compounds of technicality and suggestiveness, as the following example.

6

"About fifteen hundred pounds weight of artificial and compound magnets are so disposed and arranged as to be continually pouring forth in an ever-flowing circle, inconceivable and irresistably powerful tides of the magnetic effluvium, which every philosophical gentleman knows, has a very strong affinity with the electrical fire. These magnets, too, being pressed give that charming springiness – that sweet undulating, tittulating, vibratory, soul-dissolving, marrow-melting motion, which on certain critical and important occasions, is at once so necessary and so pleasing: and the bed is constructed with a double frame; so that the inner frame, which moves on an axis, pivot or center, can be so raised at the bottom of the bed, as in a moment, to be converted by the gentlemen into such an inclined plane, as that he can follow his lady down-hill, as it is called, which is certainly the most favourable posture for the great business of conception, or propagation, in difficult cases of corpulency, or where the want of retentive firmness is the principal cause of the barrenness."

The bed was guaranteed to cure sterility and such was Dr Graham's power of salesmanship that a duke was reputed to have paid 500 guineas for the privilege of using it. After a time, the normal charge seems to have settled down to a mere £50 a night.

Such, then, were the "doctor" and the "Temple" when Emily Hart encountered them at the end of 1780. How the meeting was brought about is uncertain, though it is reasonable to suppose that a showman such as Graham would have employed the eighteenth-century equivalent of "talent-scouts" to hang around the alehouses in search of possible "goddesses".

It is generally accredited that Emily did, for a short time, pose in the tableaux at the Temple of Health. Hilda Gamlin, writing at the end of the nineteenth century, tries to disassociate Emily from such shameful behaviour, although, strangely enough, she still gives a description of Dr Graham and his Temple. Pettigrew, however, who wrote a life of Nelson, and who knew several of Emma's early contemporaries, is quite definitely of the opinion that she did, in fact, perform in some way. What, on the other hand, is frequently, incorrectly and, more often than not, maliciously asserted is that Miss Hart posed in the nude. While the Temple of Health was at the house in the Adelphi, the entertainment was on a comparatively high moral level, innuendo and suggestion apart, as Graham was out to attract fashionable society. His goddesses wore draperies and some form of diaphanous decorum was maintained. When, in the following spring, after Emily had left, he was obliged to cut down expenses and moved to Schomberg House, in Pall Mall, the whole establishment was rearranged on a cheaper basis;

cheaper, that is to say, and nastier. The Temple was now the "Temple of Hymen" and one of the features there was a "Hebe Vestina" or "High Priestess" who appears to have assisted by reading, or reciting, some of the lectures, assisted by "the rosy, athletic and truly gigantic goddess of Health and Hymen, on the celestial throne". As there is no suggestion in any of the many portraits of Emma which are in existence, that she ever sat for any painter in any form of undress and as there is no evidence at any stage of her life that she was ever wanton in the manner of her dress, it is extremely unlikely that she would have acted out of character during her short appearance at the Temple of Health. What is more likely is that she sang (most willingly) and that she was fascinated by the idea of posing before an audience. In fact, it can hardly be going too far to suggest that her famous "Attitudes" had their beginnings in that strange house in the Adelphi.

Graham would have been quick to realise that this new Miss Hart, although she was not quite sixteen, had a well-developed figure and features which were classically perfect by any standards. She must therefore be shown off to advantage, and it was here, on the stage or dais of the "great Apollo apartment", more likely than anywhere else in London, that she was seen by the wealthy, dashing Sir Harry Featherstonhaugh.

Chapter 3

Up Park

SIR HARRY FETHERSTONHAUGH was about twenty-six when he met Emily Hart in London, more than probably, as has been said, at the Temple of Aesculapius. He had come into the family estates on the death of his father, Sir Matthew, in 1774, and was the owner of that magnificently situated residence looking across the South Downs towards Portsmouth, Up Park. As a boy, to judge from early portraits, he was extremely fond of animals, and this enthusiasm had led, quite naturally, to a penchant for horses and horse racing. With rather a thin face and sandy hair, he was no Adonis, but he was wealthy, alive, full of youthful enthusiasms and, as such, attractive to Emily whose present lack of almost any sort of education made her far more appreciative of livelinesss, dash and daring in a man than any pretentions to knowledge and wit. Sir Harry, to use a modern expression, was obviously "great fun" and Emily had no hesitation in leaving London and going to Up Park with him as his mistress. It seems likely that Mrs Cadogan knew of this new turn in her daughter's fortunes, and as she could have had no great aspirations for Emily's future, thought, in her complacent way, that things could have turned out a lot worse.

The drive down from London to Up Park in a private carriage, with stops for refreshments supplied by attentive innkeepers, was a form of luxury new to Emily, and Sir Harry would hardly have considered her travelling without a new and suitable outfit of clothes. To any young girl in her position, it must have seemed that life could hardly offer more. Passing through the village of South Harting, where Sir Harry's uncle, the Rev. Ulrick Fetherstonhaugh, was rector, and toiling up the steep incline leading to the lodge gates of the big house, the carriage deposited its light-hearted occupants on the gravel drive on the east side of the house where the main entrance then was. The building had been designed by William Talman and had been erected in the reign of

9

William and Mary. Celia Fiennes, who saw it in 1694, described it as "new built, square, 9 windows in the front and seven in the sides, brickwork with free stone coynes and windows, itts in the midst of fine gardens, gravell and grass walks and bowling green, with breast walks divideing each from other and so discovers the whole to view; att the entrance a large Court with iron gates open, which leads to a less, ascending some stepps free stone in a round, thence up more stepps to a terrass, so to the house; it looks very neate and all orchards and yards convenient". By the time Emily saw it, new stables and kitchens, each connected to the house by underground passages, had been built, but the house itself was outwardly the same.

The present approach to the house and the Doric colonnade, designed by Repton, on the north side did not come into existence until after 1810. Except for this colonnade and the arcaded corridor joining it to the main body of the house, visitors to this delightful piece of National Trust property may see for themselves almost exactly what met the delighted gaze of Emily Hart on that day in 1781. This unusual state of affairs is due in part to the fact that Sir Harry, at the age of seventy, married Mary Ann Bullock, his head dairymaid, a young thing in her twenties, whom he had groomed and trained to her new duties. On his death, at the age of ninety-two, in 1846, Mary Ann continued to live in the house with her sister Frances, keeping everything just as it was, during a period when many great houses were going through the ravages of "improvement and redecoration" which robbed them of their original character. When Mary Ann died, in 1875, her sister maintained the house in the same order until 1895. The second reason for this fortunate state of preservation is the tireless and painstaking skill which has been employed by Sir Herbert and Lady Meade-Fetherstonhaugh in their stupendous task of restoring and repairing so much of the original fabrics and furnishings.

Looking back on the time that Emily spent at Up Park, it seems likely that had the company been of a less boisterous and sporting nature, she might have been very content to indulge herself in the more innocuous delights of acting, posing and singing before an admiring audience. However, being young and adaptable, she was only too willing to give herself up to the outdoor sport of horse riding and to the indoor one of horseplay. The fearlessness in her character enabled her quickly to cut a dash on horseback, greatly to Sir Harry's approval, and her high spirits doubtless recommended her greatly to the houseparty in general. Guests came and went and there were impromptu race meetings on the Downs and organised shooting parties. One of those invited for the shooting was the second son of the Earl of Warwick, the Hon. Charles

Francis Greville. Cast in a different mould from that of most of Sir Harry's friends, who were hare-brained and hard-riding, Charles Greville's interests lay more in the world of fashion and the Arts. He was a good-looking young man of thirty-two when Emily first saw him, considerate and intelligent, though inclined to be quiet and also rather careful when it came to the point of spending money. It would not be correct to say that he was mean, but rather that he was anxious to go as far in good society as his moderate means would allow. Emily was much attracted and Greville, for his part, was very conscious of the attractions so evident in Emily. They had serious conversations during which Greville warned her against the snares and dangers of her present "mad-cap", as she expressed it, existence.

If the traditional story that she had danced naked, on the table in the dining-room, has any truth in it (and it is not confirmed that she ever carried her own words, "I like to surprise people", to quite such lengths) then that would have made a deliciously intimate subject for discussion and admonition. As well as the good advice that Emily was given by her new friend, she was also supplied with a few franked envelopes with which to correspond with him if she should get into difficulties, and these were later to prove invaluable.

Walter Sichel, in a footnote to his biography, *Emma, Lady Hamilton*, quotes a coincidence mentioned to him by the Rev. A.J. Roberts, a former vicar of Harting. "In the registers", reads the note, "there occurs this entry for April 7th, 1781: 'Buried Francis Lyon'. The name Lyon is the only one in the registers and the 'Francis' tallies with Greville's second name." The implication that Emily had a child by Greville while she was at Up Park is hardly worth consideration as, apart from other objections, Sir Harry would hardly have consented to such an interment at a church where his uncle was rector. The present vicar, the Rev. T. Hunter, has made a more thorough search in the registers and has revealed that on 12th July 1779 the burial of Sarah Lyon took place, proving conclusively that a family by the name of Lyon must have lived in the neighbourhood. Emily is therefore exonerated. This is not to say, however, that she did not have an intrigue with Greville while she was under Sir Harry's roof. She unquestionably did, and it seems more than likely that, at some time, she took the mail coach up to London to visit him, and also called on him when she was in Town on legitimate business. Support for this supposition is to be found in the letter that Greville wrote to her after she had been finally dismissed from Up Park, and in which he says, "It gave me great concern to see you imprudent the first time you came to G from the country, and as the same conduct was repeated when you was last in town, I began to despair of your happiness, to prove to you that I do not accuse you falsely I only mention 5 guineas and half a guinea for coach ..." Fares in those days were a shilling a mile, excluding food on the journey and tips for the coachmen. The distance from Harting to London and back, plus the expenses en route, would account quite reasonably for the five guineas, and the half guinea could as easily have been spent on private hire when Emily happened to be in Town.

A question might be raised as to how it was that she was able to slip up to London without Sir Harry's knowledge. It is said that Emily stayed, for a time, at Rosemary Cottage in South Harting. As, when she was sent packing by her protector, she was given, as Greville quotes her, "barely money to get to your friends", it would not have been then. It seems much more likely that, during her year at Up Park, when, by reason of a visit from his mother or from the necessity of entertaining important friends and relations, Emily's presence would have been an embarrassment to Sir Harry, she was sent down to the village to be out of the way. On such occasions she could easily, though at some risk, have caught the London coach.

At the end of November, before she had been at Up Park for quite twelve months, Emily's gay life came to an abrupt end. She was six months pregnant and she was told to leave. It is impossible to say who was to blame for her condition. The suddenness of her dismissal and the fact that she was given no more than her fare back to Hawarden make it seem that Sir Harry considered it none of his doing. Alternatively, he could have lost control of himself during an unpleasant scene of name-calling in which Emily's quick temper, assisted by her command of the language of the fishwives and barrow-women, would have done nothing to calm him. Greville does not seem to suspect Sir Harry, for he wrote to her a little later, "Sir H. may be informed of circumstances which may reasonably make him doubt, & it is not worth while to make it a subject for altercation", which makes it look as though he knew more than he chose to commit to paper. Was Greville himself the father-to-be? Here again there is no positive proof, but two circumstances make it seem unlikely. He was certainly most generous in paying for the child's upkeep, but when his uncle married Emma, the expenses were at once transferred to Sir William, who made not the slightest demur. Furthermore, at a later date still, when the question arose of finding a situation for the "little protégée", as Greville called her, there is nothing in the wording of his letters on the subject that could possibly suggest that he felt in any way responsible.

Whoever was the cause of her distress, Emily disconsolately travelled back to her grandmother's cottage in Hawarden. It seems strange that, as her journey took her to London to catch the Chester coach, she did not call upon Greville and implore his assistance. Without half-guineas to spare for coach fares, she may have felt incapable of finding her way about the maze of confusing streets. Again, she was naturally compelled to take the very first coach available in order not to have to spend more than necessary on food and lodging.

Chapter 4

Paddington

THE HON. CHARLES GREVILLE, in January 1782, was living in Portman Square when he received Emily's *cri de coeur* in the form of an ill-spelt and pathetic letter. Sometime during 1778 he had moved from his father's house in St. James's Square and had taken the lease of a large residence in Portman Square which was then almost the most northerly piece of development in London at that point. At the time in question the square was still not completed.

He was living on an income of some £600 a year, a reasonable enough figure for a man-about-town if he was not too ambitious, but Greville was trying to cut a dash. He felt that it was time he got married and was thinking in terms of a well-endowed wife. He has already been referred to as being cautious by nature but, at this moment in his life, he was taking a gamble, in the form of a pretentious house, to improve his chances in the marriage market. As so often happens to those who are not inveterate gamblers, the attempt was proving a failure and, as a result, the house in Portman Square was becoming an embarrassment.

He exchanged long letters with his uncle, Sir William Hamilton, in Naples in which they discussed everything from politics to purchases of *objets d'art* and current scandal. In December 1774 Sir William had written: "I wish you was here, there is a fine girl, Miss St. George. Her father died yesterday, & left her clear £6000 per annum. She dances admirably, & is accomplished, le nez un peu retroussé; but I wish you was here to at her." Four years later (5th May 1778) Greville concluded a letter to his uncle with a description of his position and his feelings with regard to marriage which makes it clear that he was neither a cold-blooded heiress-hunter nor a dashing Casanova. He was, in fact, a most reasonable young man.

"Now for myself", he writes, "I told you that of all the Châteaus [*sic*] I ever build none ever lasted so long as that of my wish to settle. I have known how much happiness is to be valued & I never shall loose sight of it by matching myself with mere money; but I have now the misfortune of seeing the pleasing prospect without the hopes off attaining it, & what is worse, I begin to be miserable, & then one's chances fall cent per cent. I perhaps am talking enigmatically, as I did some time ago to Louisa, but in short I am so well with Granby Ly., the Duchess, & Ly B.C.[1] that I think they have a real friendship for me, & I am afraid of becoming serious, least I should have a short No; & to be sure the field of Titles & Fortunes are so ample that I must be very impudent to flatter myself. God knows what will become of it; but, if I should long for the £20,000 prize in the lottery, it is a possibility which my ticket entitles me to wish for untill it is drawn, & I certainly shall not despond untill she is married; because I am so much bit that I cannot find the smallest grounds to alter my wishes, for it is one thing to be amiable & to suit exactly; & unless the coincidence is complete, misery must ensue, but I think I could make her happy. I talk nonsense to you because I dare not hint it to any one; I am my own confidant, therefore wish more for you to be near me; but it is so modest a request to say – take me for mes beaux yeux without anything, in preference of all the world, that it must be such an impudent fellow as you to assist me & (as) I cannot get you I must beat & beat about, &, if I can find the opportunity of asking without risk, you shall hear of my proceedings; but I shall be a Fabius, slow & sure; there is, however, so much more chance from dashing that if I did not like her I should have a better chance."

Not long before Greville met Emily at Up Park, his uncle had said: "I find, likewise, as I imagined & foretold to yourself, that a younger brother's pretending to keep house in London is certain destruction. I know what it is for an honest man to be distressed in his circumstances, tho' your macaronis make themselves perfectly easy upon that subject, & care not who suffers by them provided they pass the day in fashionable extravagance. If you find that your house is too expensive, get rid of it as soon as you can."

Luckily for Greville, a position in the Board of Admiralty, carrying with it free accommodation in the King's Mews, came his way almost in the nick of time. Writing from Caserta on 31st October 1780, Sir William sighed with relief. "I am quite pleased," he said, "at your appointment to the Board of Admiralty particularly as it will give you a good opportunity of slipping out of your expensive house into one rent free, just as I did upon the late King's death, when I left Charles Street & went into the Mews, being circumstanced much as you are at present."

Situated as he was, Charles Greville was most certainly not on the look-out for a mistress. His finances and his social aspirations were both against such a step, but he had become fond of Emily Hart and wanted to help her as far as he could. How he heard of her plight can only be a matter of conjecture. His first letter to her is lost, but as in her reply she only thanks him for "your kind letter" it seems further proof that she had not seen him on her way through London, for then she would assuredly have had to add thanks for assistance and some slight addition to her perilously empty purse. It seems most likely that she either sent him a note by messenger while in Town or used one of the franked envelopes he had given her at Up Park. It is just possible, of course, that he could have heard from Mrs Cadogan. That the idea of keeping her was in his mind when he wrote to her is shown by the fact that he asked, with characteristic caution, for some proof of her age, receiving as a result a copy of her baptismal certificate.

Her letter to him, although it has been frequently quoted in many other biographies, is so innocent, ill-spelt and pathetic that it will stand repetition here in full:

January 1782.

My dear Grevell,

Yesterday did I receve your kind let^r. It put me in some spirits for believe me I am allmost distracktid, I have never hard from Sir H. and he is not at Lechster now I am sure, what shall I dow, good God what shall I dow, I have wrote 7 letters and no anser, I cant come to town for want of mony, I have not a farthing to bless myself with and I think my frends looks cooly on me, I think so. O G what shall I dow, what shall I dow. O how your letter affected me wen you wished me happiness. O G that I was in your posesion as I was in Sir H. What a happy girl would I have been, girl indead, or what else am I but a girl in distress, in reall distress, for Gods sake G. write the minet you get this and only tell me what I ham to dow, derect some whay. I am allmos mad. O for Gods sake tell me what is to become on me. O dear Grevell write to me. Write to me G. Adue and believe yours for ever

Emily Hart.

Dont tell my mother what distress I am in and dow aford me some comfort.

My age was got out of the Reggister and I have sent it to My Dear Charles. Once more Adue, once more adue. O you dear friend.

The enclosure reads:

"Amy(ly) Daughter of Henry Lyon of Nesse by Mary his wife, bap: the 12th of May 1765.
"The above is truly copied from the G. Neston Register by"R. Carter. Curate.

"Neston Dec. 19th 1781."

Greville's detractors, of whom he has had many, take delight in suggesting that he saw in Emily's appeal the chance of obtaining an extraordinarly attractive mistress, so to speak, on the cheap. His reply, a lengthy one and rarely given in full, is referred to as niggardly, cheese-paring and having a wily caution about it. This is grossly unfair. With an expensive establishment still on his hands and his position at the Admiralty still to be consolidated, he was in no position to take on a young mistress whom he already knew from experience to be quite wild and extravagant. He was fond enough to feel that he would like to have her with him and to help her to form a more sensible way of life, but he realised, at the same time, that he must make it clear from the start that she would not be permitted to repeat her Up Park antics. He therefore wrote the following firm and sensible letter:

Jan. 10th 1782.

My dear Emily,
I do not make apologies for Sir H's behaviour to you & altho I advised you to deserve his esteem by your good conduct, I own I never expected better from him, it was your duty to deserve good treatment, & it gave me great concern to see you imprudent the first time you came to G: from the country, & as the same conduct was repeated when you was last in town, I began to despair of your happiness, to prove to you that I do not accuse you falsly I only mention 5 guineas, & half a guinea for coach, but my Emily, as you seem quite miserable now, I do not mean to give you uneasiness, but comfort, & tell you that I will forget your faults & bad conduct to Sir H. & to myself & will not repent my good humor, if I shall find that you have learnt by experience to value yourself & endeavor to preserve your Friend? by good conduct & affection.
I will now answer your last letter. You tell me you think your Friends look cooly on you, it is therefore time to leave them, but it is necessary for you to decide some points *before* you come to Town.
You are sensible that for the three next months your situation will not admit of a giddy life if you had wished it, & would therefore be

imprudent to come & hunt after new connexion, or try to regain the one you gave up as lost, after you have told me that Sir H. gave you barely money to get to your friends, & has never answer'd one letter since, & neither provides for you, nor takes any notice of you; it might appear laughing at you, to advise you to make Sir H. more kind & attentive. I do not think a great deal of time should be lost, as I have never seen a woman clever enough to keep a man who was tired of her, but it is a great deal more for me to *advise you* never to see him again, & to write only to inform him of your determination. You must, however, do the one or the other.

You may easily see my Dearest Emily, why it is absolutely necessary for this point to be completely settled *before* I can move one step. If you love Sir H. you should not give him up & if you continue with him, it would be ridiculous in me to take care of his girl, who is better able to maintain her, but besides this my Emily, I would not be troubled with your connexions (excepting your mother) & with Sir H. friends for the universe.

My advice then is to take a steady resolution, try whatever you please & if Sir H. will continue your friend, or if you prefer any other friend, do not be your own enymy, & at last if everything fails, if you mean to have my protection I must *first* know from you that *you are clear of every connexion, & that you will never take them again without my consent.* I shall then be free to dry up the tears of my lovely Emily & to give her comfort, if you do not forfeit my esteem perhaps my Emily may be happy. You know I have been so, by avoiding the vexation which so frequently arises from ingratitude & caprices, nothing but your letter & your distress could incline me to alter my system, but remember I never will give up my peace, nor continue my connexion one moment after my confidence is again betray'd.

If you should come to town free from all engagements & take my advice, you will live very retired, *till* you are brought to bed. You should part with your maid, & take another *name*, by degrees I would get you a new set of acquaintance, & by keeping your own secret, & nobody about you having it in their power to betray you, I may expect to see you respected & admired. Thus far relates to yourself, as to the child, Sir H. may be informed of circumstances which may reasonably make him doubt & it is not worth while to make it a subject of altercation, its mother shall obtain it kindness from me & it shall never want.

I inclose you some money, do not throw it away, you may send some presents when you arrive in Town, but do not be on the road without some money to *spare*, in case you should be fatigued & wish to take your time: I will send Sophy anything she wishes for, give her a good many kisses & a thousand to my dearest Emily. God bless you my dearest lovely girl, take your determination soon & let me hear from you. Once more Adieu my D. Emily.

With the spring, Emily Hart came to Paddington Green. Greville had found a suitable house, pleasantly situated in the open country which was then to be found to the west of the Edgware Road. This road itself was very rough by modern standards and ran in a north-westerly direction from the turnpike at Tyburn where there still stood three wooden grandstands or "galleries" for those who wanted a good view of the execution of criminals. The first stretch of the road was then known as "Edgware Row" and was built up on the east side. It passed another turnpike after which the way to Edgware ran towards open country and there was a branch road to Harrow. In the "V" formed by these roads lay Paddington Green with its little church, its inn, its ponds and a few houses. The church was a simple country one in a very poor state of repair and buttressed on one side. A farm building stood near the porch and outside the gate of the walled churchyard were the stocks. Only a few years later the church was demolished and the present one erected a little to the south of the former site.

Greville was either fortunate or clever in finding a retreat so conveniently accessible from London and his official residence in King's Mews, which incidentally occupied a site now covered by Trafalgar Square, for Paddington Green was sufficiently off the map to guarantee the seclusion required for his purpose. There seems to be no means of deciding the position of the house in which Emily was to live from 1782 until 1786 as there are no rate books or other similar evidence which cover that particular period. It seems almost certain that sometime in 1790 Greville moved to another house on Paddington Green. His own words to his uncle, and a written remark of Sir Joseph Banks, both confirm this point. Leases of property to be seen at the London County Record Office and a map made in 1790 make quite clear the site of the house in which he lived until 1806, when he built himself a new house on the same piece of land. Its position was almost exactly that of the present house that stands on the corner of Church Street and St Philip's Place. The grounds belonging to his house were originally more extensive than can be easily visualised today as in about the year 1808 the Green was extended northward in order to improve its proportions, the residents in the neighbourhood, including Greville, contributing towards the cost. It appears probable that the house in which Emily lived was rented and that, finding Paddington Green to his liking, Greville, in later years, took the opportunity of buying a property there when a suitable one came upon the market.

In searching for evidence concerning the original house, the fact that Emily headed her letters "Edgware Road", and for that matter that Sir William refers to "Edgware Row", has no real significance since, from the point of view of postal address, any house on the open land to the west of such a definite thoroughfare could be, and in fact would be, referred to in that manner. Had Emily really been housed in one of the row of small villas built along the east side of Edgware Row, disadvantageous as it would have been from Greville's point of view, she would certainly have added the number of the house (for there is evidence that they were numbered) when she headed her letters.

The present "Greville House" which stands facing Paddington Green has no connection with either Greville or Emily, as it was not built until 1849.

Mrs Cadogan, at Greville's request, took up residence in the newly acquired establishment, happy to be with her daughter again and willing to assume the delicate role of retiring chaperon and unpaid housekeeper. It was at this stage in her life that Emily became "Emma Hart", the new Christian name having a more fashionable and a more dignified ring to it.

The menage was a success. Emma realised her good fortune and was more than ready to comply with the merest whim of her quiet and aristocratic protector whom she adored. Ready, that is to say, except for occasional outbursts of quick temper or high spirits which Greville did his best to curb and for which she became contrite almost at once. She was conscious that there was much for her to learn and she did her utmost to follow her "dear Greville's" tuition, for, as she said to him herself, "I will give myself a fair trial & follow your advice for I allways think it wright, therefore will own myself wrong & begin again on a sure fowndation that shall ensure happyness for ous boath". Greville brought his friends to the house, partly to show her off, no doubt, but also with a view of letting her practise the social accomplishments he was trying to instil into her. What local ladies there were, were encouraged to call, and arrangements were made for a music master to come and give her lessons.

In the course of encouraging her singing, Greville took her to Ranelagh, where concerts in the gardens were still a popular attraction. The musical standards of these entertainments in the Rotunda, a large structure in the grounds not unlike a small Albert Hall, had fallen off at the time Emma visited it, but, nevertheless, society notables were still to be seen there. Either her excitement or the wine she had been given went to her head, for the story is told that she burst into song in competition with one of the singers. The crowd was delighted by this unusual diversion, but poor Greville could only see it as a disgraceful outburst and Emma was taken straight home. As soon as they got back, she rushed to her room, took off her finery and came down again in her plainest dress, imploring him to keep her as she was or to be rid of her.

George Romney had been living at No. 32 Cavendish Square for some six years. He had bought the house from the executors of the late Francis Cotes, R.A., as it had a large painting room. Greville knew Romney quite well and it was most understandable that he should want to hear the painter's praises of his new mistress. Emma's appearance was a *succés fou*. Romney, who may, as has already been mentioned, have seen her before, had not at any rate seen her looking as well groomed and beautiful as this. That he wanted to paint her at once is proved by his day-book which records, within a few weeks at most of her arrival in Paddington, that his sitters for Friday, 12th March 1782, were:

> Mrs Luitridge at 1
> Capt Dalton
> Miss H^t at 11
> Mrs Rooke at ½ pt 2
> A Gent at ½ pt 3

This entry is quickly followed by "Saturday 20th March – Mrs H^t at 12". After a pause, there appear two sittings in June, nine in July, one in August and four in December. Much as Emma enjoyed hearing the famous painter's eulogies on her beauty, she was even more enthralled by the pleasure of being able to pose to her heart's content. Romney first painted her as "Nature", but it is one of his early portraits of her "In a Black Hat" that brings out, so much better than the later pictures when perhaps he improved on nature a little, the youthful charm of the fresh complexioned Emma – Sir William's "Fair Tea-Maker of Edgware Row" rather than Romney's "Divine Lady". Emma herself would naturally have revelled in the classical poses: Alope, Ariadne, a Bacchante, Calypso, Cassandra, Circe, Euphrosyne, Iphigenia, Miranda; the very basis of the Attitudes for which she was later to become famous. There is no reason whatever to suppose that there was any sort of flirtation between the painter of forty-eight and his young model of seventeen. Mrs Cadogan was more than likely to have been present as chaperon at most, if not all, of the sittings. Eighteenth-century morals may have been fairly lax, but appearances were most important.

Romney was certainly smitten by Emma, a little in love with her even as time went on, but she had eyes and thoughts for no one but her

Greville. She had offers from a number of wealthy admirers, as Greville asserts, but she was not interested in their advances. It may well be that her serious-minded protector became a little apprehensive of the enthusiasm that Emma showed for her visits to Cavendish Square for the strange gap of nearly seventeen months that Romney's day-book discloses, between 3rd August 1782 and 19th December 1783, suggests that a little jealousy on Greville's part may have been the cause of the cessation. It was not that Romney was not working during this period. He had a full programme of sittings including, as a matter of interest, Sarah Siddons who would then have been about twenty-eight and who had just made a name for herself at Drury Lane. There may have been other reasons for the hiatus, but all was well again when the appointments were recommenced and they became exceedingly frequent. The exact number of visits cannot be computed as, most unfortunately, the diary for 1785 has been lost.

Among the letters and papers of Greville's that have survived are the household accounts that Emma kept between 27th October 1784 and 21st February 1785. That he should have kept, to the end of his life, this souvenir of his mistress is a touching indication of a sentimental trait in his character. One can only guess that early extravagances, with the connivance of such a competent housekeeper as Mrs Cadogan, made Greville insist that proper accounts be kept. The accounts, which are given in full in the Appendix, make fascinating reading. They give an all-over impression of comfortable living, while Emma's spelling, never her strong point, amuses and, at the same time, gives a clue, here and there, to her not-over-precise pronunciation. The item which appears on the third day, "Poor Man ½d", has often been quoted to demonstrate her generosity. It is far more likely that the entry was made in a vain attempt to make the accounts balance! As no more "poor men" are mentioned, the subterfuge was plainly unsuccessful and one can be sure that the genuinely needy, of whom Emma would have been an experienced judge, would have received a considerably larger sum from her own purse. Greville seems to have been content to contribute five guineas towards the housekeeping at fairly frequent intervals, making up deficiencies with other sums as the occasion warranted. It also appears that two servants at a time were kept in the house.

Emma, her mother and the maids between them managed to make household affairs run smoothly and to Greville's satisfaction. At the end of 1784, during the period of the preserved accounts, he concluded a letter with a reference to Emma, saying: "She is very well & there is not in the parish so tidy a house as ours, it being Christmas day."

Sir William Hamilton visited the Paddington house almost as soon as Greville took it, as he was in England in 1782. His first wife, Catherine (of whom he said, "I have realy found a lasting comfort in having married – something against my inclination – a virtuous, good-temper'd woman with a little independent fortune …"), had died and he had brought her body home in order that she might be buried, according to her wish, at Slebeck in Pembrokeshire. In 1784, Sir William was back from Naples again; this time his visit was connected with the estates in the neighbourhood of Milford Haven which he had inherited from his wife. He saw much of Emma, as a great deal of his time was spent with Greville. He was then fifty-four and in Emma's view, therefore, quite an old man, but a kindly and lovable one. He appreciated her good looks and her honest friendliness and went out of his way to make a fuss of her, calling her the "fair tea-maker of Edgware Row". At times she replied in kind, referring to him as Pliny; a name she had heard used by his friends, who, because of their art collecting, called Sir William and Greville, Pliny the Elder and Pliny the Younger.

In June, the two men were to go on a long business trip together and so it was decided that Emma, who was suffering from an infection on her knees and arms, should benefit by some sea-bathing. Accordingly, she and her mother went off by coach to Chester, to call first on Mrs Kidd at Hawarden who was looking after "little Emma" and then to go on, with the child, to a suitable place by the sea.

The letters which Emma wrote to Greville during the time he was away are so descriptive of her feelings, so enchanting and so naïve that it would be foolish to try to put into other words what she herself says.

Chester Satturday Morn. (June 12th 1784)

My dear Greville,

I have had no letter from you yett which makes me unhappy. I cant go to Abbergelly as it is forty miles & a very uncumfortable place & I am now going to Parkgate as it is the only place beside high lake (Hoylake) I can go to, but I will try to go there. Pray my dear Greville, do write directly & lett it be left at the post office, Parkgate tell calld for. God bless you, write. I have got my poor Emma with me & I have took leave of all my friends. I have took her from a good home & I hope she will prove worthy of your goodness to her & her mother. I should not write now tell I got to Parkgate only I want to hear from you. Pray write my dear Greville directly & send me word how to bile that Bark for parting with you made me so unhappy I forget the Book. I cant stop to write for the coach is waiting. My dear Greville dont be angry but I gave me

Granmother 5 guines for she had laid some out on her & I would not take her awhay shabbily; but Emma shall pay you. Adue, my ever dear Greville & believe me, yours ever truly,

Emma Hart.

I will write on Monday again. My love to Sir W. & say everything that you can, I am low-spirited so excuse me my dear Greville, I wish I was with you. God bless you.

*   *   *

Addressed to: – Mr Greville, M.P.
Haverfordwest, Pembrokeshire, (by London)
Parkgate, June the 15th 1784.

My dearest Greville,
  You see by the date where I am gott & likely to be & yett it is not through neglect of seeking after other places for I have & as to Abbergely it is 40 miles & so dear that I could not with my mother & me & the child have been there under 2 guines & a half a week; it is grown such a fashionable place and High Lake as 3 houses in it & not one of them as is fit for a Christan, the best is a Publick house for the sailers of such ships as is obligded to put in there so you see there is no possibility of going to either of those places. Has to where I am, I find it very comfortable considering from you. I am in the house of a Laidy whoes husband is at sea, she & her Granmother live to gether & we board with her at present tell I hear from you. The price is high but the wont lodge any body without boarding and as it is comfortable decent & quiet I thought it would not ruin ous tell I could have your oppionon which I hope to have freily & without restraint as believe me you will give it to one who will allways be happy to follow it. Lett it be what it will, as I am sure you would not lead me wrong & tho my little temper may have been sometimes high believe me, the have allways thought you in the right in the end, when I have come to reason. I bathe & find the water very soult; here is a great many Laidys batheing, but I have no society with them as it is best not, so pray my dearest Greville, write soon & tell me what to do as I will do just what you think proper & tell me what I am to do with the child for she is a great romp & I can hardly master her. I dont think she is ugly, but I think her greatly improved, she is tall, good eys & brows & all to gether she will be passible, but she has over grown all her cloaths. I am makeing and mending all as I can for her.

24

Pray my dear Greville do lett me come home as soon as you can for I am all most broken hearted being from you, endead I have no pleasure nor happiness. I wish I could not think on you, but if I was the greatest laidy in the world I should not be happy from you so dont lett me stay long. Tell Sir Wm. everything you can & tell him I am sorry our situation prevented me from giving him a kiss but my heart was ready to break but I will give it him & entreat if he will axcept it. Ask him how I looked & lett him say something kind to me when you write. Endead my dear Greville, you dont know how much I love you & your behaiver to me wen we parted was so kind, Greville, I dont know what to do, but I will make you amends by my kind behaiver to you for I have grattude and I will show it you all as I can, so dont think of my faults Greville think of all my good & blot out all my bad, for it is all gone & berried never to come again, so good by, my dear Greville, think of nobody but me for I have not a thought but of you & praying for you & for ous to meet again. God bless you & believ me, yours truly & affectionately

Emma H^t.

P.S. Poor Emma gives her duty to you. I bathe her & the people is very civel to ous. I give a guinea & half a week for ous all to gether but you will tell me what to do. God bless you, my dear, dear Greville, I long to see you for endead, I am not happy from you tho I will stay if you like tell a week before you go home, but I must go first. I have had no letter from you & you promised to write to me before I left home. It made me unhappy but I thought you might not have time. God bless you, once more goodby.

Derect for me at Mrs Darnwoods, Parkgate, near Chester & write derectly, take care of the whoman.

* * *

Parkgate, June 22 1784.

My ever dear Greville,

How teadous does the time pass a whay till I hear from you. I think it ages since I saw you & years since I heard from you. Endead, I should be miserable if I did not reccolect on what happy terms we parted, – parted yess, but to meet again with tenfould happiness. Oh, Greville, when I think on your goodness, your tender kindness, my heart is so full of grattatude that I want words to express it. But I have one happiness in vew which I am determined to practice & that is eveness of temper &

25

steadyness of mind, for endead I have thought so much of your aimable goodness when you have been tried to the utmost that I will, endead I will, manege myself & try to be like Greville – endead I can never be like him. But I will do all I can towards it & I am sure you will not desire more. I think if the time would come over again I would be differant. But it does not matter, there is nothing like bying expearance, I may be happyer for it hearafter & I will think of the time coming & not the time past, except to make comparrasons to shew you what allterations there is for the best – so my Dearest Greville, dont think on my past follies, think on my good little as it has been & I will make you amends by my kind behavior; you shall never repent your partiality – & if you had not behaived with such angel like goodness to me at parting it would not have had such affect on me. But I have done nothing but think on you since & O Greville, did you but know when I do think, what thoughts – what tender thoughts, you would say Good God & can Emma have such feiling senceibility – no. I never could think it, but now I may hope to bring her to conviction & she may now prove a valluable & aimable whoman – true, Greville & you shall not be disapointed. I will be every thing you can wish. But mind you Greville, your troo great goodness has brought this at bear, for you dont know what I am. Would you think it Greville – Emma – the wild unthinking Emma is a grave thoughtful phylosopher. Tis true Greville & I will convince you I am when I see you. But how I am running on – I say nothing abbout this guidy wild girl of mine: what shall we do with her, Greville, she is as wild & as thoughtless as somebody when she was a little girl, so you may gess how that is. Whether you will like it or no there is no telling but one comfort is she is a little afraid of me. Would you believe on satturday whe had a little querel, I mean Emma & me & I did slap her on her hands & when she came to kiss me & make it up I took her on my lap & cried. Now do you blame me or not, pray tell me. Oh Greville, you dont know how I love her, endead, I do, when she comes & looks in my face & calls me mother. Endead, I then truly am a mother for all the mothers feilings rise at once & tels me I am or ought to be a mother, for she has a wright to my protection & she shall have it as long as I can & I will do all in my power to prevent her falling into the errors her poor once miserable mother fell into. But why do I say miserable. Am not I happy abbove any of my sex, at least in my sittuation, does not Greville love me, or at least like me, does not he protect me, does not he provide for me, is not he a father to my child. O why do I call myself miserable: No, it whas a mistake & I will be happy, chearful & kind & do all as my poor abbilitys will let me to return the Fatherly goodness & prottection he has shewn. Again, O my dear Greville, the reccolection of past scenes brings tears in my eys, but the are tears of happiness. To think of your goodness is two much. But once for all, Greville, I will be grateful. Adue.

It is near batheing time & I must lay down my pen and I wont finish tell I see when the post comes whether there is a letter; he comes in abbout one a clock. I hope to have a letter to day.

I must not forgett to tell you my knees is well as I may say there is hardly a mark & my elbows is much better. I eat my vittuels very well & I am quite strong & feil hearty & well & I am in hopes I shall be very well; you cant think how soult the watter is & there is a many Laidys bathing here. But, Greville, I am obliged to give a shilling a day for the batheing house & whoman & twopence a day for the dress: it is a great expence & it fretts me wen I think of it. But wen I think how well I am & my elbows likely to gett well, it makes me quite happy for at any rate it is better than paying the docter. But wright your oppionon freily & tell me what to do. Emma is crying because I wont come & bathe, so Greville, adue tell after I have dipt. May God bless you, my dearest Greville & believe me faithfully, affectionatly & truly yours only

Emma H^t.

Thursday Morning.

& no letter from my dear Greville. Why, my dearest G- what is the reason you dont wright. If you knew my uneaseyness you would. You promised to wright before I left Hawerden & I was much disapointed you did not, but thought you might not have a oppertunity being at Wandower Hill. I have sent 2 letters to Haverford West & has never had no answer to them & it is now 3 weeks since I saw you. Pray, my dearest Greville, wright to me & make me happy for I am not so att present, tho my arms is most well. I think if I could but hear from you I should be happy, so make me happy, do pray. Give my dear kind love & compliments to Pliney & tell him I put you under his care & he must be answerable for you to me wen I see him. I hope he has not fell in love with any raw boned Scotch whoman whoes fortune would make up for the want of Beauty & then he may soon through her in a decline – Mum – for he is fond of portraits in that whay & then he must be fond of orraigenals & it will answer every purpose. But dont put him in mindof it for fear. But after all, say everything you can to him for me & tell him I shall allways think of him with grattude & remember him with pleasure & shall allways regret loesing is good company. Tell him I wish him every happiness this world can afford him, that I will pray for him & bless him as long as I live. But I am wrighting tis true, but I dont know when you will ever gett it for I cant send it tell I hear from you & the post wont be in tell to morro afternoon & I am in hopes I shall have a letter to morrow. Pray my dear Greville, lett me go home soon. I have been 3 weeks & if I stay fortnight longer that will be 5 weeks you know & then this expense is about 2 guineas a week with washing & batheing whoman & evry thing & I think a fortinight or 3 weeks longer I shall not have a spot for you can scarce descovr any thing on my knees and arms.

*   *   *

Friday morning, 12 a clock (June 25)

With what impatience do I sett down to wright tell I see the postman, but sure I shall have a letter to day. Can you, my dear Greville, no you cant have forgot your poor Emma allready, endead, tho I am but for a few weeks absent from you, my heart will not one moment leave you, I am allways thinking of you and could allmost fancy I hear you see you & think, Greville, what a disapointment when I find myself decieved & even has never heard from you. But my heart wont tell me scold you, endead, it thinks on you with two much tenderness, so do wright, my dear Greville, dont you remember how you promised, dont you reccolect what you said at parting how you should be happy to see me again. O Greville, think on me with kindness, think how many happy days, weeks & years, I hope, we may yett pass & think out of some that is past, there as been some little pleasure as well as pain & endead, did you but know how much I love you, you would freily forgive me any former quarels for I now suffer for them & one line from you would make me happy, so pray do wright & tell me when you will be returning as I shall be happy to see you again, for whilst Emma lives, she must be gratefully & ever affectionately yours,

Emma Hart

P.S. This shall not go tell I have a letter from you which I hope to have in half an hour. Adue, my dear, kind Greville.

*   *   *

Sunday Morning (June 27)

My dear Greville, I had a letter on Friday from my granmother & she sent me one from you that had been there a fortenight. I am much oblidged to you for all the kind things you say to me & tell Sir Willm I am much oblidged to him for saying I looked well. I hope he will allways think so, for I am proud of is good word & I hope I shall never forfeit it, I will at least study to reserve it. I am in hopes to have a letter from you, for it is a great comfort to me to hear from you & my dear Greville, it is now going on a month since I saw you, but I think how happy I shall be to see you again, to thank for your kindness to my poor Emma & me. She shall thank you Greville, she shall be greatful, she shall be good & make you amends for all the trouble her mother has caused you, but how I am to make you amends God knows, I shall never have it in my power, but Greville, you shall have no cause to complain, I will trye, I will do my utmost & I can only regret that fortune will not put it in my power to make a return for all the kindness & goodness you have shewd me. Good by, my dear Greville, God will bless you for me, I can only had my kindest wishes for you. Emma is much oblidged to you for remembering her & she hopes you will give her a oppertunity of thanking you personally for your goodness to her. I think you wont be disapointed in her, tho mothers – Lord bless me, what a word for the gay wild Emily to say – should not commend, but leave that for other people to do.

*   *   *

(June or July 1784)

Unkind Greville, yes I have got your letter but why do you scold me; if I wrote scral & ill, it was with thinking with two much kindness on you. You have mad me unhappy by scolding me; how can you when you know my dispotion, when you know it breaks my heart to be scolded & speacily by Greville, but I wont think you meant it ill-natured, tho you have maid me unhappy & if you had killd me, your kindness to my poor Emma would make me forget it for, endead, my Dear Greville, I love you two well to neglect you in any one point, so pray forgive me – & has to your goodness in regard to agreaments, endead I will come in to all as you propose: I will give her up to you intirely; do what you will with her, I here sollemnly say that I will never break from my word. You shall take her, put her there where you propose, lest any quarels, tho I hope there will be none – hope she shall stay whear you propose putting her. Lett what will happen I give her up to you to act as you think proper by her. Take her, Greville & may God reward you for it, tho her Mother cant. All as I desire is that if you will lett me take her home when I go to stay tell you come to see her whilst

29

she is there. Nobody shall see her, tho neither you nor I need be ashamed of her, but if you dont like that, I will give it up, so you see, my Dearest Greville, what confidence I put in you now. Scold me, unkind Greville, how can you do so. Pray wright to me derectly & wright kind. Give my Dear kind love to Sr Willm say everything from me that you can for endead I love him. I should not now wright in such a hurry only if I dont send it of by 4 oclock I cant send it of tell Tuesday, so dont think that I cant spare a hour, yes, 6 hours, all my whole life I could spare to do any thing for Greville, so God bless you, my dear Greville. Mrs Ladmore is gone to live at Chester or I should have gone there, that is my reason as I am at Mrs Downwards, but it is the cheapest place I could gett for she thinks nothing a truble, she eat soult watter 4 or 5 times a day for me to wash my elbows in, but pray lett me come to town before you if it is only a day or two, you know my reason. It may be some comfort to you peraps to know that my elbows & knees is allmost well & I never was better in my life, so Greville, if you will be happy to see me, you will find me in good health, handsome & fonder & kinder to you than ever. So my dearest cruil Greville, why did you scold me, I would not have scolded you at so great distance, but I will forgive you & I say again you shall see me every thing you can wish & I will be allways yours ever affectionatly & sincerely

E. H.   Adue.

*   *   *

Parkgate. July the 3rd 1784.

I was very happy, my Dearest Greville, to hear from you as your other letter vexd me, you scolded me so, but it is over & I forgive you. I am much oblidged to you for all the kind things you say to me & I am very happy to think we shall meet soon again, happy, good humerd & chearfull. I will be so & I think there is no fear of you. You dont know, my Dearest Greville, what a pleasure I have to think that poor Emma will be comfortable & happy & Greville, if she does but turn out well, what a happyness it will be & I hope she will for your sake. I will teach her to pray for you as long as she lives & if she is not grateful & good it wont be my fault but what you say is very true, a bad dispotion may be made good by good example & Greville would not put her any whear to have a bad one. I come in to your whay a thinking Hollidays spoils children: it takes there attention of from there scool, it gives them a bad habbit, when the have been a month & goes back, this does not pleas them & that is not wright & the do nothing but think wen the shall go back again. Now Emma will never expect what she never had, so I hope she will be very good, mild & attentive & we may have a deal of comfort. O Greville if her poor mother had ever had the luck & prospect, mearly in haveing a good edducation that she has, what a whoman might she have been, but I wont think. All my happiness now is Greville & to think that he loves me makes a recompense for all, for if he did not love me would he be so good, kind & affectionate, No, tis imposible, therefore I will have it so. I have said all as I have to say abbout Emma yet, only she gives her duty & I will now tell you a little abbout my self. I have not took but 2 of those things from Mr W – as the sea watter has done me so much good. I have drunk a tumbler glas every morning fasting, walked half an hour & then bathed & breakfasted. I have had the tang apployd to my knees & elbows every night going to bed & every day washd them twice a day in sea water & they are just well, therefore, as long as I stay I had better go on in my old whay for I can take Mr W's prescription at home, but not sea water, tang etc. I am very well, looks well, has a good appetite & is better than ever I was in my life. I have no society with anybody but the mistress of the House & her mother & sister. The latter is a very genteel yong lady, good nattured & does every thing to pleas me; but still I would rather be at home, if you was there. I follow the old saying, home is home if ever so homely. I must go to diner therefore will say no more but that I long to see you & dear Sir W. Give my kind, kind love to him, tell him next to you I love him abbove any body & that I wish I was with him to give him a kiss. Dont be affronted Greville, if I was with you I would give you a thousand & you might take as many as you pleased for I long, I mean I long to see you. I sopose you will scold next. Adue. I hope to have a letter from you this next week. We have been a month from home today, Greville, its a great wile. My mother gives her comp[ts] to you & Sir W & say every thing that is kind or will render me dear to him; to more than you can say my heart with gratiude assents & I must ever remain yours ever affectionately & sincerely

E. H.

P.S. Good by, my dear Greville, I hope we shall meet soon, happy & well. Adue. I bathe Emma & she is very well & grows & her hair will grow very well on her forehead & I dont think her nose will be very snub, her eyes is blue & pretty, but she dont speak through her nose,

31

but she speaks countryfied, but she will forget it. We squable sometimes, still, she is fond of me & endead I love her for she is senceble, so much for beauty. Adue. I long to see you.

*   *   *

Edgware Road
Tuesday August 10, 1784.

I received your kind letter last night & my Dearest Greville I *want words* to *express* to you how *happy* it made me, for I thought I was like a lost sheep & everybody had forsook me. I was eight days confined to my room, very ill, but am, thank God, very well now, & a deal better for your kind instructing letter & I own the justness of your remark. You shall have your appartments to your self, you shall read, wright or set still just as you pleas, for I shall think my self happy to be under the seam roof with Greville & do all I can to make it agreable with out disturbing him in any pursuits that he can follow, to employ him self in at home or else whare, for your absence has taught me that I ought to think my self happy if I was within a mile of you, so as I could see the place as contained you, I should think myself happy abbove my shear, so, my Dear G, come home & you shall find your home comfortable to receave you, you shall find me good, kind, gentle & affectionate & every thing you wish me to do I will do for I will give myself a fair trial & follow your advice for I allways think it wright, therefore will own myself wrong & begin again on a sure fowndation that shall ensure happyness for ous boath. Dont think Greville, this the wild fancy of a moments consideration, it is not. I have thoughraly considered everything in my confinement & *I say nothing now but what I shall practice.*

I must now inform you abbout my illness My Dear Greville. I had a rash out all over me and a fevour & I should have been worse if I had not had the rash out, but I think I am better for it now for I look fair & seems better in health than I was before. I dare say I should have been very dangerously ill iff it had not come out. Pray my Dearest Greville, do come to see me as soon as ever you come in to town, for I do so long to see you, you dont know & it will make me so happy. But I mean if you should come to town before diner, do come because I now you will come at night. I have a deal to say to you when I see you. Oh Greville, to think it is nine weeks since I saw you. I think I shall die with the pleasure of seeing you. Endead, my Dearest Greville, if you knew how much I think of you, you would love for it, for I am allways thinking on you, of your goodness, in short Greville, I truly love you & the thought of your coming home so soon makes me so happy I dont know what to do. Good by, my ever Dearest Greville, may God preserve & bless you for ever, pray yours ever affectionately & sencerely

Emma

My kind love to Sr Wm & tell him if he will come soon, I will give him a thousand *kisses*, for I do love him a little. Emma is very well & is allways wondering why you dont come home; she sends her duty to you. Good by, My Dearest Greville, pray, pray come as soon as you come to town. Good by. God bless you. O how I long to see you. Adue.

*   *   *

These letters are evidence enough to refute any suggestions that Greville was unkind or parsimonious where Emma was concerned. He had her welfare very much at heart even if, perhaps, he found her devotion, genuine though it was, a little too effusive.

However, at the beginning of 1785 he was giving some thought to the planning of his future. The house in Cavendish Square had been sold in 1784, but the expenses of his present establishment were by no means inconsiderable. The idea of a comfortable and settled married life was still in his mind and, devoted as he was to Emma, he had the feeling that he did not wish to remain tied to a mistress for the rest of his life. His sentiments are expressed in a letter to his uncle in which he writes:

Emma is very grateful for your remembrance. Her picture[2] shall be sent by the first ships – I wish Romney yet to mend the dog. She certainly is much improved since she has been with me. She has none of the bad habits which giddiness & inexperience encouraged, & which bad choice of company introduced. She has much pride, & submits to solitude rather than admit of one improper acquaintance. She is naturally elegant, & fits herself easily to any situation, having quickness & sensibility. I am sure she is attached to me or she would not have refused the offers, which I know have been great; & such is her spirit that, on the least slight or expression of my being tired or burthened by her, I am sure she would not only give up the connexion but would not even accept a farthing for future assistance.

This is another part of my situation. If I was independent I should think so little of any other connexion that I never would marry. I have not an idea of it at present, but if any proper opportunity offer'd I should be much harassed, not know to manage, or how to fix Emma to her satisfaction, & to forego the reasonable plan which you & my friends have advised is not right. I am not quite of an age to retire from bustle, & to retire to distress & poverty is worse. I can keep on here creditably this winter.

It has been suggested by a number of writers that Greville was a wily and consequently a rather unpleasant man with his eye on the main chance. They submit that, not wishing to forgo his inheritance should his uncle remarry, he determined to use his devoted Emma as a bait which would effectually take Sir William's mind off the subject of matrimony. But one must be fair to him. He had known for years that he would be his uncle's heir and, at a time when the first Lady Hamilton could reasonably be expected to outlive her husband, his affectionate references to her in his letters do not savour of ill-will towards her on that count. There is no question of his sincere devotion to his uncle or of his desire to do anything that would not contribute to Sir William's happiness. He knew well enough that his uncle had always taken great pleasure in the company of women and that, now he was free, he would obviously continue to do so to a correspondingly greater extent. To provide him with a mistress could hardly, especially in those days, be considered as a gambit that would have any lasting effect.

Greville was, without doubt, a most kind-hearted man and the idea of putting Emma out into the street in order to retrench his finances – an act which would not have been thought the least unusual – was quite abhorrent to him. His ambition to live his life to the full was a strong and a natural one but, situated as he was, he could see himself stuck fast in Paddington from a social point of view. He considered making Emma an allowance and his estimate of £100 per annum, considering the present-day value of that sum then, was an extremely generous one. However, being mindful of the pricks of jealousy and irritation that he had experienced at times from the mild form of philandering that had gone on when Sir William was in the Edgware Road house, the idea of a ready-made solution to the problem would have struck him almost at once. Even so, as anyone else in a similar position would have realised, it was a delicate matter and would have to be approached with considerable tact. Had he not been so fond of Emma and had her fate been of no consequence to him, he could have made a bold suggestion to Sir William in his next letter and if it fell flat, so much the worse for his mistress. But he was fond of Emma – very fond.

The excerpts from his correspondence which follow are not picked out to suit the foregoing argument. They contain every word in the voluminous letters he wrote to his uncle that has any bearing on Emma.

King's Mews, 10 March 1785

You have not wrote to me this great while. They say here that you are in love. I know you love variety, & are a general flirt, & of the 60 English, what with widows & young married ladies, an amateur may be caught. Some have said you have had the gout. I say I neither know whether your heart or feet are lightest, but that I believe them both sound; & altho' Harry Harpur[3] says he was witness to the deluge of blood of boars that flowed around you, I know that your heart is neither calous to friendship nor to beauty. I hope I shall ever have the usual share of the one & I shall as readily give up as much as you chuse to bestow on beauty. I do not consider them as incompatible guests in a good heart, & it must be a very interested friend indeed who does not sincerely wish everything that can give happiness to a friend. I sincerely wish that happiness to you. I am from frequent experience convinced that I can judge for you & you for me, at least suppose cases in which we should think alike, & on those cases in which comfort may arise you are more than myself able to realise suppositions by experiment; for the limited experiment I make I know to succeed, altho' from poverty it cannot last. If you did not chuse a wife, I wish the tea-maker of Edgware Row was yours, if I could without banishing myself from a visit to Naples. I do not know how to part with what I am not tired with. I do not know how to contrive to go on, & I give her every merit of prudence & moderation & affection. She shall never want, & if I decide sooner than I am forced to stop from necessity it will be that I may give her part of my pittance, & if I do so it must be by sudden resolution & by putting it out of her power to refuse it; for I know her disinterestedness to be such that she will rather encounter any difficulty than distress me. I should not write to you thus if I did not think you seem'd as partial as I am to her. She would not hear at once of any change, & from no one that was not liked by her. I think I could secure on her near £100 a year. It is more than injustice to all I can do, but with parting with part of my virtu I can secure it to her, & content myself with the remainder. I think you might settle another on her & I think you would be as comfortable as I have been & am. I am not a dog in the manger; if I could go on I would never make this arrangement, but to be reduced to a standstill & involve myself in distress further than I could extricate myself, & then to be unable to provide for her at all, would make me miserable from thinking myself very unjust to her, & as she is too young & handsome to retire into a convent or the country, & is honorable & honest, & can be trusted: after reconciling myself to the necessity, I consider where she could be happy. I know you thought me jealous of your attention to her; I can assure you her conduct entitles her more than ever to my confidence. Judge then, as you know my satisfaction on looking at a modern piece of virtu if I do not think you a second self, in thinking that by placing her within your reach I render a necessity, which would otherwise be heartbreaking, tolerable & even comforting. Yours ever, …

*   *   *

King's Mews, 5 May 1785

I have received your letter; I have no doubt of your kind wishes towards me, therefore the interest you take in my situation is by me very sensibly felt. If I could have thought that no line could be taken but that of making E do the honors of your house, I confess I never should have dreamt of it; this is a line so different from what I have practised that I should be among the first to lament that you adopted an unwise plan. I tell you fairly that your expressions of kindness to E, & the comfort you promised to her in case anything happened to me, made such an impression on her that she regards you as her protector & friend, & in moments of her thinking your goodness she related to me your last conversation, & I concluded that your regard to me had been the only reason for your not making present offers. You know that from giddiness & disipation she is prudent & quiet, & that, surrounded with temptations, I have not any the least reason to complain of her, & my attentions do not lead me to make a parade of her, or a sacrifice of my amusements or business. The secret is simple; she has pride & vanity. I have for some years directed them to her happiness. I have shewn her that creditable & quiet people will respect her from being totaly clear from all the society & habits of kept women; she does not wish for much society, but to retain two or three creditable acquaintances in the neighbourhood. She has avoided every every appearance of giddiness, & prides herself on the neatness of her person & on the good order of her house; these are habits both comfortable & convenient to me. She has vanity & likes admiration; but she connects it so much with her desire of appearing prudent, that she is more pleas'd with accidental admiration than that of crowds, which now distress her. In short, this habit, of three or 4 years aquiring, is not a

36

caprice, but is easily to be continued. If you had given her any of your villas, only making it a decided part that she had a home distinct from your house, whether her visits were frequent or rare it was immaterial, her home would be distinct; & yet if, as you say, you could not resist taking (her) into your house entirely, you certainly would vary so entirely from my ideas & plan, that I could not follow you. You would lose the greatest advantage from her disposition; she is not led by interest but by kindness, & she appreciates favors from the intentions. If you gave everything at once you would be like the prodigal, depriving yourself of the means of shewing attention; as to the duties of the connexion, it is madness to be a slave to pleasure, & if she did not expect more than you chuse, & had not reason to doubt fidelity, there would be no fear on that head, & as to running after other men, if once she has taken a line, & is sensible of good intentions towards her, she may be trusted, & ten times more if left entirely to herself. She is now but 20. An early experience makes a strong impression, and if giddiness, or avarice, or vanity could run away with her, she would not have improved, & resisted great offers & strong solicitations. She also finds that a quiet life has restored health & improved her looks. What you say is true that so beautiful a person cannot be long without a protector; there is no doubt of that, but it is not her wish to run the gantlet, & for the present I do not see that I should better myself much by putting her in that situation. If things remain as they are I shall, to be sure, be much straitned in finances. I shall be so whether she remains or not, & literary her expences are trifling; yet when income is very small a trifling expence is felt. But, above all, I own that I think I lose opportunities of settling to advantage; when home is comfortable other pursuits are less interesting, & to sink into a retreat of this sort at my time of life is what in others I should condemn. You may say that at yours it may also be absurd; every man to his idea. At your age a clean & comfortable woman is not superfluous, but I should rather purchase it than acquire it, unless in every respect a proper party offer'd. Would your friends have thought L^{y}C a more prudent connexion than E? I know the sentiments of all your friends, & my delicacy prevented my writing on that subject, but I can assure you they feel very happy at the departure of L^{y}C. I am not sorry, though I should have been so if it had been Mrs D. instead of L^{y}C.[4] Your brother spoke openly to me, that he thought the wisest thing you could do would be to buy Love ready made, & that it was not from any interested wish, as he was perfectly satisfied with the fortune he had, that it was enough for his family & that he should be very glad to hear you declare openly your successor, & particularly so if you named me; I write without affectation or disguise. If you find me either reserved or artful you may despise me; but in opening my heart & thoughts do not impute conceal'd designs. I wish you every happiness in this world & long life to enjoy it. I protest, I do not think the odds in our lives are proportioned to the difference of our years. You have spoke kindly of your intentions towards me, & you have shewn a readiness to assist me in every thing that I could in reason expect; I am very sensible & very grateful. I mentioned the assistance I wished enjoining me in a bond to Ross; when that is done, I will, as your security, assign over my whole collection of minerals, which have cost me three times the amount of the security. I therefore distinguish favor & business, & I should never have a wish to tax your goodness by drawing from you during your life any thing. I will speak out also in relation to my future assistance, & there is only one case in which I should wish to know your intentions & build upon them, which is in case I ever should by any such declaration of yours obtain the consent of the relations of a lady whose fortune would enable us to live comfortably, &, by the future provision which after your death you should settle on us, insure a provision for children if any there should be.

In my present situation, suppose a lady of 30,000 was to marry me, the interest of her fortune would not provide equal to her pretentions & also provide a saving for a provision for children, jointure, etc; & having nothing to settle, how could I expect a prudent family to adopt me? On the other hand, if such a provision could be applied to our living, & your goodness should insure me at a future period an estate which would come hereafter, there is no doubt that a lady with such a fortune might not reject me; therefore, I fairly own that the only supposition in which I should ever wish to have the kind intentions you have made known to several of our friends made any ways certain, would be that it could be the means of my being married to a lady of at least £30,000. I would not wish to have your decision for a less ample fortune, because a less fortune would not at present enable me to live comfortably, & I never would permit your goodness to be exhausted, which might be the case if you adopted me a beggar, & my principle is that you have not too much, that you have no reason to deprive yourself of any comfort of life, &, if you should shew me a preference which at one or another time you must shew to somebody, that you should not do it in a hurry; & the only case in which I could wish it to be fix't in my favor is that which will enable me while you live to prosper & appear in a line of life creditable & comfortable to myself, & that without any charge to you while you can enjoy your property, & that all my happiness should be owing to you would only add to my obligation to you, but not to the affection & regard which I now feel.

I shall only add to this long letter that taking E. is no part of the request, tho' it is not impossible I should put the question to a lady now totally inaccessible, whose fortune is what I mention; therefore I do not write idly… .

P.S. If I had wrote over my letter, or taken a copy, you would have had a better composition; but, as I had no wish to conceal any private thought, I wrote as they occurred, & if you dislike my frankness I shall be sorry, for it cost me a little to throw myself so open, & to no one's friendship could I have trusted myself, but to yours from which I have ever been treated with indulgence & preference.

*   *   *

No date (June 1785)

… My next door neighbour in Portman Square was Ld Middleton, of Nottinghamshire. I had the good fortune to please them, & have cultivated their friendship. There is one son & 2 daughters.[5] The eldest married last year, the youngest presented only this winter. You know me sufficiently to know that beauty & disposition are both requisites, & the youngest in both respects is beyond the reasonable mark for a younger brother. I understood their fortunes to be 30, but since find the eldest had only 20,000… .

Now let me say a few words about future plans & Emma.

If my letter should produce an offer from them, it is obvious we must part, if there should be no offer, I cannot go to a formal proposal; & I have fully stated that I *must* vary my plans, & reduce my establishment, which is beyond my means. I do not say one word of Emma; you know that, added to her looks, so cleanly & sweet a creature does not exist, & she is handsomer than when you saw her. What you say of Naples is true. As I told you in my former letter, every inconvenience must be of your own making. Give her one of your villas, or rather take a small retired house on the Hill at Naples, very small; she will not want to go about, & going to dine, or at any other hours, to your villa or house, when it may be convenient, will make a party of what by another plan would be dayly habit; & you know well enough that with women, no matter what is done, a change is necessary, if it was only as a mark of attention. As to Englishmen, there is nothing to fear; left to herself, she would conform to your ideas. She never has wished for an improper acquaintance; she has dropt every one she thought I could except against, & those of her own choice have been in a line of prudence & plainess, which, tho' I might have wished for, I could not have proposed to confine her; & if you can find only one or two acquaintances, & let her learn music or drawing, or anything to keep her in order, she will be as happy as if you gave her every change of disipation. She is no fool, but there is a degree of nature in her, that she has the same pleasure in a retired & confined life as in a more extensive one, & she has no difficulty in confining herself; & yet she has natural gentility & quickness to suit herself to anything, & takes easily any hint that is given with good humor. I have often heard people say you may do anything by good humor, but never saw any one so compleatly led by good nature, & I believe she would die before she yielded to ill-treatment. If you could form a plan by which you could have a trial, & could invite her & tell her that I ought not to leave England, & that I cannot afford to go on, & state it as a kindness to me if she would accept your invitation, she would go with pleasure. She is to be 6 weeks at some bathing place, & when you could write an answer to this & enclose a letter to her, I could manage it, & either by land, by the coach to Geneva, & from thence by *Veturine* forward her, or else by sea. I must add that I could not manage it so well later; after a month's absence, & absent from me, she would consider the whole more calmly. If there was in the world a person she loved so well as yourself after me, I could not arange with so much sans froid; & I am sure I would not let her go to you, if any risque of the usual coquetry of the sex being likely either to give uneasiness or appearances.... .

*   *   *

11 November 1785.

On my return to town, I found the menage just as I expected. Emma had been much alarm'd and distress'd with her mother's illness. It was not so severe an attack as I understood it to be when I informed you of it from Cornwall, but anything which the faculty stile paralysis is alarming, & I left her by no means recover'd. You may suppose that I did not increase Emma's uneasiness by any hint of the subject of our last correspondence; at any rate, it cannot take place before the spring, & she goes on so well & is so much more considerate & aimiable than she was when you saw her, & also improv'd in looks, that I own it is less agreable to part; yet I have no other alternative but to marry or remain a pauper; I shall persist in my resolution not to lose an opportunity if I can find it, & do not think that my idea of sending her to Naples on such an event arises from my consulting my convenience only. I can assure you she would not have a scarcity of offers, she has refused great ones; but I am sure she would prefer a foreign country with you to any other connexion at home, & I would not expose you to any risque. I know that confidence & good usage will never be abused by her, & that nothing can make her giddy. I was only ten days with her when I was call'd away to be Mayor of Warwick; it was not kindly meant, but it will turn out well... .

During my short stay in town I saw Hamilton[6] twice; once I call'd on him & the next I brought him to dine with Emma. He says he has not seen anything like her in G.B., & that she reminds him of a person at Rome whom he admired much, tho she was deficient in the beauties of the mouth, & that Emma's is both beautiful & uncommon. He has been meditating for a subject; he says he shall not rest untill he has prevail'd on her to sit; you may suppose she was flatter'd, & she told him she put him at once on her list of favorites, because you had spoke of him as a person you regarded, & also because he bore your name. I am told he has lately settled with his brother to take an annuity of £500 a year to give up the estate for ever, I think he will do wisely. He finds the expences of London very high, he was obliged to give 4 guineas a week for a painting room for 2 months certain, and 2½ guineas for lodging, which made six guineas ½ p^r week, without fire or victuals. His health is not the worse; on the contrary, his journey to England, & from thence to Scotland, has improved his looks... .

*   *   *

No date. (3 December 1785)

My dear Hamilton, as you have fully communicated your sentiments to me, & you know mine relative to Emma, I shall not enter further on that subject than to explain to you the occasion of your receiving the enclosed (a letter from Emma, quoted later) & my arrangements & opinion on the occasion. The absolute necessity of reducing every expence to enable me to have enough to exist on & to pay the interest of my debt without parting with my collection of minerals, which is not yet in a state of arrangement which would set it off to its greatest advantage, occasion'd my telling Emma that I should be obliged on business to absent myself for some months in Scotland. She naturally said that such a separation would be very like a total separation, for that she should be very miserable during my absence, & that she should

41

neither profit by my conversation nor improve in any degree, that my absence would be more tolerable if she had you to comfort her, & that she wished you was not so far off, as she would ask you to take her as a guest during my absence, as there was not a person in the world whom she could be happy with, if I was dead, but yourself, & that she certainly would profit of your kind offer if I should die, or slight her, & that was the consideration which often had comforted her when she look't forward to the chances which might separate us. I told her that I should have no objection to her going to Naples for 6 or 8 months, and that if she realy wished it I would forward any letter she wrote. On my return in the evening, she gave me the enclosed, & she has settled every thing in her own mind that she will go with her mother only, & if you cannot send any person so far as Geneva that she would settle in London with Desjeans[7] the Swiss carrier to convey her & her mother to Geneva in their diligence, & from there in a two-wheeled chaise to Rome, but that, a guide from Geneva being most comfortable, she proposed it. That she would not fear being troublesome, as she would be perfectly satisfied with the degree of attention you should from choice give her, & that she should be very happy in learning music & Italian, etc, while your avocations imploy'd you, provided she was under your roof & protection. I told her that she would be so happy that I should be cut out, & she said that if I did not come for her or neglected her, she would certainly be grateful to you; but that neither interest nor affection should ever induce her to change, unless my interest or wish required it, & that you could comfort her, altho' she made all the distinction of the difference of age, but that she had seen enough to value a real friend whenever she could find one, and that you had shown more real kindness to her than any person in the world beside myself, & therefore you was, after me, the nearest her heart.

I embraced the opportunity and the mode she approved, as it would soften the severity of a separation which is absolutely necessary. I would not lead you in any scrape, you know that. I have weaned her from disipation, by giving a stimulus to her pride, & made her conduct suitable to my retired stile by leading her by good humour and confidence. She had good natural sense & quick observation, & perfectly to be depended on; she is anxious of the good opinion of my friends, & has not a bad acquaintance in the world. She may be trusted by you anywhere, if you talk fairly to her your reason to wish her to avoid any thing you dislike, altho' she may wish for it, she will have a pleasure in giving it up to you if asked kindly, & you may leave her every opportunity of doing it unknown to you, & she never will abuse your confidence. She likes admiration, but merely that she may be valued, & not to profit by raising her price. I am sure there is not a more disinterested woman in the world, if she has a new gown or hat, etc, it is easy to make a little novelty go far, & all that pleases her is to have that little such as sensible and genteel people wear, & of the best quality, & I declare to you that the little excesses which I have experienced were never devoted to follies, but were given to poor relations in the country, for whose care she professes herself grateful, insomuch that I had only to scold her for not having made me supply that demand instead of making herself bare of pocket money.

You will be able to have an experiment without any risque; if it should not turn out as I expect, she will have profited by seeing a little of foreign parts; she will have improved herself & she may come home. I know that you are above acting unkindly to any woman, but particularly to a pretty woman, & your kindness to me & to her has already made you anticipate my request, & you offer'd generously to assist me in providing something for her. I do not see why you should not find some reward for your generosity when I no longer can continue my connexion from the state of my finances. I hope I shall be the more able to do something for her, & believe me, if either by marriage or office I shall become more at my ease, my first concern shall be to provide for her, whether she is with you or not. You need not fear domestic duty, women always require what men give them reason to expect, & very often they take omission of duty as proof of inconstancy, or of neglect, or diminution of affection, & therefore resent it. She has a good constitution, yet is delicate, & I think that her looks improved as well as her health since I considered myself an over-match for her, & as I consider you as my heir-aparent I must add that she is the only woman I ever slept with without having ever had any of my senses offended, & a cleanlier, sweeter bedfellow does not exist.

If I have an opportunity I will send her clothes by sea, that she may avoid trouble on the road; but if no ships go at that time she shall carry them; she has a good stock of everything, & I shall add some linnen, which is rather wanted. I find that the journey, all expences included, to Geneva for the 2 will amount to 30gs. I shall have every thing ready for setting out, & have got the refusal of 2 places in the coach which will set out the end of Feby. or the beginning of March at furthest, & Desjeans is close to Saussure,[8] & you might desire him to be of use to her if you cannot spare Cottier. And now I come to the last part of this subject; you know we are not accountable to the world further than not to offend against *bienséance*; on that principle I have acted with her. I have never told our story, therefore my conduct has never been judged from my own statement. People who do not live with us are as indifferent to us as we to them, & unless we make ourselves purposely the subject of general observation, that class leave us to ourselves.

Those who know us take us with more discretion, if they are in confidence, & we only open on a subject guardedly & in general terms, they will have discretion not to renew enquiry; those who are not in intimacy cannot take the liberty, and, if they do, remain unsatisfied. I wish, in the case of Emma, that you will use only your discretion, a young person under your protection is all that is necessary; and, altho' all the world should know both her & me, they will, according to their several dispositions, investigate the nature of the connexion, & without any agreement you will find Emma discrete, for she endeavours to gain as much consideration as possible, & tho' perfectly natural is not a sieve – is pleased if she thinks all the world not in her secret.

I am sorry that you have had the trouble to receive the Bond twice, & you will perhaps have reason to think me capricious; but Mrs McKenzie has beg'd me to let her pay off Ross,[9] and take the bond for the whole in his room; … .

I will write again soon, but I pray write by return of post to me & Emma. *You* must enable me to pay their journey, & you must say to her that you shall be happy to receive her, & hope to make her comfortable at Naples. Your last letter arriv'd the day after she had wrote her letter, & she beg'd the bottom of my letter which related to her. I am sure, if she had received your compliments & enquiries before she had written, her letter would have been a rhapsody of gratitude. She has not a doubt of the pleasure you will have to receive her, & as she will be ready to set out when your answer comes, let Cottier be at Geneva or within reach of Desjeans, at Geneva by the 10th or 15th of March.

Yours ever, etc.

*   *   *

The concern that Greville shows for Emma's kind treatment and well-being, in spite of his decision to end the connection, is remarkable. Admittedly she was being kept in good hands and might, with a less kind-hearted protector, have fared very much worse – had she not been duped into going to Naples. All the same, the poor girl's letter to Sir William, which seems quite unsuspecting, is pathetic.

Edgware Road, London. 3 December 1785.

My dear Sir William, emboldened by your kindness to me when you was in England, I have a proposal to make that I flatter myself will not be disagreable to you. Greville (whom you know I love tenderly) is oblidged to go for four or five months in the sumer to places that I cannot with propriety attend him to, & I have too great a regard for him to hinder him from pursuing those plans which I think it is right for him to folow; & I know it is necessary for him to keep up his connexions in the world; – and as you was so good as to give me encouragement, I will speak my mind. In the first place, I should be glad if I was a little more improved than what I am, and as Greville is oblidged to be absent in the sumer he has out of kindness to me offer'd, if you are agreable, for me to go to Naples for 6 or 8 months, and he will at the end of that time fetch me home, and stay a while there when he comes, which I know you will be glad to see him.

He therefore proposes for me to sett of the first of March next, as he will sett of then for his entended tour in Scotland, and I could not bear the thought of staying at home by my self when I know if I come to see you (which will be the greatest pleasure on hearth, Greville excepted) I shall be improving my self and making the time pass agreable; at the same time he thinks for me to go by the Geneva coach, and if you will lett your man that was in England with you meet me there to conduct me to Naples, I shall be glad; and if you will allot me an appartment in your house that I might be under your protection while I am there, and lett Greville occupye those appartments when he comes, you know that *must* be; but as your house is very large, and you must, from the nature of your office, have business to transact and visiters to see, I shall always keep my own room when you are better engaged or go out, and at other times I hope to have the pleasure of your company and conversation, which will be more agreable to me than any thing in Italy. As I have given you an example of sincerity, I hope you will be equaly candid and sencere in a speedy answer, as we are confined for time, and no further correspondance will be necessary, as you may depend on me, if you approve of it, setting of from London at the time I mentioned in the former part of this letter, and I shall be perfectly happy in any arrangements you will make, as I have full confidence in your kindness and attention to me, and shall long for the time when I can assure you in person how much I am, my dear Sir William, your oblidged humble servant, or affectionate Emma, which you like best.

*   *   *

The die was cast and on 20th January 1786 Greville was informing his uncle that Emma was seriously preparing for the first of March and that he would "engage places tomorrow". There is a suggestion that Emma had her suspicions about what was going on. Possibly her mother had come to her own conclusions and had dropped a hint, for Greville's letter goes on: "She has always said that if ever she was to part she might be weaned by degrees; she talks of the chances of our not meeting again, & that on the least neglect she will accept your offers, & that she will by her conduct merit your kindness. She must have in her mind a stronger impression of the chances than she expresses but she says that she would not put herself in the reach of chances with any person but yourself, and she does not say this from compliment, but from her heart."

And so Emma and her mother were to set off for Naples, accompanied part of the way by the painter Gavin Hamilton, little knowing what the future held in store.

Chapter 5

Naples

EMMA'S JOURNEY to Naples was to have started on 1st March but, in order that Gavin Hamilton could accompany her and her mother as far as Geneva, they waited a few days longer. Greville provided fifty pounds for the trip, giving thirty guineas to the painter for the ladies' fares and the remainder to Emma for incidental expenses en route. They travelled quite light, as a trunk had been sent on in advance. By selling a statue and some of his pictures, Greville had settled the outstanding bills connected with Emma's residence at Edgware Row and was, no doubt, feeling easier as regards his future expenditure even if he was still a little worried over his mistress's future. On 12th March he wrote another long letter to his uncle, imploring him to use her kindly and to "draw the line neatly & adhere to that which is reasonable".

While Emma was on her way and tasting the thrill of a new experience, Sir William was pleasantly occupied with a visit from the Hon. Anne Seymour Damer (the "Mrs D." referred to by Greville in his letter of 5th May 1785), a widow of thirty-eight of artistic talent whose company he enjoyed.

Writing just a day before Emma's arrival in Naples, Sir William informed his nephew that "I had an account of the arrival of our friend at Geneva the 27th of last month (March), so that she may be here in a day or two. The prospect of possessing so delightfull an object under my roof soon certainly causes in me some pleasing sensations, but they are accompanied with some anxious thoughts as to the prudent management of this business; however, I will do as well as I can, and hobble in and out of this pleasant scrape as decently as I can. You may be assured that I will comfort her for the loss of you as well as I am able, but I know, from the small specimen during your absence from London, that I shall have at times many tears to wipe from those charming eyes, & which if shed for any other but yourself, might give me jealousy. Now

47

that you have had the resolution of taking this necessary step, you will, I dare say, turn your mind seriously to the improving your fortune, either by marriage or getting again into employment. You shall hear from me as soon as she arrives..." The letter ends with a short postscript, "The trunk is arrived".

Even allowing for the absence of her "dear Greville", to be confronted on her twenty-first birthday with the magnificent expanse of the Bay of Naples and to be greeted most effusively by an old friend who happened to be, at the same time, the British Ambassador, must have been a momentous occasion for Emma. Naples was still a gay city, a centre of the Arts and a port of call for all the fashionable, well-connected and moneyed Englishmen and their families who were making tours in Europe. The British Embassy at the Palazzo Sessa was comfortable and well-appointed. To quote Goethe, "The rooms which he (Sir William) has had furnished in the English style are most delightful, and the view from the corner room, perhaps, unique. Below you is the sea, with a view of Capri, Posillipo at your right, with the promenade of the Villa Reale between you and the grotto; on the left an ancient building which belonged to the Jesuits, and beyond it the coast stretching from Sorrento to Cape Minerva. Another prospect equal to this is scarcely to be found in Europe – at least, not in the centre of a great and populous city."

Emma had a great fuss made of her on her arrival and was taken round to see some of the sights within the first few days. Her lack of general education precluded her from taking overmuch interest in travel or in places, for in the letter she wrote to Greville four days after she had arrived, she says nothing whatever about her journey out from England. Parties and people, the grander the better, appealed to her much more, and, with her beauty, her fresh complexion and her youth, she was a sensation in Naples from the time she set foot in it. Bearing in mind that she writes with only four days' experience of her new surroundings, there can be little doubt that Emma wrote a great deal for effect and, like so many rather flamboyant young ladies, she wrapped her inexperience in a mass of self-confident overstatement. Even her professions of love for Greville which were naturally at this time still genuine, are given a somewhat theatrical flourish. She wrote:

Naples, April the 30th 1786.

My Dearest Greville,
    I arrived at this place the 26th & I should have begun to write sooner but the post does not go out tell to morro & I dreaded setting down to

write for I try to apear as chearful before Sr Wm. as I can & I am sure to cry the moment I think of you, for I feil more & more unhappy at being seperatted from you, & if my total ruin depends on seeing you, I will & must in the end of the sumer, for to live without you is impossible. I love you to that degree that at this time there is not a hardship opon hearth, either of poverty, hunger, cold, death, or even to walk barefooted to Scotland to see you, but what I would undergo. Therefore, my dear, dear Greville, if you do love me, for God sake & for my sake, try all you can to come hear as soon as possible. You have a true freind in Sr. Wm. and he will be happy to see you & do all he can to make you happy & for me, I will be everything you can wish for. I find it is not either a fine horse or a fine coach or a pack of servants or plays or operas can make me happy, it is you that as it in your power, either to make me very happy, or very miserable. I respect Sr. Wm. I have a great regard for him as the uncle & freind of you & he loves me, Greville, but he can never be any thing nearer to me than your Uncle & my sincere freind, he never can be my lover. You do not know how good Sr. Wm. is to me, he is doing every thing he can to make me happy, he as never dined out since I came hear & endead to spake the truth he is never out of my sight, he breakfastes, dines, supes, & is constantly by me, looking in my face, I cant stir a hand, a legg, or foot but what he is marking as graceful & fine & I am sorry to say it, but he loves me now as much as ever he could Lady Bolingbroke,[10] endead, I am sorry, for I canot make him happy, I can be civil, oblidging, & I do try to make my self as agreable as I can to him, but I belong to you, Greville & to you onely will I belong & nobody shall be your heir apearant. You do not know how glad I was to arrive hear the day I did, as it was my Birthday & I was very low spirited. Oh God, that day that you used to smile on me & stay at home & be kind to me, that that day I should be at such a distance, but my comfort is I rely on your promise & September or October I shall see you, but I am quite unhappy at not hearing from you, no letter for me yet Greville, but I must wait with patience. We have had company most every day since I came, some of Sr Wm's freinds. They are all very much pleased with me & poor Sir W. is never so happy as when he is pointing out my beauties to them. He thinks I am grown much more ansome than I was, he does nothing all day but look at me & sigh. Yes, last night we had a little concert, but then I was low, for I wanted you to partake of our amusement. Sr Thomas Rumbold[11] is hear with is son who is dying of a decline, it is a son he had by is first wife & poor young man, he canot walk from the bed to the chair & Lady Rumbold, like a tender hearted rretch is gone to Rome to pass her time there with the English & as took the coach &

all the English servants with her & left poor Sr Thomas hear with is heart broken waiting on is sick son. You cant think what a worthy man he is, he dind with ous & likes me very much & every day as brought is carridge or phaeton, which he as bought hear, & carried me & my mother & Sr W. out & shows ous a deal of civelaties, for you are to understand I have a caridge of Sr. Ws, a English one painting & new livereys & new coach man, foot man & the same as Mrs Damer for of her own, for she did not go with us. If I was going abbout in is carridge they would say I was either is wife or mistress, therefore as I am not or ever can be either, we have made a very good establishment of 4 rooms very pleasant, looking to the sea, our boat comes out to day for the first time & we shall begin to bathe in a day or two & we are going for one day or two to Caserta. I was at Pasilipo yesterday, I think it a very pretty place. Sr W. as given me a camels shawl like my old one. I know you will be pleased to hear that & he as given me a beautiful goun, cost 25 guineas, India painting on wite sattin, & several little things of Lady Hamiltons & is going to by me some muslin dresses loose to tye with a sash for the hot weather, made like the turkey dresses, the sleeves tyed in fowlds with ribban & trimed with lace, in short he is all ways contriving what he shall get for me. The people admires my English dresses, but the blue hat, Greville, pleases most. Sr W. is quite enchanted with it. Oh, how he loves you. He told me he had made is will & left you every thing belonging to him; that made me very happy for your sake. Pray, my dear Greville, do write me word if you want any money. I am affraid I distressd you but I am sure Sr W. will send you some & I told him he must help you a little now & send you some for your jurney hear & he kissd me & the tears came into is eyes & told me I might comand any thing for he loved ous boath dearly & oh, how happy shall I be when I can once more see you, my dear, dear Greville. You are every thing that is dear to me on hearth & I hope happier times will soon restore you to me for endead I would rather be with you starving, than from you in the greatest splender in the world. I have onely to say I enclose this I wrote yesterday & I will not venture myself now to wright any more for my mind & heart is so torn by differant passions that I shall go mad, onely Greville, remember your promise, October. Sr Wm. says you never mentioned to him abbout coming to Naples at all, but you know the consequence of your not coming for me. Endead, my dear Greville, I live but on the hope of seeing you & if you do not come hear, lett what will be the consequence, I will come to England. I have had a conversation this morning with Sr Wm. that has made me mad. He speaks half I do not know what to make of it, but Greviile, my dear Greville, wright some comfort to me, pray do, if you love me, but onely remember you will never be loved by any body like your affectionate & sencere

Emma

P.S. Pray, for God sake wright to me & come to me, for Sr W. shall never be any thing to me but your freind.

In order to assess Emma's true feelings when she had become installed under Sir William's wing at Naples, it is essential to read as much between the lines of her letters to Greville as along them. She had plenty of time for letter writing, and, according to her, when she wrote on 22nd July, she had already written "fourteen" letters to him. This may be a figure of speech or a statement of fact, but whichever is the case, no letters have been preserved. Writing now, three months after her arrival, she announces that she has been away from him "going of six months" (actually no more than five) and launches into a great deal of sentiment about missing him and beseeches "my much loved Greville" to let her have "onely one line from your dear, dear hands".

"As soon as I know your determination", she writes, "I shall take my own mesures. If I dont hear from you & that you are coming according to promise, I shall be in England by Cristmas at farthest, dont be unhappy at that, I will see you once more for the last time. I find life is unsuportable with out you. Oh my heart is intirely broke. Then for God sake, my ever dear Greville, do write mee some comfort. I dont know what to do, I am now in that state I am incapable of any thing". Throughout her life she is very prone to echoing the "what shall I dow?" theme that she started after her dismissal from Up Park. It seems to appeal to her sense of the melodramatic, but what she really appears to be missing in Naples is the feeling of security that she had in Edgware Row and this becomes evident as she continues, "I have a language master, a singing master, musick, etc, etc, but what is it for, if it was to amuse you I should be happy, but Greville, what will it avail me. I am poor, helpeless & forlorn. I have lived with you 5 years & you have sent me to a strange place & no one prospect, me thinking you was coming to me; instead of which I was told I was to live, you know how, with Sir W. No. I respect him, but no, never, shall he peraps live with me for a little wile like you & send me to England, then what am I to do, what is to become of me."

The second half of this letter does not give the impression that she is quite so "forlorn" as she would have Greville believe. She continues:

If I have spirits, I will tell you something concerning how we go on, that will make my letter worth paying for. Sr Wm. wants a picture of me the sise of the Bacante for his new appartments & he will take that picture of me in the Black gown at Romneys & I have made the bargain with him that the picture shall still be yours if he will pay for it & he will & I have wrote to Romney to send it. Their is two painters now in the house painting me; one picture is finished. It is the size of the Bacante setting in a turbin, a turkish dress, the other is in a black rubin hat with fethers, blue silk gown etc. but as soon as these is finished ther is two more to paint me & Angelaca[12] if she comes, & Marchmont is to cut a head of me for a ring. I wish Angelaca would come for Prince Draydrixton (Dietrichstein) from Veina is hear & dines with ous often & he wants a picture of me – he is my cavaliere servente or chechespeo which you like. He is much in love with me. I walk in the Villa Reale every night, I have generally two princes, two or 3 nobles, the English minister & the King, with a crowd beyound ous. The Queen likes me much & desired Prince Draydrixton to walk with me near her, that she might get a sight of me, for the Prince when he is not with ous, he is with the Queen & he does notthing but entertains her with my beauty, the accounts of it etc. etc. But Greville, the King as eyes, he as a heart & I have made an impression on his heart, but he told the Prince, Hamilton is my freind & she belongs to his Nephey, for all our freinds knows it and the Prince desires his best compliments to you. I must tell you a peice of gallantry of the K. on Sunday. He dined at Paysilipo & he allways comes every Sunday before the Casina in his boat to look at me—we had a small deplomatic party & we was sailing in our boat. The K. directly came up, put his boat of musick next us & made all the French horns & the wole band play, he took off his hat & sett with his hat on his knees all the wile & when we was going to land, he made his bow & said it was a sin he could not speak English, but I have him every night in my train at the Villa or oppera etc. etc.

(Here the letter stops and is continued later in the day)

I have been to Pompea etc. etc, and we are going next week round the Islands Corprea, Ischea, Sormenta etc. etc. We shall be a whay a little wile. I should feil pleasure in all this if you was heare, but that blessing I have not & so I must make the best of my lot. God bless you, I would write a longer letter but I am going to Paysylipo to diner & I have a conversazyeone to night & a concert. I bathe every day. I have not any irruptions & what will surprise you I am remarkably fair that every body says I put on red & wite. We have no English hear but Lord

52

Hervey who is a lover of mine. I had a letter from Sr. Thomas Rumbold last week who is coming hear in October & desired me to write him what I wanted from England & he would bring it me. I am pleased with the fate of Fitzgerald,[13] it shews the very little partialty they have in England for the rich. In Naples he would not have suffered. "We have had dreadful thunder & lightenen; it fell at the Malteese minister just by our house & burnt is beds & wines etc. etc. I have now perswaded Sr. Wm. to put up a conducter to his house; the lava runs a little but the mountain is very ful & we expect an irruption every day. I must stop or else I should begin & tell you my ideas of the people of Naples, in my next I will. But Greville, flees, & lice their is millions. I shall write you an Italian letter soon. God bless you. Make my compliments to your brother & all your freinds thats my freinds. Pray write to yors ever, with the truist & sincere affecton

Emma

God bless you write, my ever dear, dear Greville.

To Emma, who was naturally in complete ignorance of the state of affairs in Naples, the magnificence of the Court, the balls, the levees and the entertainments in general seemed impressive indeed. King Ferdinand was to her a "King" without qualifications. She did not see him, for instance, with the eyes of Mrs Piozzi, who commented, "This prince lives among his subjects with the old Roman idea of a window before his bosom, I believe. They know the worst of him is that he shoots at birds, dances with the girls, eats macaroni, and helps himself to it with his fingers, and rows against the watermen in the bay, till one of them burst out o'bleeding at the nose last week with his uncourtly efforts to outdo the king, who won the trifling wager by this accident – conquered, laughed, and leaped on shore, amidst the acclamations of the populace, who huzzaed him home to the palace, from whence he sent double the sum he had won to the waterman's wife and children, with other tokens of kindness. Meantime, while he resolves to be happy himself, he is equally determined to make no man miserable... .The truth is the jolly Neapolitans lead a coarse life; but it is an unoppressed one."

Ferdinand III of Sicily and IV of Naples and the I of the two Sicilies was, in fact, boorish and not over-intelligent. He left the management of the kingdom entirely to his queen, Maria Carolina, a sister of Marie Antoinette, who took her duties very seriously, and considered her husband as a "right good fool". Hunting was the king's great passion and these expeditions he organised to the point, one might say, of animal massacres. Sir William, who was himself fond of shooting and was expected to attend the royal hunting parties, considered Ferdinand's sport nearer to carnage, and in consequence, distasteful. He had frequently seen, he said, a heap entirely composed of offal or bowels reaching as high as his head and many feet in circumference. "The King," he told Wraxall, "rarely misses a shot; but when he is tired with killing, then commences another operation. He next dissects the principal pieces of game, of which he sends presents to favoured courtiers, or distributes it among his attendants. In order to perform this part of the diversion, he strips, puts on a flannel dress, takes the knife in hand, and, with inconcievable dexterity cuts up the animal. No carcass-butcher in Smithfield can exceed him in anatomical ability; but he is frequently besmeared with blood from head to foot before he has finished, and exhibits an extraordinary spectacle, not easily imagined."

To judge from her portraits, the Queen had austere though well-bred features, but Lady Anne Miller describes her as follows: "Her Majesty is a beautiful woman, she has the finest and most transparent complexion I ever saw; her hair is of that glossy light chestnut I so much admire; it is by no means red; her eyes are large, brilliant, and of a dark blue, her eyebrows exact and darker than her hair, her nose inclining to the aquiline, her mouth small, her lips very red (not of the Austrian thickness), her teeth beautifully white and even, and when she smiles she discovers two dimples, which give a finishing sweetness to her whole countenance; her shape is perfect: she is just plump enough not to appear lean; her neck is long, her deportment easy, her walk majestic, her attitudes and action graceful." Maria Carolina was not quite so perfect as Lady Anne Miller thought but, at any rate, she was quite attractive and decidedly animated. She had a large family, and when not occupied with looking after it, or attending to matters of state with the assistance of her Minister of the Marine and of War, Sir John Acton (an English soldier of fortune whose adventurous career had deposited him in Naples), she found time for an intrigue or two amongst her courtiers. In view of the close attachment she was later to have for Emma, and to the exaggerated gossip that circulated about this friendship, it may be well to state that the Queen was by nature given to having intimate women friends, though not, as Napoleon later suggested, to the point of lesbianism. Before Emma's time, the Princess of Belmonte and the Marchesa di San Marco had both been close favourites.

Just over a week after her last letter to Greville, Emma wrote to him again in much the same strain. She was still berating him for his apparent indifference, while seeing herself just a little as a tragedy queen, and she provides, as before, an interesting insight into her activities; but in the postscript there is the very first warning of things to come. The idea of *making* Sir William marry her is not at all what one would have expected from the good-natured Emma of the Edgware Row period. Generosity was a trait that never deserted her, but the sweetness in her character was to diminish gradually as time went on. After only four months in her new surroundings, she was beginning to appreciate the greater sense of freedom, the added importance and the insidious attraction of continuous flattery. At this moment of writing she might still have been willing to resume a quiet life with Greville, had the opportunity been offered, but she was very soon to pass that point. She wrote:

Naples, 1st of August 1786.

I have received your letter, my dearest Greville, at last, and you dont know how happy I am at hearing from you, however I may like some parts of your letter, but I wont complain, it is enough I have paper that Greville as wrote on, he as foldet up, he wet the wafer – happy wafer, how I envy thee to take the place of Emmas lips, that she would give worlds had she them, to kiss those lips, but if I go on in this whay I shall be incapable of writing. I onely wish that a wafer was my onely rival, but I submit to what God & Greville pleases. I allways knew, I have ever had a forebodeing, since I first begun to love you, that I was not destined to be happy, for their is not a King or prince on hearth that could make me happy without you; so onely consider when I offer to live with you on the hundred a year Sir Wm. will give me, what can you desire, and this from a girl that a King etc, etc, etc, is sighing for. As to what you write to me to oblidge Sr. Wm. I will not answer you for Oh if you knew what pain I feil in reading those lines whare you advise me to W.... . nothing can express my rage, I am all madness, Greville, to advise me, you that used to envy my smiles, now with cooll indifferance to advise me to go to bed to him, Sr. Wm. Oh, thats worst of all, but I will not, no I will not rage for if I was with you, I would murder you & myself boath. I will leave of & try to get more strength for I am now very ill with a cold.

I wont look back to what I wrote. I onely say I have had 2 letters in 6 months nor nothing shall ever do for me but going home to you. If that is not to be, I will except of nothing, I will go to London, their go in to every exess of vice, tell I dye a miserable broken hearted wretch & leave my fate as a warning to young whomin never to be two good, for, now you have made me love you, made me good, you have abbandoned me & some violent end shall finish our connexion if it is to finish, but, Oh Greville, you cannot, you must not give me up, you have not the heart to do it, you love me I am sure & I am willing to do everything in my power that you shall require of me & what will you have more and I onely say this the last time, I will either beg or pray, do as you like.

I am sorry Lord Brook[14] is dead and I am sinecerly sorry for Sr James & Lady Peachey, but the W- - - - -k family wont mind it much. We have been 7 weeks in doupt wether he was dead or no for Sr. Wm. had a letter from Lord Warwick & he said Lord B. was better, so I suppose he must have had a relapse. Poor little boy, how I envy him his happiness. We have a deal of rain hear & violent winds, the oldest people hear never remember such a sumer, but it is luckey for us. The Queen is very poorly with a cold caught in the Villa Reale & mine is pretty much like it. We dont dine at Passylipo today on the account of my cold. We are closely besieged by the K. in a round a bout maner, he comes every Sunday to P- - - - - -po but we keep the good will of the other party mentioned abbove & never gives him any encouragement. Prince Draydrixton's our constant freind, he allways enquiries after you, he desires his compliments to you; he speaks English, he says I am a dymond of the first waiter & the finest creature on the hearth, he attends me to the Bath, to the walk etc. etc. etc. I have such a head ake today with my cold I dont know what to do. I shall write next post by Sr. Wm, onely I cant lett a week go without telling you how happy I am at hearing from you. Pray write as often as you can & come as soon as you can & if you come we shall all go home to England in 2 years & go throug Spain & you will like that. Pray write to me & dont write in the stile of a freind but a lover, for I wont hear a word of a freind, it shall be all love & no freindship. Sr. Wm is our freind, but we are lovers. I am glad you have sent me a Blue Hat & gloves; my hat is universaly admired through Naples. God bless you, my dear Greville prays your ever truly and affectionate

Emma Hart

P.S. Pray write for nothing will make me so angry & it is not to your interest to disoblidge me, for you dont know the power I have hear, onely I never will be his mistress. If you affront me, I will make him marry me. God bless you for ever.

In October, Greville was still concerning himself with Emma's ultimate fate. He clearly did not visualise her staying with his uncle indefinitely and he was a little worried as to how she should be settled when she returned to England. Sir William had evidently shown no intention of allowing the affair to become in any way permanent either, for Greville says, "Your proposed provision exceeds your promise..." Later on in the same letter he continues:

"But you have now rendered it possible for her to be respected & comfortable, & if she has not talked herself out of the true view of her situation she will retain the protection & affection of us both. For, after all, consider what a charming creature she would have been if she had been bless'd with the advantages of an early education & had not been spoilt by indulgence of every caprice... . If she will put me on the footing of a friend, which she says I always have assumed, she will write to me fairly on her plans, she will tell me her thoughts, & her future comfort shall be my serious concern; but she must not think that I can resume that close connexion, & live as I did with her. In the first place I cannot afford it; in the next, it would keep me out of the world, & would ruin me & herself; whereas, if she acts wisely and kindly to herself & to me, she will take up a new line, live independant, & consult me as a friend, & either settle for life or adopt any line which she shall see is favourable & agreable... . The plan I propose is to make Mr Rornney her trustee, & vest your grant in him for her benefit; & I will consider further & write to you when I have form'd my opinion, & it will be much better that the plan is generally discussed & aproved before it is executed; it is her peace & comfort, & not those of caprice or convenience which I consider, & I shall not be obliged to vary one sentiment I ever impressed on her mind; all that I have to shew is that the period I long ago foretold has arrived, & that her pride need not suffer by its arrival, because the sentiments with which I began with her were less favorable than those I part with, & either were sufficient to make me interested in her welfare; & altho' I am firm in my resolutions, I ever wish to sacrifice much temper to avoid the use of it; for with women it is cruelty to act with the necessary firmness which the intercourse of business with men requires; & when she has the provision you give her fix't, she has her carrier (career) open either of retirement or of the world". In a further long letter to Sir William written a month later, he goes over much the same ground again, moralising rather tediously on the ways of women, and concluding with his view that, "Without any other plan she must wait events, & the difficulty will be to reject improper offers; &, if a journey homewards should give a favorable one, it should not be lost; but, at any rate, she will have the good sense not to expose herself with any boy of family; she must look to from 25 to 35, & one who is his own master."

Sir William was happy enough with things as they were. In July of that year he added a postscript to a letter to his friend, Sir Joseph Banks:[15] "A beautiful plant called *Emma* has been transplanted here from England & at least has not lost any of its beauty."

In September, he added a further comment:

"My visitor, for you must know I have *one*, is as handsome as ever & in tolerable spirits considering all – it is a bad job to come from the Nephew to the Uncle but one must make the best of it & I long to see poor Charles out of his difficulties."

At the end of December and during the first few weeks of the New Year (1787) Sir William was away on one of the royal hunting parties. Emma's letters to him both by their frequency and their content leave no room for doubt that the uncle had now supplanted the nephew in her affections. As Sir William was perhaps too kind to take her to task for her spelling, she let it rip. She writes first from Caserta where the royal family had their out-of-town palace.

December 26th 1786. Caserta.

Pray don't scold me for writing to you, for endead I can't help it, and I should have been ashamed to have wrote to you without an excuse for doing it, therefore Smith as returned the letter I sent to town, & I told Cottier that I would send it you, or else he might think I was so much in love I could not be 3 days without sending to you. But lett them think if he will; certain it is I love you & sincerely & endead I am appreensive two much for my own quiet, but lett it be. Love as its pleasures & its pains; for instance, yesterday when you went a whey from me, I thought all my heart and soul was torn from me, and my greif was excessive I assure you; to-day I am better, perche the day after to moro is friday & then I shall have you with me to make up for past pain. I shall have much pleasure and comfort, and my mind tells me you will have much pleasure to come home to me again, and I will setle you & comfort you. Pray excuse this scrall, for I expect Garly and I have wrote in a great hurry. Don A. and Hackert & Garly was here yesterday night. I saw Greffer[16] yesterday, and he said he would come this evening to play wist, but I would rather play this evening at *all fours* with you; – oh! I forgot, cribige is our game, it's all the same, you like crib. Adio, my dear Sir William; laying jokes aside, there is nothing I assure you can give me the least comfort tell you come home. I shall receive you with smiles, affection and good humer, & think had I the offer of crowns I would refuse them and except you, and I don't care if all the world knows it. If sometimes I am out of humer, forgive me, tell me, put me in a whey to be grateful to you for you(r) kindness to me, and believe me I never will abuse your kindness to me, and in a little time all faults will be corrected. I am a pretty whoman, and one can't be everything at once; but now I have my wisdom teeth I will try to be ansome and reasonable. God bless you, my ever dear friend, etc, etc, etc, etc, and believe me yours and onely yours for ever sincerly.

P.S. It thrives.
Do write 3 lines to me, and come home soon.

Naples. January 5th 1787.

I shall begin to write to you to night for the post goes of so early in the morning that we are scarce out of bed, and of a evening I am alone after 7 a clock and I feel it a pleasure to wright to you. Mr King and Lady Lanesborough[17] is gone of and nobody can tell as yet how the got a passport, but the day after the was gone Tierny received a letter from his banker with an order to pay half yearly pay to Lady L., and she was to sign the receipt, but he was not to lett them run any further. So the are gone, and Tierney is still in the lurch, for he cannot pay himself except she had signd to him, but the are gone this 3 days; the owe your taylor ninety ducats, besides General Acton's cook and many other people, and Tieniey, Clark, etc, etc, etc. In short, there innumerable villanys is more than I am able to recount to you onely, I believe you are the onely person that has acted towards them with good sence, and you have done perfectly right, and indead your foresights in this was lucky, or what trouble you might have had, but you allways do right in everything.

Curney or Cuney, your man, as been with me and beg'd you will write to Gasperino to speak to the Matre d'Hotel of the Marquis Sestes – I can't spell this names write – and tell him he shall not rise his rent nor turn him out, for he wants C. to pay him more rent or turn out, and he pays him now a great deal for his rooms, besides fifteen Carleens a year more towards the balcony, and Curney is quite distressed and he begs you will onely write 3 lines to Gasperino and it will be settled, for that fellow must be the nastys creature living, after the benefit he has had from you, to go to impose on that poor man for the sake of a few ducats more.

Satturday morning: I had Hackert, Gatty & Donker last night. Hackert was ful dres'd going to Skarvonskys. Last night the Duke of

Glouster[18] was to be there to some musick, but not the Dutches nor the children.

Gatty[19] has had it from a whoman abbout Court that the queen is very dissatisfied with the Dutches of G. for her pride and her imprudent taulk. She told the queen that when she was at Millan her son was quite in love with the Archdutches, and in every corner every day was kissing her when her father and mother was in England and on their tour, and likewise the Archduches was in love with the Prince, and would kiss his lips and smack them, and they was much together. So the queen said to her whomen, what kind of people must the A.D. have abbout her in the absence of her parents, and she did not understand kissing there lips and all that, and it was a pitty but her people was removed. But the D of G. did ceartainly speak imprudently, don't you think so? I don't wonder the Q. does not like her; for a whoman of the queen's sence and understanding to see her behave so proud, and then when she did speak to speak such stuf, I don't wonder at her not liking her. Gatty had it from the first hands, and you have it as I had it from him. He sends his compliments to you, and everybody that knows you does the same. The French Ambassador had his house on fire last night; one room was very much on fire, and if they had not got timely assistance it would have gone bad with them.

I have just received your kind letter. I am glad you had such sport. I wish I had been at your post, I should like to see you shoot, tho' I am afraid I should have two much compassion. But I hope you will every day have luck to repay you for the loss of my kisses. God bless you, my dearest dear Sir W., and believe me yours, more then my own or any person's else, sincerely and affectionately.

January 8th 1787

I don't know how you like this excessive cold wether; but I do think I never felt much colder in Inghilterra; for to-day it was impossible to keep one's self warm; and I pittied you much, for if you have not a good sport you must be frose with standing still. The ice is lying abbout the streets in Naples, just as it is in London the hardest frosts there is. I now see that every thing you say is true: for you told me to stop tell Jany, and then I should fell, and to-day as fuly proved it.

I was at Coletalino's today. She will make a very great likeness and very pretty it will be. It shall not be two naked, for it would not be so interesting, and as you will have it in a box, it will be seen a great deal, and those beautys that only you can see shall not be exposed to the common eyes of all, and wile you can even more than see the originals, others may gess at them, for the are sacred to all but you, and I wish the wos better for your sake. But I should not know how to mend them if I could tho' you don't like sugar loaves.

Mr Greffer was here yesterday and 2 of his children. He enquired for you abbout money, and I told him, if he could stop or go to Borch or Marn Bem (?), but he says he will make shift tell he sees you, and I think he is right, if he can, for I would not go to those creatures for a grain, tho' it is a pitty you should be trubled with them. – Skaveranky gives a diner to-morro to all his musick people, even the harpscord tuner, at Torre-del-Greco. All the Coletalinos go there, and I fancy there will be a fine mess of them altogether, for I don't hear of any body of fashion that is going. But he will be master of the Band, and the will flatter him, and he will be in his kingdom come. It is a pitty he is so od, for I believe he as a good heart. He has given Hackert the finest new sattin dress lined with sable, besides a hundred guineas a-pece for 2 little pictures, that I should think twenty enough for them, for I am of your opinion, I would pay for good things, but not for bad ones, and the are pretty but not fine painting.

I have Galluchy from nine to ten, from ten to twelve at the Coletalinos, from twelve to one my lesson, and between 2 and 3 my diner. I dine frequently upstairs, for Gasperino said a fire in that room must be to air it well, and the diner is cold before it gets to our room. So I have my diner very comfortable endead. For if you was to know how kind everybody behaves to me, you would love them.

Tuesday morn: – I have just received your kind letter, my dear Sir Wm. But how I was frightened in reading abbout those men. Sure they wont die. Oh Lord! endead I never will bite your lips nor fingers no more. Good God! What a passion the must have been in, but there ought to be some punishment to prevent them from such dreadful work. I am sorry you had not any sport. To stay out in the cold yesterday must be enugh to kill you. How I wish'd to give you some warm punch, and settle you in my arms all night, to make up for your bad day.

I wish you would tell me something to say to Cune or Curney your man, in answer to what I wrote to you, or will you write to Gasperino to tell Sesos Maitre d'Hotel the shall not take his room from him. I am sorry to trouble you. But, as he asked me, I could not denigh to write to you. Adio and believe me, Yours, etc.

P.S. – I am sorry you don't hear of coming home. But patienzza.

January 10th 1787

I had hardly time to thank you for your kind letter of this morning, as I was buisy prepairing for to go on my visit to the Convent of S. Romita; and endead I am glad I went, tho' it was a short visit. But tomorrow I dine with them in full assembly. I am quite charmed with Beatrice Acquaviva. Such is the name of the charming whoman I saw to-day. Oh, Sir William, she is a pretty whoman. She is 29 years old. She took the veil at twenty, and does not repent to this day, though, if I am a judge in physiognomy, her eyes does not look like the eyes of a nun. They are airways laughing, and something in them vastly alluring, and I wonder the men of Naples would suffer the onely pretty whoman who is realy pretty to be shut in a convent. But it is like the mean-spirited ill taste of the Neapolitans. I told her I wondered how she would be lett to hide herself from the world, and I dare say thousands of tears was shed the day she deprived Naples of one of its greatest ornaments. She answered with a sigh, that endead numbers of tears was shed, and once or twice her resolution was allmost shook, but a pleasing comfort she felt at regaining her friends, that she had been brought up with, and religious considerations strengthened her mind, and she parted with the world with pleasure, and since that time one of her sisters had followed her example, and another – which I saw – was preparing to enter soon. But neither of her sisters is so beautiful as her, tho' the are booth very agreable. But I think Beatrice is charming, and I realy feil for her an affection. Her eyes, Sir William, is I don't know how to describe them. I stopt one hour with them, and I had all the good things to eat, and I promise you they don't starve themselves. But there dress is very becoming, and she told me that she was allowed to wear rings and mufs and any little thing she liked, and endead she displayd today a good deal of finery, for she had 4 or 5 dimond rings on her fingers, and seemed fond of her muff. She has excellent teeth and shows them, for she is allways laughing. She kissed my lips, cheeks and forehead, and every moment exclaimed "charming fine creature", admired my dress, said I looked like an angel, for I was in clear white dimity and a blue sash. She admired my hat and fine hair, and she said she had heard I was good to the poor, and generous and noble minded. "Now", she says, "it would be worth wile to live for such a one as you. Your good heart would melt at any trouble that befel me, and partake of one's greef or be equaly happy at one's good fortune. But I never met with a freind yet, or I ever saw a person I could love tell now, and you shall have proofs of my love". In short I sat and listened to her, and the tears stood in my eyes, I don't know why; but I loved her at that moment. I thought what a charming wife she would have made, what a mother of a family, and what a freind, and the first good and amiable whoman I have seen since I came to Naples for to be lost to the world – how cruel! She gave me a sattin pocketbook of her own work, and bid me think of her, when I saw it and was many miles far of; and years hence when she peraps should be no more, to look at it, and think the person that give it had not a bad heart. Did she not speak very pretty? but not one word of religion; but I shall be happy today, for I shall dine with them all, and come home at night. It is a beautiful house and garden, and the attention of them was very pleasing. There is sixty whomen and all well-looking, but not like the fair Beatrice. "Oh Emma", she says to me, "the brought here the Viene minister's wife, but I did not like the looks of her at first. She was little, short pinch'd face, and I received her cooly. How different from you, and how surprised was I in seeing you tall in statue. We may read your heart in your countenance, your complexion, in short, your figure and features is rare, for you are like the marble statues I saw, when I was in the world". I think she flattered me up, but I was pleased. –

Thursday morning: I have just receved your kind letter, and I am pleased and content that you should write to me, tho' it is onely one or two lines a day. Be assured I am grateful. I am sorry you had bad sport, and I shall be most happy to see you at home, to warm you with my kisses, and comfort you with my smiles and good humer, and oblidge you by my attentions, which will be the constant pleasure of, my Dear Sir William, your truly affectionate, etc.

P.S. Cuny's duty to you, and thanks abbout the Marquis Sesos – (you may look big upon it.)

Naples, Sunday Night, January (17)87.

Endead, my Sir Wm, I am angry. I told you one line would satisfie me, and when I have no other comfort then your letters, you should not so cruely disapoint me; for I am unhappy, and I don't feil right without hearing from you, and I won't forgive you; no, that I won't. It is a very cold night, and I am just returned from Hart's. He was very civil to me; there was an Abbé and a very genteel man, a friend of Andreas, and an Englishman I did not know; but they was all very polite, and such a profusion of diner that it is impossible to describe. I sett next to Hart, who would help me to every thing, and poor man could not see, but to the best of his power paid me a number of compliments, and produced me as a specimen of English beauty. After diner he, fetched an Italian song, that was made on Lady Sophi Ferner fourty years past, and he had translated it to English and would sing it; and when he came to dymond eyes and pearl teeth, he looked at me and bid the others look at me; and he is going to dedicate the English to me, and oh! you can't think, just as if he could see me, and as if I was the most perfect beauty in the world. Endead, I heard the Abbé say to the others I was perfectly beautiful and elagantly behaved in my manners and conversation. And so the all admired me. But Hart is quite gone. He is come to see me to-night. Poor Tierny is very poorly.

Monday morning: Oh, thank you, my dear Sir William, for your letter. Endead, I forgive you and am sorry I scolded you. The wind made me so sleepy that I slept till eight a clock, and was fast asleep when Vinchenzo brought your letter, and I read it in bed, and gave it a good hug. But I wished you had been there. But I gave it a kiss or 2. But I hope you will believe me sencere when I write to you; for endead, everything flows from my heart, and I cannot stop it. I am glad you had some good sport. I should like to see that that is 200 weight, for it must be a fine one; but the other 2, that got of wounded, the must be somewere in great pain. Adio, my dear Sir William. Lying in bed so long as made me hurry as this goes in half a minet. I was in bed last night at 8 a clock and slept till eight this morning.

(January 18th 1787) "Monday Morning"

Oh, my dearest Sir William, I have just received your dear sweet letter. It has charmed me. I don't know what to say to you to thank you in words kind enough. Oh, how kind! Do you call me your dear freind? Oh, what a happy creature is your Emma! – me that had no freind, no protector, no body that I could trust, and now to be the freind, the Emma, of Sir William Hamilton! Oh, if I could express my self! if I had words to thank you, that I may not thus be choaked with meanings, for which I can find no utterance! Think only, my dear Sir William, what I would say to you, if I could express myself, only to thank you a thousand times. Mr Hart went awhay yesterday with his head turn'd; I sung so well Handell's 3 songs, Picini, Paisiello, etc, that you never saw a man so delighted. He said it was the most extraordinary thing he ever knew. But what struck him was holding on the notes and going from the high to low notes so very neat. He says I shall turn the heads of the English. He was so happy with Gallucci. He made great frendship with him. Gallucci played solo some of my solfegos and you whold have thought he would have gone mad. He says he had heard a great deal of me. But he never saw or heard of such a whoman before. He

64

says when he first came in, I frightened him with a Majesty and Juno look that I receved him with. Then he says that whent of on being more acquainted, and I enchanted him by my politeness and the manner in which I did the honors, and then I made him allmost cry with Handels; and with the comick he could not contain himself, for he says he never saw the tragick and comick muse blended so happily together. He says Garrick would have been delighted with me. I suppose he makes to-day a fine work all over Naples. But your ideas of him are the same as mine. We boath think alike of him. He taulks too much for me.

I hope you have received the letter and news I sent you yesterday. I told you Gatty is here. He is enchanted with me. He says I sing to please him better than anybody. He says the progress I make he could not have believed. He sat and listened with so much pleasure, and his neice was very much pleased. She is gone to Don Andrea's house. Gatty is here, and he says I am so accomplishd, so kind, speaks Italian so well, that he sitts 2 hours together and taulks to me. Him and Don Andrea dines with me today. I thought as you was not at home that Don Andrea would be company for him. His neice dined with us yesterday. But today she is to dine with the wife of Don A-, and the are to come in the evening to hear me sing. Yours, etc.

"Caserta, Thursday Morning" (1787)

I can't be happy till I have wrote to you, my dearest Sir William, tho' it is so lattely I saw you. But what of that to a person that loves as I do. One hour's absence is a year, and I shall count the hours and moments till Saturday, when I shall find myself one more in your kind dear arms, my dear Sir William, my friend, my All, my earthly Good, every kind name in one, you are to me eating, drinking and cloathing, my comforter in distress. Then why shall I not love you? Endead, I must and ought, whilst life is left in me, or reason to think on you. I believe it is right I should be separated from you sometimes, to make me know myself, for I don't know till you are absent how dear you are to me: and I wont tell you how many tears I shed for you this morning, and even now I can't stop them, for in thinking of you my heart and eyes fill.

I have had a long walk since I wrote the other side, and feel better for it. I have had a long lesson, and am going now to have another, for musick quiets my mind, so that I shall study much tell I see you. I can't finish this subject tell I have thanked you, my dearest Sir William, for having given me the means of at least amusing myself a little, if in your absence I can be amused. I owe everything to you, and shall for ever with grattitude remember it. Pray, one little line, if you have time, just that I may kiss your name. I hope you will have had news from England. Take care of your dear self, and that is all that's requested from Yours, etc.

P.S. I send you a thousand kisses, and remember last night how happy you made me, and I tell you Satturday night I shall be happier in your presence unmixed with thoughts of parting.

A letter from his uncle (16 February 1787) made it clear to Greville that he need have no worries over Emma for the present.

"Our dear Em", wrote Sir William, "goes on now quite as I cou'd wish, improves daily, & is universally beloved. She is wonderfull, considering her youth & beauty, & I flatter myself that E. and her mother are happy to be with me, so that I see my every wish fulfilled."

For the next few years life was like a fairy story for Emma. Sir William, in spite of the disapproval of his nephew and also of his niece, Mrs Dickenson, had started to allow Emma to act as his hostess at the Embassy. A little to his surprise and greatly to his delight, she managed her duties very well. Her impulsive friendliness and her charm helped her to ride over any awkward situations, and the fact that she was eagerly learning Italian both flattered the Neapolitans and helped to distract attention from her imperfect command of her own language. Awe for the sudden heights to which she had risen acted as an invaluable controlling force. Had she been less impressed by the company surrounding her she would soon have become boisterous and probably tactless, but, as it was, with the exception perhaps of a few English visitors, all were delighted by her reticence, her grace and her beauty. The Queen, who must have been more than a little apprehensive when she learnt that the British Ambassador's mistress was being allowed her head, was pleased to find that she need have no worries, and went out of her way to show her approval. Emma, according to report, is supposed to have lent a deaf ear to tentative advances by King Ferdinand and to have informed the Queen of her predicament, thereby confirming her Majesty's good opinion of her.

The Duke of Gloucester, when visiting Naples, had been curious about what he had heard of Emma and in a note to Sir William, said, "You may depend upon us at Caserta about twelve on Sunday. I am sorry your little friend does not come to town today, but I hope you will bring her next week before I go, that I may have the pleasure of seeing her."

Greville had now dwindled in Emma's thoughts to the proportions of an old flame. She still looked back on the Edgware Road days with affection and she was happy to have a correspondent to whom she could pour out her tales of success and excitement. In August she wrote him an enormously long letter, at a time when she was as happy and as carefree as she was ever to be in her life.

Naples, Agosto 4 (1787)

Alltho you never think me worth writing to, yet I cannot so easily forget you and when ever I have had any particular pleasure, I feil as tho I was not right tell I had communicated it to my dearest Greville, for you will ever be dear to me and tho we cannot be to gether, lett ous corespond as freinds. I have a happiness in hearing from you and a comfort in communicating my little storieys to you, because I flatter myself that you still love the name of that Emma that was once very dear to you, and, but for unfortunate evels might still have claimed the first place in your affections, and I hope still you will never meet with any person that will use you ill, but never will you meet with the sincere love that I shew'd you, dont expect it for you canot meet with it, but I have done, onely think of my words, you will meet with more evels than one as Sir Wm. says, that one is the devile. We have been to Sorrento on a visit at the Duke Saint de Maitre for ten days. We are just returned, but I never passed a happier ten days, except Edg-re R-d. In the morning we bathed and returned to a fine sumer house where we breakfasted. But first this sumer house is on a rock over the sea that looks over Caprea, Ischea, Procheda, Vesuva, Porticea, Paysilipo, Naples etc, etc, etc, & the sea all before ous, that you have no idea of the beautes of it. From this little Paridise, after breakfast we vewd the lava running down 3 miles of Vesuvua and every now & then black clouds of smoak rising in to the air, had the most magnificent apearance in the world. I have made some drawings from it, for I am so used to draw now, it is as easey as a.b.c. For when we are at Naples we dine every day at Villa Emma at Paysilipo and I make 2 or 3 drawings. Sir William laughs at me and says I shall rival him with the mountains now. After breakfast I had my singing lession for Sir Wm. as took a mutton (musician) in to the house, but he is one of the best masters in Italia; after my lesson we rode on asses all about the Country, paid visits & dined at 3 and after diner saild about the coast, returned & dress'd for the conversazioni. We had Sir Wm's band of musick with ous, and about dark the concert in one room, and I satt in a nother & received all the nobility who came every night whilst we was there and I sung generally 2 searrous songs & 2 bufos, the last night I sang fifteen songs, one was a recatitive from a opera at St Carlos, the begining was Luci belle sio vadoro, the finest thing you ever heard, that for ten minutes after I sung it, their was such a claping that I was oblidged to sing it over again, and I sung after that one with a tambourin in the character of a young girl with a raire-shew, the pretist thing you ever heard, in short, I left the people at Sorrento with their heards turned. I left some dying, some crying & some in despair. Mind you theis was all nobility as proud as the Devil, but we humbled them. But what astonished them, was that I should speak such good Italian, for I paid them, I spared non of them, tho I was civil and oblidged every body, one asked me if I had left a love at Naples that I left them so soon, I pulld my lip at him, so says, I pray do you take me to be an Italian whoman that as four or five differant men to attend her. Look Sir, I am English, I have one cavelere servant & I have brought him with me, pointing to Sir Wm; but he never spoke a nother word after for before he had been offering him self as cavelere servante. He said I was una donna rara. We are going up Vesuvua to night, as there is a large eruption, and the lava runs down allmost to Porticea; the mountain looks beautiful. One part their is nothing but cascades of liquid fire, lava I mean, red hot, runs in to a deep cavern that it is beautiful, but I fancy we shall have some very large eruption soon, as large as that of 67: I wish we may. We dine to day at 2 a clock, so sett of at four. We shall get on our asses at Porticea and arrive at the top just at dark & so be at Naples abbout 2 a clock to morrow morning. Sir Wm. is very fond of me & very kind to me; the house is ful of painters painting me. He as now got nine pictures of me & 2 a painting: Marchant is cutting my head in stone, that is in camea for a ring, there is a nother man modeling me in wax & another in clay. All the artists is come from Rome to study from me that Sir Wm. as fitted up a room that is calld the painting room. Sir Wm. is never a moment from me. He goes no whare without me, he as no diners, but what I can be of the party, no body comes with out the are civil to me; we have allways good company. I now live up stairs in the same apartments whare he lives and my old apartments is made the musick rooms whare I have my lessions in the morning & our house at Caserta is fitting up elaganter this year, a room making for my musick and a room fitting up for my master as he goes with ous. Sir Wm. says he loves nothing but me, likes no person to sing but me and takes delight in all I do and all I say so we are happy.

Sunday morning.

We was last night up Vesuvus at twelve a clock and in my life I never saw so fine a sight. The lava runs a bout five mile down from the top, for the mountain is not burst as ignorant people say it is, but when we got up to the Hermitage there was the finest fountain of liquid fire falling down a great precipice & as it run down it sett fire to the trees and brush wood so that the mountain looked like one entire mountain of fire. We saw the lava suround the poor Hermits house & take possesion of the chapel not withstanding it was coverd with pictures of saints & other religios preservitaves against the fury of nature. For me I was inraptured. I could have staid all night there & I have never been in charity with the moon since for it looked so pale & sickly & the red hot lava served to light up the moon for the light of the moon was nothing to the lava. We met the Prince Royal on the mountain, but is foolish tuters onely took him up a little whay & did not lett him stay 3 minuets, so when we asked him how he liked it he said Bella ma poca roba when if the had took him five hundred yards higher he would have seen the noblest sublimest sight in the world, but poor creatures, the where frightened out of their sences & glad to make a hasty retreat. O I shall kill myselfe with laughing. Their has been a prince paying ous a visit. He is sixty years of age, one of the first families here and as allways lived at Naples & when I told him I had been to Caprea he asked me if I went their by land; onely think what ignorance. I staired at him and asked who was his tutor.

I left of in a hurry and as not wrote this ten days as we have been on a visit to the Countess Mahoney at Ische 9 days and are just returned from their. We went in a hired vessel & took all Sr Wms. musicians, my harpsicord & master, 4 servants & my maid. I think I never had such a pleasant voyage any where. The Countess came down to the sea shore to meet ous, she took me in her arms & kissd me, thanked Sir Wm. for bringing her the company of so beautiful & lovely whoman. She took ous to her house where there was a full conversazione & tho I was in a undress, onely having on a muslin chemise very thin, yet the admiration I met with was surprising. The Countess made me set by her & seemed to have pleasure to distinguish me by every mark of attention & the all allowd the never had seen such a belissima creature in all their life. I spoke Italian to most all, a little French to some that spoke to me in French. The obligded me to sing but I got such aplause that for ten minuets you could not hear a word. I sung four songs, two Rondos, a Duetto & a bravoro song of St Carlos. The Countess gave a great diner the day after to the noblesse of the place whare I was & in the evening an accadema of musick, where there was others sung, but I gott all the aplause again. I sung one little Italian air that the all cried, but one priest that whas their was so in love with me that Sir William was oblidged to give him my picture in a snuffbox & he carries the snuffbox in his breast:

this is a priest mind you. So everyday we stayd we had parties of pleasure & the poor Countess cried when we came a whay & I am now setting for a picture for her in a turkish dress, very pretty. I must tell you I have had great offers to be first whoman in the Italian opera at Madrid where I was to have six thousand pound for 3 years, but I would not engage as I should not like to go into Spain with out I knew people their & I could not speak their language, so I refused it & a nother reason was that Galini as been hear from the opera house at London to engage people & tho I have not been persuaded to make a written engagement, I ceartainly shall sing at the Pantheon & Hanover Square, except something perticuler happens for Galini says he will make a subscription concert for me if I wont engage for the Opera, but I wishd to consider of it before I engage. Sir William says he will give me leave to sing at Hanover Square on the condition Galini as proposed, which is 2 thousand pounds. Sir William as took my master in to the house & pays him a great price on purpose that he shall not teach any other person. Their was some of the oficers in Captain Finches ship that came to our concert whare I sung; they says Miss Hamilton is a fool in singing in comparison to me, & so says Sir William, but I dont know; it is a most extraoirdary thing that my voice is totaly alterd, it is the finest soprana you ever heard, that Sir William shuts his eyes & think one of the Castratos is singing & what is most extraordinary that my shake or tril, what do you call it, is so very good in every note, my master says that if he did not feil & see & no that I am a substance, he would think I was an angel. I have now gone through all difficculties. I solfega at first sight & in reccatative famous. Sir William is in raptures with me; he spares neither expence nor pains in any thing. Our house at Caserta is all new fitted up for me, a new room for my master, a musick room for me. I have my French master, I have the Queens dancing master 3 times a week, I have 3 lessons in singing a day, morning eight a clock, before dinner & the evening & people makes enterest to come & hear me; my master goes to England with ous & then I give up one hour in the day to reading the Italian, their is a person comes a purpose & for all this their is now five painters & 2 modlers at work on me for Sir Wm. & their is a picture going of me to the Empress of Russia, but Sir William as the phaeton at the door after I have had my first singing lesson & dancing & he drives me out for 2 hours & you will say thats right, for as I study a deal, it is right I should have excercise, but last night I did do a thing very extraordinary. We gave yesterday a deplomatic diner, so after diner I gave them a concert, so I sent the coach & my compliments to the Banti who is first whoman at St Carlos & desired her to come & sing at my concert, so she came & their was near sixty people, so after the first quartett I was to sing the first song; at first I was in a little fright before I begun, for she is a famous singer & she placed herself close to me, but when I begun all fear whent a whay & I sung so well that she cried out, just God, what a voice, I would give a great deal for your voice; in short, I met with such aplause that it allmost turned my head. The Banti sung one song after me and I asure you every body said I sung in a finer stile than her. Poor Sir Wm. was so inraptured with me, for he was afraid I should have been in a great fright and it was of consequence that evening for he wanted to shew me of to some Dutch officers that was there, that is with a sixty gun ship & a frigate. The Comodore whoes name is Melvile was so inchanted with me that tho he was to depart the next day, he put it of & gave me a diner on board that nealy surpasses all description. First Sir Wm. me & mother went down to the mole where the long boat was waiting, all mand so beautiful, their was a comodore & the Captain & four more of the first officers waited to conduct ous to the ship. The 2 ships was dresd out so fine in all the collours, the men all put in order a band of musick & all the marrine did their duty & when we went on board twenty peices of canon fired, but as we past the frigate she fired all her guns that I wish you had seen it; we sett down thirty to dine, me at the head of the table, mistress of the feast, drest all in virgin wite & my hair all in ringlets reaching all most to my heals. I assure you it is so long that I realy lookd and moved an angel, Sir Wm. said so. That night their was a great opera at St Carlos in honor of the King of Spains name day, so St Carlos was illumanated and every body in great galla. Well, I had the finest dress made up on purpose as I had a box near the K & Queen. My gown was purple sattin, wite sattin peticoat trimd with crape & spangles, my cap lovely from Paris, all wite fethers, my hair was to have been delightfully dressd as I have a very good hair dresser, but for me unfortunately, the diner on board did not finish tell half past five English, then the Comodore & Sr. Win. would have a nother bottle to drink to the Belle ocche of the loveliest whoman in the world as the cald me. At least, I wisperd to Sr. Wm. and told him I should be angry with him if he did not gett up to go as we was to dress & it was necessary to be at the theatre before the royal party so at last the put out the boat, so after a salute from the 2 ships of all the guns we arrived on shoar with the Comodore & five princapal officers and in we all crowd in one coach which is large. We just got in time to the opera, the Comodore went with ous and the officers came next and attended my box all the time and behaved to me as tho I was a Queen.

You must know this letter as been begun abbove 4 months and I have wrote a little at a time & I now finish from Caserta where we have been five weeks. We go to Naples the 28 of this month December and stay the Carnaval their & then return to this place. I believe we shall have a great erruption soon for tho we are here 16 miles from Naples yet yesterday the mountain made such a dreadful noise just like cannons in ones ears. Sir William & me was yesterday as endead we are every day at the Queens Garden and wilst Mr Greffer & me ware talking all of a sudin their rose such black collums of smoke out of Vesuvus attended with such roaring that I was frightened and last night I went on the leads of our house hear and the throughs was such that I could see Naples by the light of the fire very plain and after the throughs the red hot cinders fell all over the mountain. The Caviliere Gatty who arrived here yesterday & is come to stay with ous a week says the day before yesterday he spoke with Padre Antoine a old priest, who lives on the mountain, who told him that in a week or fortenight a mouth would open the Portice side and carry all that place a whay, but at least their is bad signs now. I took last night one of my maids who is a great biggot to the top of the house & I shewd her the mountain but when she saw the great fire she fell down on her knees & cried out, O Janaro mio, Antoino mio, so I fel down on my knees and cried out O Saint Loola mio Look mio, but she got up in a great hurry & said ebene signora la vostro excellenza non credo in St Janaro evero, so sais I no teresa evero per me lo credo se voi prega alla Loola mia Septeso Cosa. She looks at me and said to be sure I read a great many books & must know more than her, but says she, does not God favour you more than ous, no says I. O God says she, your excellency is very ungrateful, he as been so good as to make your face the same as he made the Blessed virgins and you dont esteem it as a favour. Why says I, did you ever see the virgin, O yes says she, you are like every picture that their is of yer & you know the people at Iscea fel down on their knees to you & begd you to grant them favours in her name, & Greville, its true that the have all got it in their heads I am like the virgin & the do come to beg favours of me. Last night their was two preists came to our house & Sir William made me put the shawl over my head & look up & the preist burst in to tears & kist my feet & said God had sent me a purpose. O propo, now as I have such a use of shawls & mine is wore out Sir Wm. is quite miserable for I stand in atitudes[20] with them on me. As you know Mr Machpherson ask him to give you one for me, pray do, for mine is wore out. O pray send me 4 or 5 prints of that little Gipsey picture[21] with the hat on; Sir Wm. wants one and 2 other people I have promised. Thank you for the boxes, I was enchanted with the hats, the black one was two little but I have give it to Madam Vonvatelli, a friend of mine hear at Court, who admired it. Sir Wm. scolds me for writing so long a letter; Mind you, your Uncle Freds daughter cant sing so well as me, tell her so. Pray write to me & tell me if I shall sing at the opera or no. We shall be in London this Spring twelve months: we are going to Rome this spring.

Adio & believe me more your freind than what you are mine.

Emma

I send you a kiss on my name, its more than you deserve. Next post I write to your brother abbout Wite, as he is my freind and I have assisted them a good deal & will more. Pray give my love to your brother & compliments to Legg, Banks, Tolemach etc. etc. & tell them to take care of their hearts when I come back; as to you, you will be uterly undone but Sr Wm. allready is distractedly in love & endead I love him tenderly. He deserves it. God bless you.

Emma's forecast of a visit to England "this Spring twelve months" was a little premature, as she was to remain in Italy until 1791, but no doubt Sir William had discussed the possibility of a visit. He was delighted and impressed with the improvement in her singing and her mastery of Italian. He also helped her, by encouragement and by arranging the lighting, to make something of her original idea for entertaining their more intimate guests – her attitudes – a form of dumb-charades, one might say, for which she was later to become famous. Sir William sang her praises to Greville:

Caserta,   December 18th 1787.

We are here as usual, my dear Charles, and I am out almost every day on shooting parties, but I find my house comfortable in the evening with Emma's society. You can have no idea of the improvement she makes daily in every respect – manners, language, & musick particularly. She has now applied closely to singing 5 months, & I have her master (an excellent one) in the house, so that she takes 3 lessons a day; her voice is remarkably fine, & she begins now to have a command over it. She has much expression, & as she applies chiefly to the solfeggia, she will be grounded in musick, & there is no saying what she may be in a year or two: I believe myself of the first rate, & so do the best judges here, who can scarcely believe she has only learnt 5 months. I can assure you her behaviour is such as has acquired her many sensible admirers, and we have a good man society, and all the female nobility, with the Queen at their head, shew her every distant civility. She has wrote a volume for you, but whether she will send it or not I can not tell... .

Greville was not one to sit about doing nothing. He had not found his heiress, in fact he never did find her, but he was not put off by reverses. In 1786 he had found that the printing of some plates for a book on some of Sir William's vases would prove an expensive operation and so he bought a printing press and paper and set it up in the laundry at Edgware Row, hiring a printer to operate it. He was keeping an eye on Sir William's estates around Milford Haven for him, and now, in 1788, he was speculating in house property, having just borrowed the money to build a house overlooking Hyde Park. He had obtained £4,500 at 4½ per cent. for this project and he intended to let the place on a six-monthly lease so that he could live in it himself, should he want to, at reasonably short notice. It would appear that he was taking some risk in the matter, as he informed his uncle that "my situation is daily more critical, for my brother does not seem likely either to attend to his own or to my interest". Sir William watched his nephew's progress with concern and, in 1789, writing again to his friend Banks, he said, "Why should not Charles Greville turn his mind to the Foreign line – Lord Warwick might manage that & if he turns him out of Parliament which I suppose he will do, it is incumbent upon him to provide for him – I will labour to make up the breach between the two Brothers with whom I am as yet upon the most friendly terms but Charles to be sure is the Friend of my bosom."

Emma was now firmly established in a most satisfactory position in Naples. She was admired, fêted and flattered – and furthermore she was beginning to put pressure on Sir William and to mention marriage. He resisted her suggestions and wrote to Greville in May 1789, saying:

Emma often asks me, do you love me? ay, but as well as your new appartment? Her conduct is such as to gain universal esteem, & she profits daily in musick and language. I endeavour to lose no time in forming her & certainly she would be welcome to share with me, *on our present footing*, all I have during my life, but I fear her views are beyond what I can bring myself to execute; & that when her hopes on that point are over, that she will make herself & me unhappy; but all this *entre nous*; if ever a separation should be necessary for our mutual happiness, I would settle £150 a year on her, & £50 on her mother, who is a very worthy woman; but all this is only thinking aloud to you, & foreseeing that the difference of 57 & 22 may produce events; but, indeed, hitherto her behaviour is irreproachable, but her temper, as you must know, unequal... .

I seriously propose making you a visit next spring, as you know my affairs require my presence; how we shall manage about Emma is another question; however, I only trouble myself at present with making her accomplished, let what may come of it.

The visit to England in the spring did not materialise and in March Sir William was saying, "I wish I cou'd have come home this year, but Emma wou'd not be left, and if I did not follow up her singing with Aprile another year she wou'd remain imperfect."

Emma's singing was doubtless becoming more accomplished, but so were her ruthless attacks on Sir William's weakening defences. From what he wrote to Greville in a letter dated 21st September 1790, it sounds as if the Queen was lending a little of her weight to Emma's side in the tug-of-war:

Naples, September 21st 1790

By degrees I am running into Ross's debt, instead of his being in mine, which he was considerably when I left England. I am determined at any rate to pay all my debts, & one comfort is that I have a sufficient stock in hand to do it. The fitting up my new appartment cost me much more than I thought it wou'd – near £4000. I give Emma £200 a year to keep her & her mother in cloths & washing, and you may imagine every now and then a present of a gown, a ring, a feather, etc, and once indeed she so long'd for diamonds that, having an opportunity of a good bargain of single stones of a good water & tolerable size, I gave her at once £500 worth. She realy deserves everything, & has gained the love of everybody, &, wou'd you think it, is preached up by the Queen & nobility as a rare example of virtue. By Aprile's lessons she begins to sing in a capital stile, and has talents for both bravoura, pathetic, & buffo; but, as her voice & expression is so perfect, the pathetic is what I cultivate most, & I am sure in that she will excell any dilettante in England. Her knowledge of musick will surprise you as it does me, for I did not expect her to apply as she has done. She has grown thinner of late, & is the handsomer for it... .

With the New Year (1791) Emma knew that she had triumphed. Her letter to Greville is indeed complacent:

Naples, Jany 1791.

I received your oblidging letter on Thursday & am sensible of the part you take in my happiness & wellfare. I have not time today to answer to all the points in your letter, but will the next post. You may think of my aflictions when I heard of the Duchess of Argylles[22] death, I never had such a freind as her & that you will know when I see you & recount to you all the acts of kindness she shewd to me, for they where two good & numerous to describe in a letter: think then to a heart of sinsibility & grattitude what it must suffer, ma passiensa io ho molto. You need not be affraid for me in England; we come for a short time & that time must be occupied in buisiness & to take our last leave. I dont wish to atract notice, I wish to be an example of good conduct & to shew the world that a pretty woman is not allways a *fool*, all my ambition is to make Sir Wm. happy & you will see he is so. As to our seperating houses, we cant do it or why should we, you cant think 2 people that as lived five years with all the domestic happiness thats possible, can seperate & those 2 persons that knows no other comfort but in one anothers comppany, which is the case, I assure you with ous, tho you Bachelers dont understand it, but you cant imagjine, 2 houses must seperate ous, no, it cant be, that you will be a judge of when you see us. We will lett you in to our plans & secretts, Sir William will lett you know on what a footing we are here. On Monday last we give a concert & Ball at our hous. I had near four hundred persons, all the foreign ministers & their wives, all the first ladies of fashion, foreynors & neapolitans, our house was full in every room. I had the Banti, the tenor Casacelli & 2 others to sing. Sir Wm. dressd me in wite sattin, no coller abbout me but my hair & cheeks. I was with out powder as it was the first great assembly we had given publickly. All the ladies strove to out do one another in dress and jewels, but Sir William said I was the finest jewel amongst them. Every night our house is open to small partys of fifty or sixty men & women. We have musick, tea etc. etc. & we have a great adition lately to our party, we have a new Spanish ambassader & his wife & we as made a great frendship & we are allways together. She is charming. Think then after what Sir Wm. as done for me if I should not be the horrid wreth in the world not to be exemplary towards him. Endead I will do all I can to render him happy. We shall be with you in the Spring & return heer in Novr. & the next year you may pay ous a visit, we shall be glad to see you. I shall allways esteem you for your relationship to Sir William & haveing been the means of me knowing him. As to Sir W. I confess to you I doat on him nor I never can have any other person but him. This confession will please you I know. I will write more next post.

Emma.

If any doubts remained in Greville's mind that his former mistress was about to become his aunt they were dispelled by an urgent letter from his friend, Heneage Legge, who happened to be in Naples:

Naples, March 8th 1791.

I have long been determin'd not to quit this place without adding you to the list of my correspondents, from a thorough conviction that in the course of fourteen weeks' residence I had witness'd many scenes which could be little interesting to any body but yourself, but the result of which my real regard for you now tempts me to communicate, with an assurance that I neither have or will drop the smallest hint on the subject to any other person. In Switzerland last year I met L^d & L^{y}Elcho, who had pass'd the preceeding winter at Naples, together with the Duke & Duch^{ss} of Argyle, & assured me that, altho' Sr W.H's public situation would not permit him to declare it, there was no doubt of his being married to Mrs H., that he had presented her to them upon that ground, & that the behaviour of both parties confirm'd her belief of its being so. When we came, he immediately waited upon us with all the kindness & attention that our former acquaintance could dictate, having previously wrote me word while I was at Rome that Emma would be at all times happy to attend Mrs L. as a nurse, or contribute to her amusement as a companion. Mrs L. is not over-scrupulous in her manners or sentiments beyond the usual forms establish'd by the rules of society in her own country; but, as she was not particularly inform'd of any change in Mrs H's situation, she had no reason to think her present different from her former line of life, & therefore could not quite reconcile it to her feelings to accept these offers of friendship & service, tho' there was no doubt of their being kindly intended. Mrs L, therefore, very soon gave it to be understood that she wish'd to retain her old footing of intimacy with him, but that any other branch of the family was inadmissable, which has certainly depriv'd her of much of his company, tho' he has been good in calling upon her whenever he could. To me you may be sure his companion was no objection, & few days have past in which I have not at some time found myself under his roof. The language of both parties, who always spoke in the plural number – we, us, & ours – stagger'd me at first, but soon made me determine to speak openly to him on the subject, when he assur'd me, what I confess I was most happy to hear, that he was not married; but flung out some hints of doing justice to her good behaviour, if his public situation did not forbid him to consider himself an independent man. Her influence over him exceeds all belief; his attachment exceeds admiration, it is perfect dotage. She gives everybody to understand that he is now going to England to sollicit the K's consent to marry her, & that on her return she shall appear as L^y H. She says it is impossible to continue in her present dubious state, which exposes her to frequent slight & mortification; & his whole thought, happiness & comfort seems so center'd in her presence, that if she should refuse to return on other terms, I am confident she will gain her point, against which it is the duty of every friend to strengthen his mind as much as possible; & she will be satisfied with no argument but the King's absolute refusal of his approbation. Her talents & powers of amusing are very wonderfull; her voice is very fine, but she does not sing with great taste, & Aprili says she has not a good ear; her attitudes are beyond description beautifull and striking, & I think you will find her figure much improved since you last saw her. *They* say they shall be in London by the latter end of May, that their stay in England will be as short as possible, & that, having settled his affairs, he is determin'd never to return. She is much visited here by ladies of the highest rank, & many of the *Corps diplomatique*; does the honours of his house with great attention & desire to please, but wants a little refinement of manners, in which, in the course of six years, I wonder she has not made greater progress. I have all along told her she could never change her situation for the better, & that she was a happier woman as Mrs H. than she would be as Ly H., when, more reserved behaviour being necessary, she would be depriv'd of half her amusements, & must no longer sing those comic parts which tend so much to the entertainment of herself & her friends. She does not accede to that doctrine, & unless great care is taken to prevent it I am clear she will in some unguarded hour work upon his empassion'd mind, & effect her design of becoming your aunt. He tells me he has made ample provision for her, in which he is certainly right, and with that she ought to be content. It must be unnecessary for me to caution you against ever telling them that I wrote to you on this subject, nor should I have done it, if I had not been sure that you are not apprised of the state they are in, & the unbounded influence she has gain'd over him & all that belongs to him. We leave Naples to-morrow, & should have done so long ago if an unexpected eruption of Mt Vesuvius had not given good cause of delay; it has not been a very profuse one, but full enough to gratify our curiosity.... .

Sir William follows us to Rome in a few days, but will not stay much above a week; he has had a bad cold & hoarseness, which pull'd him down a good deal, & he has hardly yet recovered the effects of it. I conclude you are still either a real or nominal inhabitant of the Mews, therefore shall direct my letter there; & after begging you to give my best compliments & regards to your brother, assure you that I am, etc.

At some time during her return journey to England, the thought must have crossed Emma's mind that, after all, her visit to Naples, although longer than she had expected, had been a decided success.

Chapter 6

Marriage

THE JOURNEY BACK to England was made in May (1791) and the happy pair, accompanied by Mrs Cadogan, made their way overland as Sir William had friends to visit in Rome, Florence, Venice and Vienna. It was necessary for him to obtain the King's permission to marry and the wedding, now that Sir William had become used to the idea and had made his rather reluctant decision, was the primary purpose of the trip. For Emma it was the sole purpose, though doubtless she had thoughts of the pleasure it would be to bathe in a sea of flattery as she sat again in Romney's studio. What her feelings were about meeting Greville again can only be conjectured. She certainly bore him no ill-will and the idea of so soon becoming Lady Hamilton may have given her the feeling that a little mischievous flaunting of her good fortune would do him no harm.

At this point it may be appropriate to mention a remark she was heard to make, on her final return to England, by Lady Elizabeth Foster. On the question of her not being received at Court, she said, "It is hard, because the examples of Lady Wellesley, Lady Yarmouth, and Lady Ferrers [Hyacinthe Gabrielle Roland, Maria Fagniani and Elizabeth Mundy, none of whom enjoyed a good reputation] are quoted, which are cases quite different from mine, for I never lived with Sir William as his mistress. I was under the protection of his roof, my mother with me, and we were married in private two years before he married me openly in England." The idea of being already married before she came to England must be taken as a permissible flight of fancy under the circumstances. Elizabeth Foster did believe it, as she suggested that if it could be proved, the Queen, who could not be expected to know such a secret, might change her opinion. Sir William, who felt the slight on his wife far more than it affected Emma, would have been ready enough to substantiate the claim – had it been true.

Arrived in London at the very end of May, Emma could hardly wait to visit the studio in Cavendish Square. Sir William was only too willing to accompany her and their first visit was unannounced, Emma wearing "a Turkish habit". Romney was delighted to see them and his day book shows that he was eager to expend more paint on recording the beauties of his favourite model. On Thursday, 2nd June, it was "Mrs H. at ½ pt 9", on Saturday, 4th June, "Mrs H. at 10" and Wednesday, 8th June, "Mrs Hart at ½ pt 9". So the sittings continued, the 11th, 14th, 17th, 19th (a Sunday), 20th, 22nd, 23rd, 25th, 27th and 29th June; and a further sixteen sittings in July. The painter wrote to his friend Hayley: "At present, and the greatest part of the summer, I shall be engaged in painting pictures from the divine lady. I cannot give her any other epithet, for I think her superior to all womankind." He began a "Joan of Arc", a "Magdalen" and a "Bacchante" and he painted her as "Cassandra". He was asked to their house to see her "Attitudes" which he admired and told her that they were "simple, grand, terrible and pathetic". Then something went a little wrong with the friendship. Emma was becoming perhaps a trifle grand in her ideas. She had met Sir William's cousin, Lord Abercorn. The Duke of Queensberry had entertained her with much flattery at his house in Richmond. It is doubtful if she realised that neither of these nobleman enjoyed good reputation or that Horace Walpole, who met her at Queensberry House was to whisper behind her back about "Sir William's pantomime mistress".

It is interesting to note that a visit to the play at Drury Lane was the occasion of a meeting between old friends, both of whom had come a long way since they last met – in the servants' hall at Dr Budd's house in Chatham Place. Emma met and chatted with Jane Powell who had now become a leading lady in the company.

While Emma enjoyed the gaiety of London, Romney had noticed what he described as "an alteration in her conduct to me. A coldness and neglect seemed to have taken the place of her repeated declarations of regard". He was left feeling miserable, when, at the beginning of August, Sir William took Emma on a visit to the West Country, which included a call on William Beckford at his house at Fonthill, in Wiltshire, and a stay in Bath.

While in Bath, they met the Duchess of Devonshire one evening and Emma was introduced. The Duchess had evidently heard of the "Attitudes", which were becoming quite famous, for she invited Emma to give a performance the next morning. Lady Elizabeth Foster was an interested spectator and wrote in her diary the following candid opinion of what she saw:

Having just seen the celebrated Mrs Hart, who by an extraordinary talent, as Lord Charlemont says, found out a new source of pleasure to mankind, I cannot forbear mentioning the impression which she made upon me. She was introduced last night to the Duchess of Devonshire by Sir W. Hamilton. She appeared to be a very handsome woman, but coarse and vulgar. She sung, and her countenance lightened up – her *Buffo* songs were inimitable from the expression and vivacity with which they were sung. Her serious singing appeared to me not good – her voice is strong, she is well taught, yet has a forced expression and has neither softness nor tenderness. Her voice wants flexibility.

This morning she was to show her attitudes. She came, and her appearance was more striking than I can describe, or could have imagined. She was draped exactly like a Grecian statue, her chemise of white muslin was exactly in that form, her sash in the antique manner, her fine black hair flowing over her shoulders. It was a Helena, Cassandra or Andromache, no Grecian or Trojan Princess could have had a more perfect or commanding form. Her attitudes, which she performed with the help alone of two shawls, were varied – every one was perfect – everything she did was just and beautiful. She then sung and acted the mad scene in *Nina* – this was good, but I think chiefly owing to her beautiful action and attitudes – her singing except in the *Buffo* is always in my mind a secondary talent and performance …

In the evening she came again but we ought to have closed with the morning. She looked very handsome certainly, and she was better draped than the first evening, but her conversation, though perfectly good-natured and unaffected, was uninteresting, and her pronunciation very vulgar. In short, Lord Bristol's remark seems to me so just a one that I must end with it: "Take her as anything but Mrs Hart and she is a superior being – as herself she is always vulgar."

I must however add, as an excuse for that vulgarity and as a further proof of the superiority of her talents that have burst forth in spite of these disadvantages, that Mrs Hart was born and lived in the lowest situation till the age of 19, and since that in no higher one than the mistress of Sir W. Hamilton.

Emma's "Attitudes" were her speciality. The idea of entertaining a roomful of people in this manner seems strange, even in the age in which she lived, when singing or playing on an instrument by amateur or professional performers was almost the only alternative to cards or dancing. It is difficult to imagine this seemingly tame form of spectacle, not unlike a dumb-charade, having the power to hold the attention of an audience for long. It was certainly original, and no doubt Sir

William's classical knowledge, added to his ardent desire for Emma to shine, made him an excellent stage manager. From the comments of many contemporary writers there seems no doubt that these exhibitions were a novel attraction. The Comtesse de Boigne, who was so far from being an admirer of Emma's that she referred to her as a "bad woman" who had "a low mind within a magnificent form", cannot help praising the "Attitudes" which she witnessed while in Naples. In a letter referring to Emma, she says:

In conformity with her husband's taste, she was generally dressed in a white tunic, with a belt round her waist, her hair down her back or turned up by a comb, but dressed in no special way. When she consented to give a performance, she would provide herself with two or three cashmere shawls, an urn, a scent-box, a lyre, and a tambourine. With these few properties, and her classical costume, she took up her position in the middle of a room. She threw a shawl over her head which reached the ground and covered her entirely, and thus hidden, draped herself with the other shawls. Then she suddenly raised the covering, either throwing it off entirely or half raising it, and making it form part of the drapery of the model which she represented. But she always appeared as a statue of most admirable design.

I have heard artists say that if a perfect reproduction had been possible, art would have found nothing to change in her. She often varied her attitude and her expression, "from grave to gay, from trivial to severe", before dropping the shawl which concluded that part of the performance.

I have sometimes acted with her as a subordinate figure to form a group. She used to place me in the proper position, and arrange my draperies before raising the shawl, which served as a curtain enveloping us both. My fair hair contrasted with her magnificent black hair, to which many of her effects were due.

One day she placed me on my knees before an urn, with my hands together in an attitude of prayer. Leaning over me, she seemed lost in grief, and both of us had our hair dishevelled. Suddenly rising and moving backward a little, she grasped me by the hair with a movement so sudden that I turned round in surprise and almost in fright, which brought me precisely into the spirit of my part, for she was brandishing a dagger. The passionate applause of the artists who were looking on resounded with exclamations of "Brava, Medea!" Then drawing me to her and clasping me to her breast as though she were fighting to preserve me from the anger of Heaven, she evoked loud cries of "Viva, la Niobe!".

She took her inspiration from the antique statues, and without making any servile copy of them, recalled them to the poetical imagination of the Italians by improvised gesture. Others have tried to imitate Lady Hamilton's talent, but I doubt if any one has succeeded. It is a business in which there is but a step from the sublime to the ridiculous. Moreover, to equal her success, the actor must first be of faultless beauty from head to foot, and such perfection is rare.

As a woman, the Comtesse had a poor opinion of Emma. "Apart from this artistic instinct", she continues, "Lady Hamilton was entirely vulgar and common. When she exchanged her classical tunic for ordinary dress she lost all distinction. Her conversation showed no interest and little intelligence."

The opinions of Lady Elizabeth Foster and the Comtesse de Boigne are so much in agreement that one is forced rather unwillingly to the conclusion that whatever charms Emma had for Sir William and later for Nelson, an unfortunate trait of vulgarity, which Greville would certainly never have tolerated, was on the increase.

Emma and Sir William returned to London on 16th August, and soon the little rift with Romney was forgotten, as, according to him, she had "resumed her former kindness", and his appointment book for 22nd August had the entry, "Mrs H. at 1". She was with him again the next day at "¼ pt 9" and three days later at "½ pt 10". The painter was overjoyed and went so far as to give a party at his house (the only occasion on which he is recorded as doing so) in her honour. "She performed in my house last week", he says, "singing and acting before some of the nobility with most astonishing power. She is the talk of the whole town, and really surpasses every thing, both in singing and acting, that ever appeared. Gallini offered her two thousand pounds a year, and two benefits, if she would engage with him, on which Sir William said pleasantly, that he had engaged her for life."

During the time that she was in England, Emma's interests in "Emma Carew", the "little Emma" of the days in Park Gate, were attended to by Greville and Mrs Cadogan, the latter visiting her ageing mother in Hawarden and making all necessary arrangements for the growing child.

The wedding day, fixed for Tuesday, 6th September, was now getting very near, but as the ceremony was to be a very quiet one, the visits to Cavendish Square were not affected by preparations. A great many of Emma's hours may have been devoted to consultation and fittings with her dressmaker, but nevertheless Romney was still able to continue his paintings. "Mrs H." was with him at 10 o'clock on Sunday the 4th, and on the 5th, the day before the event, she was there at 9 a.m.

The wedding took place at Marylebone Parish Church certainly not later than 10 o'clock. Mrs Cadogan was there and a few friends, including, almost certainly, Charles Greville. The witnesses were Sir William's relation, the Marquis of Abercorn, Mr Dutens, the secretary to the English Minister at Turin, and Dr Edward Barry, rector of Elsdon, who officiated.

In the vestry, when the ceremony was over, Emma signed her proper name – Amy Lyons – in the register which recorded that:

The Right Hon[ble] Sir Will[m] Hamilton of this Parish, Widower and Amy Lyons of the same Parish, Spinster.
Married in this Church by Licence
this Sixth Day of September in the Year One Thousand Seven Hundred and Ninety One   By me, Edw[d] Barry, M.D. Clerk.
This Marriage was solemnised   {W[m] Hamilton
between Us   {Amy Lyons

In the Presence of   {Abercorn
                                                    {L. Dutens
                                                    {Rector of Elsdon in Northumberland.

That no great stir in London society was caused by the wedding can be gauged by the following brief references to the occasion:

The Gentleman's Magazine
Sept. 6th – Sir Wm Hamilton K.B. envoy extraordinary and minister plenipotentiary to the Court of Naples, to Miss Harte, a lady much celebrated for her elegant accomplishments and great musical abilities.

The European Magazine
Sir William Hamilton K.B. Envoy Extraordinary and Minister Plenipotentiary to the Court of Naples to Miss Harte.

By eleven o'clock Emma was sitting to Romney for the last time and his day book shows the one and only entry of her new title, "Lady Hamilton". His portrait of the "Ambassadress"[23] is a charming one and shows her in what must have been her wedding dress. She wears a large crowned hat, with an upright feather at one side, held on by a scarf tied under the chin. Her dress, fashionably voluminous, had long sleeves, a coloured sash and a large cape-like collar.

Two days later the bride and groom set out on the return journey to Naples. There had been an affectionate farewell to Romney, whom

Emma was never to see again. He was affected by the parting to the extent of making no appointments until 16th October, and on one of the flyleaves of his diary for 1791 is a pathetic little note in his own handwriting: "Sir William H. was married to Emma. Sept. the 6th 1791." His health, which was far from being robust, seemed to decline more rapidly from that date.

After the wedding, a friend wrote to Sir William's niece, Mary Dickenson, "God forbid I should think a false step irretrievable, or that one vice shuts out every virtue; but Sir William Hamilton's age, family and character make one sorry he should have been so fascinated, and the example is a bad one. He, however, may be happy, and she good and grateful, and I hope they will be so." These sentiments were very much in accordance with the thoughts of most of Sir William's family and friends. Mary Dickenson herself had been friendly and kind to Emma, in spite of her mother's disapproval, and during the journey to Naples, Emma wrote to Mary, "I am so happy and feel so content, that I shall have a pleasure in writing to you, and believe me before the 6th of September I was always unhappy and discontented with myself; Ah, madam, how much do I owe to your dear uncle. I feel every moment my obligations to him and am always afraid I can never do enough for him since that moment. I say to myself, Am I his wife, and can I never separate more. Am I Emma Hamilton? It seems impossible I can be so happy. Surely no person was ever so happy as I am." Emma was revelling in a delighted sense of both achievement and security.

Leaving London so soon after the wedding was a sensible move on the part of Sir William. Emma had caused a mild sensation in social circles, her beauty counteracting to some extent the sweet smell of scandal, and it was as well to be out of the way before there were any repercussions. A letter from Strawberry Hill expressed Walpole's shrewish wit: "Sir William Hamilton has actually married his gallery of statues." Casanova, who met the Hamiltons a little later on, added his comments on the new state of affairs, by saying: "A clever man marrying a young woman clever enough to bewitch him. Such a fate often overtakes a man of intelligence when he grows old. It is always a mistake to marry, but when a man's physical and mental forces are declining, it is a calamity." As a generalisation he was not so far from the mark, but in this case he shot rather wide, as Sir William was never seriously to regret the step he had taken.

Stopping for a while in Paris on their way to Naples, Emma was able to witness the last phase of the old monarchy in France. She was present with Sir William at the Assembly when the King, virtually a prisoner after the flight to Varennes, accepted the constitution forced upon him.

Marie Antoinette received her and gave her a letter to deliver to her sister, the Queen of Naples. Although Emma, in later years, was to attempt to magnify this small service to the unfortunate Queen into an act of consequence, the real significance of the gesture was one of great kindness on the part of Marie Antoinette who wished, quite simply, to pave the way for the reception of the new Lady Hamilton at the Court of Naples.

The ominous signs of catastrophe in Paris would hardly have bothered Emma to whom the first taste of being accepted as Lady Hamilton must have been an all-enveloping thrill. Sir William was aware of a great deal that was going on but he was not the man to upset his bride's happiness by pointing to thunder clouds, and she would have been in no mood for a course in politics. To be received by the Queen of France on a throne that rocked was a great improvement, to her way of thinking, on the disregard of the Queen of England on one that did not. Her great concern, for the rest of the journey to Naples, was for the safety of the letter entrusted to her.

Maria Carolina was quite ready to welcome Emma to the Neapolitan Court, with or without a letter from her sister, and all went smoothly for the wife of the British Ambassador. Writing to Sir Joshua Banks on 27th March 1792, Sir William said: "Lady Hamilton has nothing to do with my public character but Their Sicilian Majesties are so good as to receive & treat her as any other travelling Lady of distinction – She has gained the hearts of all even of the Ladies by her humility & proper behaviour, & we shall I dare say go on well – I will allow with that 99 times in a hundred such a step as I took would be very imprudent but I knew my way here & here I mean to pass the most of the days that I can have a chance of living. Without a Woman you can have no Society at home & I am sure you will hear from every quarter of the comforts of my house."

Soon after her return to Naples, Emma wrote a letter to Romney, which he must have read with great pleasure.

Caserta, December 20th 1791.

I have the pleasure to inform you we arrived safe at Naples. I have been receved with open arms by all the Neapolitans of booth sexes, by all the foreighners of every distinction. I have been presented to the Queen of Naples by her own desire, she as shewn me all sorts of kind and affectionate attentions; in short, I am the happiest woman in the world.

Sir William is fonder of me every day, & I hope I will have no corse to repent of what he as done, for I feel so grateful to him that I think I shall never be able to make him amends for his goodness to me. But why do I tell you this? you know me enough; you was the first dear friend I open'd my heart to, you ought to know me, for you have seen and discoursed with me in my poorer days, you have known me in my poverty and prosperity, and I had no occasion to have lived for years in poverty and distress if I had not felt something of virtue in my mind. Oh, my dear friend, for a time I own through distress my virtue was vanquished, but my sense of virtue was not overcome. How gratefull now, then, do I feel to my dear, dear husband that has restored peace to my mind, that has given me honors, rank, and, what is more, innocence and happiness. Rejoice with me, my dear sir, my friend, my more than father, believe me I am still that same Emma you knew me. If I could forget for a moment what I was, I ought to suffer. Command me in anything I can do for you here; believe me, I shall have a real pleasure. Come to Naples, and I will be your model, anything to induce you to come, that I may have an opportunity to show my gratitude to you. Take care of your health for all our sakes. How does the pictures go on? Has the Prince been to you? write to me, I arn interested in all that concerns you. God bless you, my dear friend! I spoke to Lady Sutherland about you; she loves you dearly. Give my love to Mr Hayly, tell him I shall be glad to see him at Naples. As you was so good to say you would give me the little picture with the black hat, I wish you would unfrill it, and give it to Mr Duten. I have a great regard for him; he took a deal of pains and trouble for me, and I could not do him a greater favour than give him my picture. Do, my dear friend, do me that pleasure, and if there is anything from Naples command me.

We have a many English at Naples, Ladys Malmsbery, Malden, Plymouth, Carnegie, Wright, etc. They are very kind and attentive to me; they all make it a point to be remarkably civil to me. You will be happy at this, as you know what prudes our Ladys are. Tell Hayly I am allways reading his *Triumphs of Temper*; it was that that made me Lady H., for, God knows, I had for 5 years enough to try my temper, and I am affraid if it had not been for the good example Serena taught me, my girdle would have burst, and if it had I had been undone, for Sir W. minds more temper than beauty. He, therefore, wishes Mr Hayly would come, that he might thank him for his sweet-tempered wife. I swear to you I have never been once out of humour since the 6th of last September. God bless you.

Back in London, Greville was concerning himself with the welfare of little Emma Carew, now nearly ten years old. His letter to Sir William explains the situation:

No date. (10th January 1792)

I have taken a liberty with you, & I communicate it to you instead of LʸH., because I know it would give her some embarrassment, & she might imagine it unkind in me so soon to trouble you about her protégé. I had settled the Midsummer half year; & I intended to have done the same at Xmas if I could have kept my account at Mr Hoare's within bounds. I have overdrawn him £150, & my next receipt is in May. It will not, therefore, be taken ill of you that I have given Blackburn an order on Messrs. Ross & Ogilvy for £32 11s. in this form:-

£32. 11s. January 10, 1792.

Please to pay Mr Blackburn or Bearer thirty-two pounds 11s on account of Sir Wm. Hamilton, the particulars of which demand I have transmitted to him at Naples.
C.F.G.

I do not mean this necessary step to be concealed from LʸH, but I should be sorry that she considered it unkindly. You will know better than me that an early decision should be taken about her; Blackburne says she has grown, & that she has been evidently more anxious since Mrs Cadogan visited her; I think they judged well in consulting the apothecary, for growing & worms more usually affect persons of her age than great sensibility. The age of curiosity is, however, near at hand, & her future plans shou'd be settled & communicated; as every part of her history has been stated to you, there can be little difficulty to decide. The natural attachment to a deserted orphan may be supposed to increase from the length of time she has been protected. I have avoided any such sentiment by having only found the means to indulge so amiable a sentiment in LʸH.; if I could have done so longer I would, & if I could have taken care of her for life I should have personally seen the progress of it. I had full confidence in Mrs Blackburn, & in Mr B's discretion, & as Mrs Cadogan saw her situated to her satisfaction, I had only to ensure the continuance of her residence with these good people untill her plans of life could be settled.

I enclose the account that you may see the particulars of what I have allowed her, which you will continue till her plans are decided on. I cannot have an opinion what the plan should be, but that which is most agreable to LʸH. will be best; & I know that she will consider your attention on this subject as additional proof of your kindness.

The enclosed account (added up wrong by a penny) read as follows:

1791		Miss Hart.	
Half a year's board due January the 6th, 1792	£10	10	-
French	1	1	-
Music	3	3	-
Music book		10	6
Use of a pianoforte		12	-
Dancing		2	2
Writing, copy books, etc.	1	2	6
Remaining the Xmas holidays	1	1	-
Washing		1	1
Teacher & servants		15	6
Books		2	6
Hair cutting		2	6
Seat at church		6	-
Weekly allowance		4	4
Shoes	1	4	8
Filligree box for Mrs Hart by order of Mrs Cadogan	2	12	6
Packing-case		1	-
Pair of garters			8
Bonnet		18	9
6 pair of stocking		12	6
One dozen of red port wine		1	1
Apothecary's bill for the year '90.		3	6
Gloves		6	-
Pins, needles, tape, & thread		2	6
Pair of stays, 14s, & stuff skirt, 9s	1	3	
Carriage of two packing-cases for Miss Hart from London		4	2
Evans' worm powders 7s, drawing 2 teeth, 2s		9	-
4 yards ribbon for a sash, 8s & 3 flannel pettycoats, 10s		18	-
	£32	11	-

It is not at all clear at what stage the young Emma was called, or called herself, "Carew". If, while she was living with the Blackburns, near Manchester, she went by the name of Hart, it seems strange that she should change her name later to Carew. It would be more reasonable to assume, perhaps, that she was referred to, when the Blackburns wrote to Greville, as Miss Hart, but was called to her face Miss Carew.

In a letter to Horace Walpole, who had just become Earl of Orford, Sir William again uses the phrase about Emma being treated by the Queen "like any other travelling lady of distinction". He says:

Naples, April 17th 1792

... Lady H., who has had also a difficult part to act & has succeeded wonderfully, having gained, by having no pretentions, the thorough approbation of all the English ladies. The Queen of Naples, as you may have heard, was very kind to her on our return, and treats her like any other travelling lady of distinction; in short, we are very comfortably situated here.... You can not imagine how delighted L^yH was in having gained your approbation in England. She desires to be kindly remember'd to you. She goes on improving daily, particularly in musick & in the French & Italian languages. She is really an extraordinary being, & most gratefull to me for having saved her from the precipice into which she had good sense enough to see she must without me have inevitably fallen, and she sees that nothing but a constant good conduct can maintain the respect that is now shown her by every body. It has often been remarked that a reformed rake makes a good husband. *Why not vice versâ?* ...

Romney certainly did not presume on his friendship with Emma as his somewhat tardy reply to her shows. In reading his letter, it is clear that Emma was not the only one to whom correct spelling did not come easily.

No date (1792)

What must you think of my neglect of answering your kind letter? Do not accuse me of ingratitud. I wish I could express myself as I felt at the perusal of it to find your happyness so compleat; May God grant it may remain so till the end of your days. You may be assured that I have the same anxiety that Sir William and yourself should continue to think well of me, and the same desire to do everything in my power that may merit your esteem. I have waited till I could give you some account of the picter of Cassandra and some other of the pictures you were so kind as to let me see. The Cassandra[24] is at last gone to the Shakespeare Gallery. It suits.

The King and Royal Family saw it. I hav never heard from the Prince of Wales till a few days ago Mr West called and said the Prince desired him to look at the picture for His Royal Hiness. They are near finished. The lively one I have made to suit Calipso.

I am anxious to know what you would wish me to do with the picture with a bonnet as you have not mentioned it in your letter. Mr Crawford has expressed a great desire ot possessing it in preference to the other. I shall wait for your instructions. I sent, as your Ladyship required, the picter in black to du Tens.

I was lead into a thing that gives me uneasyness. I was solicited so very strongly for a letter of recommendation to your Ladyship, that I was not able to get off. The person was then in Italy, but was not informed who he was. I hope your Ladyship will forgive me for taking such a liberty, and that nothing unpleasant happened.

In the course of the year after their return from England, Sir William was taken ill. The malady seems to have been quite a serious one, even allowing for Emma's tendency to exaggerate her wifely concern when writing to Greville. The "Dear Sir" and the "my dear Mr Greville" in the letter are unkind, to say the least, considering what Greville had done for her in the past and, to a lesser degree, what he had been doing recently for the welfare of her child. Emma's character was showing signs of changing for the worse, but her kindness to her grandmother was unaltered, although the glamour and seeming importance of her new position in Naples were beginning to swamp her better nature. The letter reads:

Caserta, December 4th 1792.

Dear Sir,
I have the pleasure to inform you that Sir William is out of danger & very well considering the illness he as had to battle with. He as been 15 days in bed with a billious fever & I have been almost as ill as him with anxiety, aprehension, & fatige, the last, endeed, the least, of what I have felt & I am now doubly repaid by the dayly progress he makes for the better. Luckily we are at Caserta were his convalescence will have fair play & I am in hopes he will be better than ever he was in his life, for his disorder as been long gathering & was a liver complaint. I need not say to you my dear Mr Greville what I have suffered, endeed I was almost distracted, from such extreme happiness at once to such misery, that I felt, your good heart may imagine. I was eight days without undressing, eating or sleeping. I have great obligations to the English ladies & Neapolitans, altho we are 16 miles from Naples. Lady Plymouth, Lady Dunmore, Lady Webster & several others sent twice a day & offered to come & stay with me, & the King & Queen sent constantly, morning & evening, the most flattering messages, but all was nothing to me – what cou'd console me for the loss of such a husband, friend & protecter, for surely no happiness is like ours. We live but for one another, but I was to happy, I had imagined I was never more to be unhappy, all is right, I now know myself again & I shall not easily fall in to the same error

again, for every moment I feel what I felt when I thought I was loseing him for ever. Pray excuse me, but you who love Sir William may figure to your self my situation at that moment.

I will trouble you with my own affairs as you are so good to enterest yourself about me. You must know I send my grandmother every cristmas, twenty pounds & so I ought, I have 2 hundred a year for nonsense & it wou'd be hard I cou'd not give her twenty pounds when she as so often given me her last shilling. As Sir Wm. is ill I cannot ask him for the order but if you will get the twenty pounds & send it to her you will do me the greatest favour, for if the time passes without hearing from me she may imagine I have forgot her & I wou'd not keep her poor old heart in suspence for the world, & as she as heard of my circumstance (I dont know how) but she is prudent, therefore pray lose no time & Sir Wm. shall send you the order. You know her direction, Mrs Kidd, Hawerden, Flintshire. Cou'd you not write to her a line from me or send to her & tell her by my order & she may write to you & send me her answer, for I cannot divert myself of my original feelings. It will contribute to my happiness & I am sure you will assist to make me happy, tell her every year she shall have twenty pound. The fourth of November last I had a dress on that cost twenty five pounds as it was gala at Court & believe me I felt unhappy all the while I had it on. Excuse the trouble I give you & believe me your sincere

Emma Hamilton

Sir W as wrote you a few lines.

Sir William could see no flaws in his wife. The following March, he wrote to Greville:

Emma goes on perfectly to my mind, but she has made our house so agreeable that it is more frequented than ever, &, of course, I am at a greater expence. However, I may safely say that no minister was ever more respected than I am here, & the English travellers, as Lord Cholmondley will tell you, feel the benefit of our being so well at this Court, for Emma is now as well with the K. & Q. as I am, & of many parties with them. [He elaborated on this theme to his friend Banks when he wrote to him from Caserta on the 11th June 1793 saying:] You will be glad to hear as I am sure you must from every quarter of the prudent conduct of Emma. – She knows the value of a good reputation which she is determined to maintain having been compleatly recovered.

She knows that beauty fades & therefore applies daily to the improvement of her mind. Altho we have had many Ladies of the first rank from England here lately & indeed such as give the Ton in London, the Queen of Naples remarked that Emma's deportment was infinitely superior. She is often with the Queen who really loves her – By coming to Naples at 19 she has got the language better than I have in 28 years – She desires her kind love to you & we trust that you will one day make us a visit.

Sir William was never very accurate when it was a question of age, his own or anyone else's. Emma was, of course, twenty-one on the day she arrived in Naples.

In view of Emma's "my dear Mr Greville" there appears to have been some coolness between them while she was in London but, whether this was so or not, Greville evidently bore her no ill-feelings. Sometime in June 1793 he added to one of his letters to his uncle a little flattery for Emma's benefit. "Tell Lady H. that I hope that she does not follow the fashion of others; at the birthday the prevailing fashion was very unlike a court dress, & very unlike a Grecian dress & very unlike L^{y}H. dress, but evidently an imitation of her, & you may tell her that *her own country cloathing is far more adorning* than all the trappings of French milliners on awkward inanimate damsels."

The attentions that Emma was receiving from the Queen were due in part to the fact that her Majesty was pleased with her behaviour, her enthusiasm and her will to please, but what Emma did not really understand was that she represented to Maria Carolina a powerful liaison with England via Sir William.

In January of the present year, Louis XVI had been guillotined and although the Carnival period was about to begin, Naples went into mourning and a Requiem Mass was attended by all the Court. On 1st February, France declared war on England and Holland. The gay and carefree days of Naples were coming to an end and in the Queen's breast there was burning hatred of the French. A treaty of alliance with England was eventually signed, on 12th July. Naples was to supply 6,000 soldiers and twelve ships for operations in the Mediterranean, and there was to be no trading with France. English ships would protect Neapolitan merchantmen.

Emma's letter to Greville, written at a time when there was, even among Neapolitans, considerable concern, serves to show the shallowness of her brain. Perhaps to the distraught Queen, her gaiety acted as a stimulant.

Caserta. June 2nd 1793.

I shou'd have answerd your kind letter sooner but I have not had time to write to any of my freinds these five months, which I am sorry for, as they may accuse me of neglect & ingratitude, which if they do, it will be a wrong accusition, for I litterally have been so busy with the English, the Court & my home duties, as to prevent me doing things I had much at heart to do.

For political reasons we have lived eight months at Caserta, that is, making this our constant residence & going twice a week to town to give dinners, balls etc, etc, returning here at 2 or 3 a clock in the morning after the fatige of a dinner of fifty, & ball & supper of 3 hundred, then to dress early in the morning to go to Court to dinner at twelve a clock as the Royal familly dine early & they have done Sir Wm. & me the honner to invite us very very often. Our house at Caserta as been like an inn this winter as we have had partys that have come either to see the environs or have been invited to Court. We had the Duchess of Ancaster several days; it is but 3 days since the Devonshire familly has left us & we had fifty in familly for four days at Caserta. Tis true we dined every day at Court or at some Casino of the King for you cannot immagine how good our King & Queen as been to the principal English who have been here, particularly to Lord & L^y Palmerstone, Cholmondlys, Devonshire, Sir G & Lady Webster & I have carried the Ladies to the Queen very often, as she as permitted me to go to her very often in private, which I do & the reason why we stay now here, is I have promised the Queen to remain as long as she does, which will be toll the tenth of July. In the evenings I go to her & we are tête a tête 2 or 3 hours; sometimes we sing, yesterday the King & me sung duetts for 3 hours, *it was but bad as he sings like a king*; today the Princess Royal of Sweden comes to Court to take leave of their Majestys. Sir W & me are invited to dinner with her. She is an amiable princess & as lived very much with us; we have given her several dinners, balls etc, etc for she loves dancing dearly. The other ministers wives have not shewd her the least attention because she did not pay them the first visit, as she travels under the name of Countess of Wasa. In consequence the Queen as not asked them to dinner to day & her M^y told me I had done very well in waiting on her R.H. the moment she arrived; however the ministers wives are very fond of me as the see I have no pretensions nor do I abuse of her Majestys goodness & she observed the other night at Court at Naples we had a drawing room in honner of the Empress having brought a son. I had been with the Queen the night before *alone en famille* laughing, singing, etc. etc. etc. but at the drawing room I kept my distance & pay'd the Queen as much respect as tho I had never seen her before which pleased her much, but she shewd me great distinction that night & told me several times how much she admired my good conduct. I onely tell you this to shew & convince you I shall never change but allways be simple & natural.

You may immagine how happy my dear, dear Sir William is & I can assure you if ever I had any little teazing caprice it is so intirely gone that neither Sir William or me remembers it & he will tell you the same: endeed you cannot immagine our happiness, it is not to be described, we are not an hour in the day separable, we live more like lovers than husband & wife, *as husbands & wives go nowadays.* Good Lord deliver me & the English are getting as bad as the Italians & some few excepted. I study very hard & have made great progress in French & musick & I have had all my songs set for the viola that Sir Wm. may accompany me which as pleased him much so that we now study together; the English garden is going on very fast, the King & Queen go there every day. Sir Wm. & me are there every morning at seven a clock, sometimes dine there & allways drink tea, in short, it is Sir Wms. favourite child & boath him & me are now studying botany but not to make ourselves pedantical prigs to shew our learning like some of our traveling neighbours, but for our own pleasure. Greffer is as happy as a prince, poor Flint the messanger was killed going from hence; I am very sorry, he was lodged in our house & I had really a love for him. I sent him to see Pompea, Portici and all our delightful environs & sent all his daughters presents, poor man. The Queen as expressed great sorrow. Pray let me know if his familly are provided for as I may get something for them perhaps. Addio. Love me & believe me your sincere friend,

E. Hamilton.
Pray dont fail to send the enclosed.

The execution of her sister in France came as a terrible blow to the Queen. She was in an advanced state of pregnancy and the news was almost too much for her. She fortunately had no trouble in giving birth to another princess in December (1793), but a bitterness had entered her soul that was never to be eradicated. On a portrait of Marie Antoinette which hung in her study, she wrote: "Je poursuiverai ma vengeance jusqu'au tombeau."

On 11th September, H.M.S. *Agamemnon*, commanded by Captain Nelson, sailed into the Bay of Naples. He had come with despatches for Sir William Hamilton, which asked for troops to assist in the garrisoning of the port of Toulon. According to Southey, Sir William told Emma that he was about to introduce to her a little man who could not boast of being very handsome, but who would, he believed, one day astonish the world. "I have never before entertained an officer at my house," he said, "but I am determined to bring him here. Let him be put in the room prepared for Prince Augustus."

It must not be thought that it was love at first sight when Nelson met Emma on this occasion. After much time spent at sea, any captain in the Royal Navy, especially if his age was no more than thirty-five, would be favourably impressed by a smartly dressed and attractive woman of twenty-eight.

Nelson was actually on shore for four days and during that time he was much taken up with interviews with Sir William Hamilton and Sir John Acton. The King was anxious to see him too and meetings were arranged each day, one of the occasions requiring a drive of five and a half miles, in the royal carriage, to the palace at Portici. To return hospitality, the King was invited on board the *Agamemnon*. As the ship was not in the best of condition for such an occasion, Sir William provided food, wine and other necessaries for the banquet. At 10 a.m. on a Sunday morning, Emma and Sir William went aboard accompanied by the Bishop of Winchester with his family, Lord and Lady Plymouth, Lord Grandison and his daughter together with, in Nelson's words, "other Baronets, etc." The King was to arrive at one o'clock, but a note from shore effectively cancelled all arrangements. A French man-of-war had been seen to anchor off Sardinia with three ships under escort. The guests were hurriedly despatched ashore, what was lent from the British Embassy was returned, and H.M.S. *Agamemnon* weighed anchor and was off to sea.

Emma's attention was not greatly taken up with Captain Nelson. She cannot have forgotten him entirely, for when he wrote to Sir William from Corsica, in May 1794, after the capture of Bastia, he enclosed a note for her. It would seem that his thoughts were more for her than hers were for him. He was impressed enough to write home to his wife, Fanny, that "Lady Hamilton has been wonderfully kind and good to Josiah. She is a young woman of amiable manners and who does honour to the station to which she is raised".

Rather a pathetic aspect of the meeting was that Emma's beauty was already full-blown, for, even though she was now only twenty-eight, hers was a type of figure which in youth can best be described as "luscious" and which so soon runs to fat. In this respect, her delight in what she called "guttling" did nothing to help matters. Sir William had already remarked that, "she knows that beauty fades". The signs were there already, and in three years' time Sir Gilbert Elliot was to inform his wife that Lady Hamilton was beginning to lose her figure. When Nelson was next to see her, she would have lost at least some of her outward charm.

He, himself, which was far worse, was to lose the sight of his right eye on 10th July 1794 when engaged with a battery ashore, attacking Calvi, in Corsica. He was struck by a shower of splintering stone which hit his face and chest, and the damage caused to his eye resulted in the loss of sight for all practical purposes, although he could still distinguish light from darkness. In July 1797, still before he met Emma again, he lost his right arm as he stepped ashore during a landing at Santa Cruz on the island of Teneriffe.

That he did not spend all his free time either thinking of Emma or writing to his wife is suggested by four short extracts from the diary of Captain Fremantle, which are quoted in *A Portrait of Lord Nelson* by Oliver Warner:

December 1794. Wed. 3.
Dined at Nelson's and his dolly. Called on old Udney,[25] went to the opera with him. He introduced me to a very handsome Greek woman.

August 1795.
A convoy arrived from Genoa. Dined with Nelson. Dolly aboard who has a sort of abscess in her side, he makes himself ridiculous with that woman.

August, Sat. 28.
Dined with Nelson and his Dolly.

September, Sun 27.
Dined with Nelson and Dolly. Very bad dinner indeed.

This seems to have taken place at Leghorn.

The occupation of Toulon by the British fleet was a failure. The Republican French troops besieging the town from the landward side, were continually being reinforced, and among their numbers was a young lieutenant-colonel of artillery named Napoleon Buonaparte. By February 1794 the Neapolitan squadron had returned to base. They had fought well, but their losses were 200 dead and 400 taken prisoner and much of their equipment was lost. Naples was bitter with dis-appointment and the poor Queen more depressed than anyone. The pro-French elements in the city were doing all they could to stir up trouble and there was unpleasantness in the town to say the least of it.

Two more letters from Emma to Greville seem to show that she was unaffected by what was going on around her.

Castellamare, Sep^bre 16, 1794.

I congratulate you, my dear Mr Greville, with all my heart on your appointment to the vice chamberlainship. You have well merited it & all your friends must be happy at a change so favourable, not onely for your pecuniary circumstances as for the honner of the situation; may you long enjoy it with every happiness that you deserve & *I speak from my heart*. I don't know a better, honester or more amiable worthy man than yourself & it is a great deal for me to say for what ever I think I am not apt to pay compliments.

My dear Sir William as had the disorder that me & all Naples have had since the eruption, a violent diarea that reduced him to so very low an ebb that I was very much alarmed for him notwithstanding I thought I shou'd have gone with him, but thank God, we are here as happy as possible in the Queens palace, enjoying every comfort & happiness that good health, royall favour & domestick happiness can give us, so much so, the other day, the aniversary of our marriage, Sir Wm told me he loved me better than ever & had never for one moment repented. Think of my feelings in that moment when I cou'd with truth say the same to him. I gave here that day a little fete here. Lord & Lady Plymouth etc, etc came down here & I never saw Sir William nor never was so happy myself. I tell you this because I know you will rejoice at it. I will write soon & send to you to setle with Mrs Hackwood, but all the things were spoilt & I had no right to pay for them, but I will setle it & pray go & tell her so; for the other affair I will write to you fully and as this is a letter of congratulation, nothing shall disturb our happy ideas. I wish you cou'd send me an English riding hat, very fashionable, but I desire you to put it to Sir Wms. account. We have company to day from Naples & I cannot write more than that I am my dear Mr Grevilles ever sincere & affectionate friend,

Emma Hamilton.

P.S. Mothers love to you; she is the comfort of our lives & is our house keeper. Sir Wm. doats on her. Give my love to the Col.

Caserta, Dec^ber 18th 1794.

I have only time to write you a few lines by the Neapolitan courier who will give you this. He comes back soon so pray send me by him some Ribbands, & fourteen yards of fine muslin work'd for a gownd or fine leno: ask any lady what leno is & she will tell you & pray pay Hackwoods & put it down to Sir Williams account with his banker, he told me I might, for I have so many occasions to spend my money that my 2 hundred pounds will scarcely do for me a constant attendance at court now once & generally twice a day & I must be well dress'd. You know how far 2 hundred will go. Today we expect the Prince Augustas from Rome, he is to be lodged at the Pallace here & with us in town. Tomorrow we have a great dinner at Court for the Prince. The Queen invited me last night herself. I carried Lord Bristol to her & we pass'd four hours in an inchantment, no person can be so charming as the Queen, she is everything one can wish, the best mother, wife & friend in the world. I live constantly with her & have done intimately so for 2 years & I have never in all that time seen any thing but goodness & sincerity in her & if ever you hear any lyes about her contridick them & if you shou'd see a cursed book written by a vile french dog with her character in it dont believe one word. She lent it me last night & I have, by reading the infamous culomny, put myself quite out of humer that so good & virtus a princess shou'd be so infamously described.

Lord Bristol is with us at Caserta; he passes one weak at Naples & one with us; he is very fond of me & very kind, he is very entertaining & dashes at every thing, nor does he mind King or Queen when he is inclined to shew his talents. I am now taking lessons from Willico & make a great progress, nor do I slacken in any of my studys. We have been here 3 months & remain four or five months longer. We go to Naples every now & then, I ride on horseback. The Queen has had the goodness to supply me with horses, an equery & her own servant in her livery every day, in short, if I was her daughter she cou'd not be kinder to me & I love her with my whole soul.

My dear Sir William is very well & as fond of me as ever & I am, as women generally are, ten thousand times fonder of him than I was & you wou'd be delighted to see how happy we are, no quarelling, nor crossness nor caprices, all nonsense is at an end & every body that sees us are edified by our example of conjugal & domestick felicaty. Will you ever come & see us; you shall be receved with kindness from us boath for we have boath obligations to you for having made us acquainted with each other. Excuse the haist with which I write for we are going to Capua to meet the Prince Augustus. Do send me a plan how I cou'd situate little Emma, poor thing, for I wish it.

E. Hamilton.

Greville was not idle in the matter of little Emma. He had had an interview with Mr Blackburn and wrote his impressions to Sir William.

January 5th 1795.

... I have begun my duty, and, notwithstanding, my income is encreased, I retain the same establishment and residence at Paddington. My room in the King's Mews makes this possible, & I have had sufficient experience to know that to be independent I must be prudent. The addition of a carriage would be a *luxe*, but the consequent increase of establishment and the expence would not stop there, & with the necessary expences of Court dress & attendance it would suit to anticipate receipt which only come when due the fourth quarter... .

You mentioned some time ago that the young protégé of L^y Hamilton should meet your assistance on proper occasion. I told you then I wished you to consult L^{y}H. as to what she advised, & that she was too young to be put to anything. Blackburn brought me an account of £29 for her board, etc, which I shall, as before, desire Ross & Ogilvie to pay. I enquired particularly about her; she will not be tall or handsome, but of a good disposition. I had mentioned to Blackburn the impropriety of raising her expectations, & she has no one idea to act or think upon beyond the quiet & retired life which she passes with Mrs Blackburn, whose daughters are near her age & are educated with her. I told B. that I conceived something would be decided this Spring, & if she is to be put in a way to help herself it cannot be as you suggested by giving a sum once for all; a premium is given during the period of learning, & after that time a sum may enable them to derive benefit. If in the interval any good sort of man, either with a profession or fortune, would marry, a moderate dot may have its effect. All this I write because within six months I wish you to consider & decide – both on L^{y}H. & on her éleve's account... .

The Queen was now putting all her despairing trust in the English. She had become on the most intimate terms of friendship with Emma, partly because the British Ambassador and his wife represented her life-line to England and perhaps a great deal more, because Emma was always cheerful, unafraid and encouragingly patriotic. The next letter to Greville shows that Emma was beginning to realise that her position was becoming more important politically. She was more thrilled than serious about it, however.

Caserta, April 19th 1795.

I write in a hurry as I have a vast deal to do and the Queen as just sent to me that a Courier is go of for England this afternoon. Poor Sir William as been in bed 8 days with a billious fever and was better but woud get up yesterday which as thrown him back and to day he is not so well, but the doctor who is in the house with me says their is no danger. I am very uneasy and not well myself as I have not been in bed since he was taken ill. He was allways subject to billious atacks, but after this illness I hope he will be better than he as been for some time for the quantity of bile he as discharged these days past is incredable and he is naturaly of a strong healthy constitution. We are going to get good sadle horses as we live much in the country; riding will do him good and is very good for billious complaints.

You never answer'd my letter by the last courier nor sent me what I wanted, so I will not trouble you with any more comissions, but try to find out somebody else *who will be more attentive to me.* My ever dear Queen as been like a mother to me since Sir William as been ill; she writes to me four or five times a day, and offered to come and assist me; *this is friendship.*

I have seen letters that the King of england is not pleased with this Court and Sir William because they did not leave Castilcicala with them. Sir W. did all he cou'd and he does not care wether they are pleased or not, as they must be very ungratefull to a minister like him that as done so much to keep up good harmony between the 2 Courts and as done more business in one day than another wou'd have done in ten, owing to the friendly footing he is on here with their Majestys and ministers, so if they are out of humer they may be, but between you and me, I have spoke a great deal to the Queen about the consequence it is to them to have a person of Castilcicalas abilitys and being beloved in England there and I believe he will return from a letter I had from the Queen this morning; and yesterday she said they wou'd do their utmost, but I can assure you Sir Wm. did all he cou'd to have him kept in England, so dont let them blame the best and most worthy man living, for they have no minister like him.

I have had Lady Bath with me here 2 days. I carried her to the Queen. She is very shy, but she took a great fancy to me as I put her at her ease and did the honners of a ball for her that she gave at Naples. She envited all the Neapolitan ladies of the first distinction and I was to present them and she took a *nervous* fit and wou'd not come out of her room for 3 hours. At last I got her out and brought her in to the room between me and Lady Berwick and I carried the ladies who were dancing one by one to her in a corner and she took such a liking that we are very great friends. Sir James seems a worthy good man, but Sir Wm. says he wou'd not have her with all her money, however I like her for I think she as a great deal of good about her. You was to have married her I think I heard. However, the Queen was very civil to her as she is to every body I carry to her. I have had a very bad billious fever this winter, near dying, but it was owing to fatige when Prince Augustus was with us, dancing, supping etc, etc, etc. Send me some news, political & private for against my will *owing to my situation here* I am got in to politicks and I wish to have news for our dear much loved Queen, whom I adore nor can I live without her, for she is to me a mother, friend & everything. If you could know her as I do how you wou'd adore her, for she is the first woman in the world, her talents are superior to every womans in the world and her heart is the most excellent and strictly good and upright, but you'l say it is because I am so partial but ask every body that knows her. She loves england and attached to our ministry and wishes the continuation of the war as the onely means to ruin that abominable french council.

Addio. Love to Machperson. Tell him I will write next post; I have received his. Poor Macaully is in a sad way by the villany of that vile Mackinnon.

Ever yours
Emma Hamilton.

During Sir William's illness Emma had been acting to some extent as his secretary as is shown by several documents in Italian and French that are copied in her handwriting. She still found time to write to Greville:

Casino Merala Sotto S. Elmo , Saturday 16th of May 1795.

Dear Sir,

I have onely time to say 2 words as the Courrier is going of. Sir James Douglas died yesterday & Macauley thinks their is a possibility of his getting the Consalship with enterest, which wou'd set his affairs a little to right; if it is possible do help him by speaking to somebody in power. Do you know Lord Grenville, 2 words to him wou'd do and they cannot make an excuse that it is given away as they don't know of poor Sir James death, so pray do your utmost for I wish of all things that poor Macauly may get it & do for god sake pay Mrs Hackwood my debt. I wrote to you in Jany last to beg of you to do so, but I am affraid my letters never got to you. Get the money from Ross & Ogilvey & let it be done emediatly, tho she does not deserve it, as the things are all spoilt & I never cou'd make use of any one thing. We go tomorrow to Caserta for ten days as the Queen as beg'd to see me & Sir W. as not yet seen their Majestys since his illness; therefore tomorrow we dine at Actons & go to Court in the evening were Sir Wm. will be receved with open arms by all. This air as done him a great deal of good & he is better than he as been for some years. The Queen as offered me to go to her Pallace of Castelamare which I believe we shall in the summer. In short, we are so happy, our situation here is very flattering in the publick character & in private we are models for all husbands & wives. This will give you pleasure I am sure. Remember me to the Col. tho he never thinks of me. Is the princess of Wales handsome, how can red hair be handsome. You are in the midst of *feats*. We shall next year as our princess Royal comes. In haiste. Yours sincerely

Emma Hamilton.

In 1796, George, Earl Macartney, was in Naples. He was a diplomat and had been sent to Russia in 1764 and to China in 1792. One can only wonder what he thought of the following letters which he received from the wife of the British Ambassador.

No date (February 1796)

I have this moment received a letter from my adorable Queen. She is arrived with the King. She has much to do to persuade him; but he approves of all *our prospects*. She is *wore out* with fatigue. To-morrow I will send you her letter. God bless you.

No date (February 1796)

I have been with the Queen this morning, and she desires so much to see you that I have appointed to carry you to her this evening at half past seven. She will be alone, and you will see her in her family way. You will be in love with her, as I am. Sir William is to go with us; shall we call on you or will you drink tea with us? – let me know. What a charming morning I have past; our discorse was on you, we could not have a better subject. We will go to the opera to-morrow, but I would give up all operas for *my Queen of Hearts*. She expects you with impatience. Addio, Caro Milord, ever yours,

No date (February 1796)

I have just received a letter from the Queen to put of the party till Sunday next on account of the weather, therefore, my dear Lord, you must dine with Sir William and self; pray do, at your hour; name it, bring your Secretary and tuter, not a sole more. We will shew your our house and all its fine prospects, and all in hand. Ever yours,

P.S. Go to Portici, and send me word what hour you will dine – ours is 3 o'clock.

No date (February 1796)

You will see by the enclosed I have just received from the Queen, my dear Lord, that there is a fatility about the opera; but I am sure you will think with me our dear Queen is worth all the operas in the world, so we will call on you at half past seven, for with Royalty one must be rather before one's time than after. Send me back my letter when you have read it, for I never shew Royal letters to anyone – first, for fear of showing pride, for you know I have none; and, last, for many reasons. How could you think we shou'd be angry with you – you are not amiable. Ever yours sincerely

Emma.

Sometime in August little Emma is again the subject of a letter from Greville to his uncle.

No date (August 1796)

... I was led to expect a line from L^yH. relative to the little protégé whose education you have paid for since your marriage. I have not misunderstood your intention, viz., that you wished to put her unto some trade, & by a benefaction once for all to settle her. I am surprised that it should be hinted more had been done than was necessary or required. L^yH. was better apprized than I was as to the whole, Mrs C. having been with the child to Mrs Blackburn's & the expectation of seeing her friends was perhaps a little imprudently hinted to it, for she has never forgot the impression, & tho' she has outgrown the memory of persons her mind has I find been, for a young person, very reserved; &, tho' I have not seen her for many years, I have had every attention & desired Blackburn to give her no high ideas, & I am convinced the economy & prudence of the family she is in cannot be exceeded, for Blackburn & his wife have now no other scholar, & has a very small income, which with prudence & the aid of Emma's board make out a decent living. I inclose an answer which Mr B. received on my saying that she must chuse a situation, & from various difficulty I have said that during the present half-year the option must be made; you will see that she is desirous to do anything, & has sense enough to see the difficulty of her situation. I do not find that she is handsome; Blackburn says that she has very large eyes & a sensible look, & small, but very active, sometimes ailing, but not sick, supposed to be worms. I hope you will excuse my tardiness in relieving you from this charge. I have thought a little money might be an inducement for a clergyman to marry her, & then I might help him on; but, if she does not make an impression on a good sort of man, I am sure I cannot find one for her; & then I do not know whether you would approve such aid. I enclose the last account, by which you will have all before you & may give me your clear decision. I am still uncertain of her history, but I believe her to be niece to Mrs C., & that her parents are alive; this she should know, for her age is now such as to make it proper to give her at least the comfort of knowing, or the certainty that she cannot be the better from receiving the information, neither of which I am able to give, unless LʸH. will inform you, or communicate to me her wishes... .

Pray let me hear from you; my kindest remembrance to Lady Hamilton, tell her your accounts make her appear as I wish her to be – the subject of praise; to Mrs Cadogan pray remember me kindly... .

Emma has at last realised that the position in Naples is becoming decidedly unpleasant. This is evident from her next letter to Greville, from which it also appears that her frequent and close associations with the Queen have caused her to assume what she considers to be a grand manner and to borrow Her Majesty's royal "we".

Naples. Sepᵇʳ 21st 1796.

We have not time to write to you as we have been 3 days & nights writing to send by this courier letters of *consequence* for our government. They ought to be gratefull to Sir William & *myself in particular* as my situation at this court is *very extraordinary* & what no person as as yet arrived at, but one as no thanks & I am allmost sick of grandeur. We are tired to death with anxiety & God knows were we shall soon be & what will become of us if things go on as they do now. Sir Wm. is very well, I am not but hope when the cold wether comes on & we go to Caserta,

I shall be better. Our house, breakfast, dinner & supper is like a fair & what with attendence on my adorable Queen I have not one moment for writing or any thing comfortable. I however hope soon to get quiet & I then will write you fully. Pray setle Hackwoods accounts, Sir Wm. desires it & send me by the bearer a dunstable Hat & some Ribbands or what you think will be acceptable. Pray do you never think on me. He is *our* Courrier so pray do not spare him. In haist, ever your sincere
                                                                                    Emma Hamilton

I have now tonight an assembly of 3 hundred waiting.

The grandeur that Emma found so tedious was certainly going to her head.

By the summer of 1795 the prospects of the Kingdom of the Two Sicilies appeared extremely poor. French arms were now being brought to bear on Italy and the chances of the kingdom of Naples being able to withstand any onslaught were so slight as to be negligible. Charles of Spain, King Ferdinand's brother, had every intention of changing sides and was writing earnest letters to Ferdinand to persuade him to follow suit. Ferdinand himself was inclined to favour the idea as he felt it would be gratifying to be able to counter the opposite policies of his Queen which were upheld by Hamilton and Acton. The British Government was inclined to suggest that Naples should make its own peace with Buonaparte's armies and thus free them from the necessity of keeping ships in the Mediterranean. They knew well enough from reports which had been received from their agents in Spain that some sort of alliance was likely between Spain and France.

Sir William's continued ill-health put Emma into a more definite role of go-between from the Queen to Sir William, and she was kept busy copying letters and carrying information to her husband and running back, so to speak, with any news received in letters from Nelson. It was during this period that she alleges she persuaded the Queen to allow her to copy a secret document from the King of Spain to Ferdinand and which she says that she sent by courier to the English Foreign Secretary, Lord Grenville. At a much later date, Nelson did his utmost to back up his story, as it was only natural that he would, but, although the whole business is far from clear, it seems almost certain that whatever Emma may or may not have sent by courier (whose expenses she estimated at £400 when she later tried to claim them from the British Government), the same courier appears to have carried other letters from Sir William and Sir John Acton which contained similar information about the Spanish alliance. The matter is not one of importance. The Queen herself was so ardent to co-operate with the English that any vital knowledge that she was able to glean would certainly be forwarded to London by one means or another, whether Emma handled it at any stage or not. The only point that is crystal clear is that Emma felt very important. By the end of September the government in England were fully aware not only of the Franco-Spanish alliance but of the terms of the pact by which the Spanish forces were ranged on the side of France.

Chapter 7

Nelson

IN APRIL 1798, Nelson, now an Admiral, was once again ready to put to sea after being in England for just over six months, during which he had been most tenderly nursed back to health by his wife. On board the *Vanguard*, he wrote rather testily to Fanny about discrepancies in the packing of his things, but he ended the letter by saying, "Nothing in the world can exceed the pleasure I shall have in returning to you"; a forecast that was to prove rather wide of the mark.

By May, he was in the Mediterranean on the lookout for supply ships bound for Marseilles and Toulon. A little later the *Vanguard* was dismasted in a storm and her accompanying frigates ran for shelter back to Gibraltar where they expected the disabled *Vanguard* would return for repairs. The flagship, however, taken in tow by the *Alexander*, had reached Sardinia. Here, at the port of St Pietro, her damage was repaired and the day after he put to sea again, Nelson learned from a passing merchant ship that Buonaparte had sailed from Toulon (the day before the storm) with a fleet of thirteen ships-of-the-line and 400 transports.

Now the hunt was on in earnest, but Nelson's squadron was badly handicapped. The missing frigates, being small fast vessels, would have been invaluable in carrying out a sweeping search for the enemy. Joined by Captain Troubridge with further vessels, Nelson received instructions from Admiral St Vincent for the chase, with the added comment that he should "open a correspondence with His Majesty's Ministers at every Court in Italy, at Vienna and Constantinople, and the different Consuls on the coasts of the seas you are to operate in". As a result, one of the letters written was addressed to Sir William Hamilton. It was a formal request, suitable to be shown to the Chief Minister at the Court of Naples, Sir John Acton, for the loan of frigates or other small ships from the Neapolitan Navy.

On 17th June (1798) the squadron anchored in Naples Bay, outside territorial waters, and Nelson sent Troubridge in the *Mutine* into the harbour to speak with Sir William Hamilton and to see what assistance could be arranged. The result was not encouraging. King Ferdinand dared not allow Neapolitan vessels to assist in tracking down the French fleet for fear of upsetting the rather shaky state of truce that then existed with France. Sir John Acton nevertheless furnished Troubridge with an informal order to all governors of Neapolitan and Sicilian ports to turn a blind eye to British ships taking on water and stores.

While awaiting Captain Troubridge's return, letters came out from shore for Nelson from both Sir William and Emma. Emma's note read:

(17 June 1798)

My dear Admiral, – I write in a hurry as Captain T. Carrol stays on Monarch. God bless you, and send you victorious, and that I may see you bring back Buonaparte with you. Pray send Captain Hardy out to us, for I shall have a fever with anxiety. The Queen desires me to say everything that's kind, and bids me say with her whole heart and soul she wishes you victory. God bless you, my dear Sir, I will not say how glad I shall be to see you. Indeed, I cannot describe to you my feelings on your being so near us. Ever, Ever, dear Sir, your affte. and gratefull Emma Hamilton.

In a second note, she enclosed a letter of the Queen's, presumably addressed to herself, and scrawled hastily:

Dear Sir, I send you a letter I have this moment received from the Queen. *Kiss it*, and send it back by Bowen, as I am bound not to give any of her letters, Ever yours, Emma.

Nelson answered with formal gallantry, rather relishing the reference to "kissing" which in the circumstances and the period would have been considered as verging on the risqué.

My dear Lady Hamilton, I have kissed the Queen's letter. Pray say I hope for the honor of kissing her hand when no fears will intervene, assure her Majesty that no person has her felicity more at heart than myself and that the sufferings of her family will be a Tower of Strength on the day of Battle; fear not the event, God is with us. God bless you and Sir William, pray say I cannot stay to answer his letter, Ever yours faithfully, Horatio Nelson.

Learning that the French had taken Malta, Nelson anticipated that they would then make for Alexandria. He sailed at once for Egypt with all speed, but, without knowing it, he was too quick. The port was empty except for a Turkish man-of-war, four frigates and the usual collection of merchant ships of varying nationality. Disconsolately he returned to Syracuse, where he was refused entry by the port authorities. He wrote a strong letter of complaint to Sir William saying that he had understood that private orders at least would have been given for his reception. He added that he complained "as a public man" and that every personal courtesy had been shown him. He informed Lord St Vincent that he was getting water and such refreshments as the place afforded, although in a second letter he said that "Our treatment in the Sicilian Ports is shameful. If they had the force, this Governor says, they are bound by their orders to prevent our entry. Acton has promised to send orders. None has been sent. What [do you] think of this?" Emma, who had written to him again, received an answer containing her share of the Admiral's indignation.

My dear Madam,

I am so hurt at the treatment we received from the power we came to assist and fight for, that I am hardly in a situation to write a letter to an elegant body: therefore you must on this occasion forgive my want of those attentions which I am ever anxious to shew you. I wish to know your and Sir William's plans for coming down the Mediterranean, for if we are to be kicked at every port of the Sicilian dominions, the sooner we are gone, the better. Good God! how sensibly I feel our treatment. I have only to pray that I may find the French and throw all my vengeance on them.

Next day, however, a further letter, in a different vein, arrived for Sir William, concluding with the usual respects for his Lady and announcing that Nelson was now ready to sail with the first favourable wind from "this delightful harbour, where our present wants have been most amply supplied, and where every attention has been paid to us". Rather paradoxically, but perhaps to cover up for the unofficially helpful authorities in Syracuse, Nelson added a final sentence "But I have been tormented by no private orders being given to the Governor for our admission."

It was later to be stated, both by Emma and by Nelson when putting forward a claim that the British Government should make some sort of financial award to her for her services to them in Naples, that the watering of Nelson's ships was effected only by Emma's astuteness in persuading the Queen of Naples to act in defiance of her husband's intentions. It is natural that the then famous national hero should wish to associate his mistress with his successes, even if facts had to be twisted in the process. There is no doubt that Emma realised that the victualling of the fleet was important. All the same the situation would have been far clearer to the Queen whose hatred of the French would have held her back from no action that would be to their disadvantage. She certainly ranted to Emma over the delaying and pusillanimous councils of the King and his anti-British Secretary of State, the Marquis de Gallo, and Emma agreed enthusiastically; but whether Maria Carolina wrote private letters to pave the way for Nelson or not, the only fact of importance seems to be that the Governor of Syracuse considered he had no official orders countermanding his instructions to deny his port to the British. If anyone is to be praised for acting on their own initiative it would seem to be the Governor. Fortunately the incident is not one that has any serious repercussions on Emma's life, for by the time the claims were made money was running through her hands like water, and it may be passed over in much the same way as the memorials to Parliament on the subject were passed over by the British Government.

Nelson's second approach to Alexandria was as disappointing as the first. As no French ships were to be seen in the harbour, he gave the signal to turn eastwards. Rather despondently, in the Ward Room and on the mess-decks, officers and ratings sat down to their midday meal. The sudden easing of tension was an anti-climax, but it was not to last. A mast-head look-out had spotted the enemy in Aboukir Bay, and the atmosphere at once became electric again. The French fleet was at anchor in tricky shoal water for which the British had no proper charts. Nelson was determined to attack. The thought of a night action in uncharted shallow waters in no way daunted his courage. He rose from table with a remark which had a decidedly egotistical flavour. "Before this time tomorrow," he said, "I shall have gained a Peerage or Westminster Abbey." His seamen had not quite the same alternatives before them, but they were tough fighting men inspired by their leader and would not have thought critically of the words had they heard them. At 5.30 p.m. Nelson signalled that he intended to engage the enemy. He banked on the fact that if a French 74 could swing at anchor, an English one would have room to get on the shore side of her where her gun ports were probably not cleared for action.

It is not proposed to describe the battle, as this book is concerned only with events in the life of Emma Hamilton. To her, the Battle of the Nile was a great victory, a crowning glory for Horatio Nelson and a great destruction of French ships. A dissertation on naval strategy would have been beyond her comprehension. She would far rather have listened to a recital of Mrs Hemans' poem, inspired by the battle, which begins, "The boy stood on the burning deck ..." had it been written at the time. Suffice it to say, therefore, that on the night of 1st August 1798 a hard fought naval engagement brought sadly needed battle honours to England, the first serious setback to the plans of Napoleon and, as a subsidiary issue, enormous relief to the Court of Naples.

During the battle Nelson received a wound on his forehead which, for a time, he feared to be a fatal one. However, on being examined by the surgeon, Michael Jefferson, he was assured that the injury was only superficial.

On 8th August Nelson wrote to Sir William informing him of the victory and two young officers, William Hoste and the Hon. Thomas Capel, were sent in the *Mutine* brig to Naples with the news. They arrived on Monday, 1st September, and delivered their despatches to the British Embassy. The King and Queen, the Court and all Naples went mad with joy, with the exception of the pro-French element who were forced to lie very low.

Taking several days, as she frequently did, to write a long letter, Emma addressed Nelson:

Naples, September 8, 1798.

My dear, dear Sir,
How shall I begin, what shall I say to you. 'tis impossible I can write, for since last Monday (when she first heard the news) I am delerious with joy, and assure you I have a fevour caused by agitation and pleasure. God, what a victory! Never, never has there been anything half so glorious, so compleat. I fainted when I heard the joyfull news, and fell on my side and am hurt, but well of that. I shou'd feil it a glory to die in such a cause. No, I wou'd not like to die till I see and embrace the Victor of the Nile. How shall I describe to you the transports of Maria Carolina, 'tis not possible. She fainted and kissed her husband, her children, walked about the room, cried, kissed, and embraced every person near her, exclaiming, Oh, brave Nelson, oh, God bless and protect our brave deliverer, oh, Nelson, Nelson, what do we not owe to you, oh Victor, Savour of Itali, oh, that my swolen heart cou'd now tell him personally what we owe to him!

You may judge, my dear Sir, of the rest, but my head will not permit me to tell you half the rejoicing. The Neapolitans are mad with joy, and if you wos here now, you wou'd be killed with kindness. Sonets on sonets, illuminations, rejoicings; not a French dog dare shew his face. How I glory in the honner of my Country and my Countryman! I walk and tread in the air with pride, feiling I was born in the same land with the victor Nelson and his gallant band. But no more, I cannot, dare not, trust myself, for I am not well. Little dear Captain Hoste will tell you the rest. He dines with us in the day, for he will not sleep out of his ship, and we Love him dearly. He is a fine, good lad. Sir William is delighted with him, and I say he will be a second Nelson. If he is onely half a Nelson, he will be superior to all others.

I send you two letters from my adorable queen. One was written to me the day we received the glorious news, the other yesterday. Keep them, as they are in her own handwriting. I have kept copies only, but I feil that you ought to have them. If you had seen our meeting after the battle, but I will keep it all for your arrival. I coo'd not do justice to her feiling nor to my own, with writing it; and we are preparing your appartment against you come. I hope it will not be long, for Sir William and I are so impatient to embrace you. I wish you cou'd have seen our house the 3 nights of illumination. 'Tis, 'twas covered with your glorious name. Their were 3 thousand Lamps, and their shou'd have been 3 millions if we had had time. All the English vie with each other in celebrating this most gallant and ever memorable victory. Sir William is ten years younger since the happy news, and he now only wishes to see his friend to be completely happy. How he glories in you when your name is mentioned. He cannot contain his joy. For God's sake come to Naples soon. We receive so many Sonets and Letters of congratulation. I send you some of them to shew you how much your success is felt here. How I felt for poor Troubridge. He must have been so angry on the sandbank, so brave an officer! In short I pity those who were not in the battle. I wou'd have been rather an English powder-monkey, or a swab in that great victory, than an Emperor out of it, but you will be so tired of all this. Write or come soon to Naples, and rejoin your ever sincere and oblidged friend,

Emma Hamilton.

The Queen as this moment sent a Dymond Ring to Captain Hoste, six buts of wine, 2 casks, for the officers, and every man on board a guinea each. Her letter is in English and comes as from an unknown person, but a well-wisher to our country, and an admirer of our gallant Nelson. As war is not yet declared with France, she cou'd not shew herself so openly as she wished, but she as done so much, and rejoiced so very publickly, that all the world sees it. She bids me to say that she longs more to see you than any woman with child can long for anything she may take a fancy to, and she shall be for ever unhappy if you do not come. God bless you my dear, dear friend.

My dress from head to foot is alla Nelson. Ask Hoste. Even my shawl is in Blue with gold anchors all over. My earrings are Nelson's anchors; in short, we are be-Nelsoned all over. I send you some Sonets, but I must have taken a ship on purpose to send you all written on you. Once more, God bless you. My mother desires her love to you. I am so sorry to write in such a hurry. I am affraid you will not be able to read this scrawl.

Miss Ellis Cornelia Knight, who was staying in Naples with her mother, kept a journal through the pages of which frequent glimpses of the Hamiltons may be seen. She provides a description of the *Vanguard's* arrival in the following words:

22nd September 1798.

In the evening, went out with Sir William and Lady Hamilton, music, etc, to meet Admiral Nelson, who in the Vanguard, with the Thalia frigate (Captain Newhouse), was seen coming in. We went on board, about a league out at sea, and sailed with him: soon after us, the King came on board, and stayed till the anchor was dropped. He embraced the Admiral with the greatest warmth, and said he wished he could have been in the engagement, and served under his orders; and that he likewise wished he could have been in England when the news of the victory arrived there. He went down to see the ship, and was delighted to perceive the care taken of a wounded man, who had two to serve him, and one reading to him. He asked to see the hat which saved the Admiral's life, when he was wounded in the head with a splinter. The Queen was taken with a fit of ague when she was coming on board with the Princesses. Commodore Caraccioli came soon after the King, and many of the Neapolitan nobility. It happened to be the anniversary of our King's coronation. The Admiral came on shore with us, and said it was the first time he had been out of his ship for six months, except once on board the Lord St Vincent. The Russian Ambassador and all the Legation came out to meet him. When we landed at the Health Office, the applauses and the crowd of people were beyond description. Admiral Nelson is little, and not remarkable in his person either way; but he has great animation of countenance, and activity in his appearance: his manners are unaffectedly simple and modest. He lodges at Sir William Hamilton's who has given him the upper apartment. The whole city is mad with joy.... . In the evening, went to visit the Admiral, at Sir William Hamilton's, where there was a grand illumination. The Neapolitans have written up "Vittoria" and "Viva Nelson" at every corner of the streets.

Nelson's own description of his arrival had a decidedly romantic flavour about it which can scarcely have been to the taste of the recipient of the letter, for it was addressed to Lady Nelson, Round Wood, Ipswich, Suffolk:

September 25th.

The poor wretched *Vanguard* arrived here on the 22nd. I must endeavour to convey to you something of what passed, but if it was so affecting to those only who are united in bonds of friendship what must it be to my dearest wife. My friends say everything which is most dear to me in this world. Sir William and Lady Hamilton came out to sea attended by numerous boats with emblems etc. My most respectable friends had really been laid up and seriously ill, first from anxiety and then from joy. It was imprudently told Lady Hamilton in a moment. The effect was a shot. She fell apparently dead and is not yet perfectly recovered from severe bruises. Alongside my honoured friends came, the scene in the boat appeared terribly affecting. Up flew her ladyship and exclaiming: "Oh God is it possible" fell into my arms more dead than alive. Tears however soon set matters to rights, when alongside came the King. The scene was in its way affecting. He took me by the hand, calling me his deliverer and preserver, with every other expression of kindness. In short all Naples calls me "Nostra Liberatore" for the scene with the lower classes was truly affecting. I hope one day to have the pleasure of introducing you to Lady Hamilton. She is one of the very best women in this world. How few could have made the turn she has. She is an honour to her sex and a proof that even reputation may be regained, but I own it requires a great soul. Her kindness with Sir William to me is more than I can express. I am in their house, and I may tell you it required all the kindness of my friends to set me up. Her ladyship if Josiah was to stay would make something of him and with all his bluntness I am sure he likes Lady Hamilton more than any female. She would fashion him in 6 months in spite of himself. I believe Lady Hamilton intends writing you.

May God Almighty bless you my dearest Fanny and give us in due time a happy meeting. Should the King give me a peerage I believe I

116

scarcely need state the propriety of your going to court. Don't mind the expense. Money is thrash. Again God Almighty bless you.

Ever your most affectionate Horatio Nelson.

You cannot write to Naples by common post. The Admiralty or Secretary of State is the only way.

It was an extremely foolish letter to write and poor Fanny's heart must have sunk when she read it. Her son, Josiah, in spite of her husband's statement to the contrary, did not like Emma, and he was soon to give expression to his feelings. For twenty-three days Nelson stayed in Naples, which he thought of privately as a court of fiddlers and poets, whores and scoundrels, feted by the populace, flattered by every attention from the Royal Family, and assiduously nursed to health by Emma. He relished each moment of his well-earned glory and Emma, by being with him on every occasion she could, basked in the reflection of that glory. Action, movement and excitement suited her temperament. The luxury she enjoyed as the Ambassador's lady in Naples was a pleasant change after the hardships of her early life, but it was continuing to spoil her character, and Sir William's kindly indulgence had done nothing to help it. He would have been better advised to have kept her on as short a rein as his nephew had done. Her nature craved excitement and in recent years it was only Vesuvius that had supplied the need. Now, the Battle of the Nile and the arrival of the naval hero of the occasion stirred her passions. Her attentions, with which Nelson found himself overwhelmed, were so pleasing to him that he gave no thought to the inadvisability of such a connection, which was soon to start the tongues of scandal wagging in London and to cause a growing disapproval of Emma in persons who had previously been full of her praises. Troubridge was conscious that his revered Admiral, now raised to the peerage, was going too far, and Josiah Nisbet was not long in realising that his mother was not being fairly treated.

On the 28th, Nelson found the time to write further to Fanny. He was not quite so naive and foolish as before, but he still could not resist referring to Emma as often as possible. The goodness of Sir William and Lady Hamilton, he said, was beyond everything he could have expected or desired. Her preparations for celebrating his birthday were enough to fill him with vanity and "good Lady Hamilton" was preserving all the papers as the highest treat for Fanny. He even repeated his words about Lady Hamilton "fashioning" Josiah in six months. Apart from Emma's praises, he was not exactly reticent in his own. He quoted an additional verse to "God save the King" which had been written in his honour, as he thought Fanny would like to sing it. It went:

Join we great Nelson's name
First on the roll of fame
Him let us sing
Spread we his praise around
Honour of British ground
Who made Nile's shores resound
God save the King.

On 1st October he wrote again. This time there was less about Emma, though more probably than Fanny wanted. She had to read that "The continued attention of Sir William and Lady Hamilton must ever make you and I love them and they are deserving of the love and admiration of all the world", and that, "My pride is being your husband, the son of my dear father and in having Sir William and Lady Hamilton for my friends". If she was pleased to hear that on her husband's fortieth birthday eighty people dined at Sir William's, 1,740 came to a ball and 800 supped, she could have done without the information that Lady Hamilton had said that the rostral column erected under a magnificent canopy in their garden was never to come down while they remained in Naples. Fanny was not told, however, that Josiah had got drunk at the birthday party and had become abusive. Before he was forcibly removed from the scene, he had made it quite clear that he strongly disapproved of his stepfather's indiscreet behaviour.

Towards the end of November the Neapolitan army under General Mack, who had been sent from Vienna for the purpose, marched against the French. No declaration of war was made and Ferdinand was not altogether enthusiastic over this drastic step, the dangers of which had been pointed out to him by the British Government. However, he had been brought to agree rather grudgingly with the forceful arguments of his Queen, backed by the Hamiltons and Acton whose opinion was that as Naples was bound to be invaded by Buonaparte, it was best to strike first. Nelson fully supported the idea and, with Emma acting most conveniently as his interpreter, gave opinions and encouragement that were perhaps a little outside his sphere. He was to assist by landing troops behind the French lines at Leghorn, and although the whole operation was badly managed, the Neapolitan army marched almost unopposed to Rome, which it occupied without a fight, the French General, Championnet, having withdrawn his troops. By 7th December the boot was on the other foot. General Championnet had concentrated his forces and was returning to Rome. King Ferdinand had to make an unceremonious exit and with bedraggled remnants of his army made his way back to Naples again.

Nelson, arriving back from Leghorn, learned that the whole operation had turned out a fiasco.

For a few days Naples was in a turmoil of despondency, religious fervour and depression. The King had determined to stay in the city and await the French onslaught. The Queen, with the assistance of Nelson and the Hamiltons had made other plans. She commenced packing up clothes and valuables and sending them under cover of darkness to the British Embassy from whence Emma passed them on to parties of Nelson's seamen, who took them on board the ships in the harbour.

For some time Nelson had realised that it might be necessary to evacuate the Royal Family at short notice. He had, in fact, told Emma so on 3rd October. The populace was becoming restive and strongly anti-French. On one occasion an excited mob had called for Ferdinand and his family to appear on the balcony of the palace. To placate them they came out, but were distressed to see an elderly man in the crowd, who had been a royal courier, clubbed and stilettoed to death, having been mistaken for a French spy. Whether Emma happened to be present on the balcony or not, she would have been sufficiently aware that the Neapolitans were in an ugly mood and that there was danger inside the city and on its approaches. It says much for her personal courage that she worked so efficiently in assisting these preparations for the flight of the King and Queen.

Arrangements were made to take the Royal Family on board the *Vanguard*. All was done with the utmost secrecy, as, if the Neapolitans were to discover that their King and Queen were about to leave them to their fate, they would obviously become quite out of hand. The first move was made when the ships, loaded with jewels, plate and currency to the value of £2,500,000 took up positions further out in the Bay so as to be out of range of the forts, in case of trouble. Admiral Caracciolo, who understandably resented the way in which he was overshadowed by Nelson, felt it a slur on his ships that the Royal Family was to sail in the *Vanguard*, although he had to admit that his vessels were undermanned and that in spite of offers of double pay many of his seamen had deserted because of anxiety for the welfare of their families.

Sir William had obtained Nelson's permission to send on board H.M.S. *Colossus*, which was bound for England, crates of the best pictures and vases from his collection, and for some time the interior of the Palazzo Sessa had had a somewhat desolate appearance. Emma was fully occupied with her duties on the Queen's behalf and was, no doubt, enjoying the sense of urgency and importance that went with them, so that she would have been unlikely to have given much thought to the

119

effect that the impending disaster would have on her own position. She was not given to introspection and under the circumstances it was just as well.

Rumours were beginning to spread around the city that the King and Queen were leaving. Time was now very short, but by 21st December all was set for the embarkation. Cornelia Knight's mother had already received a note which read:

To Lady Knight.   Naples   December 20th   1798.
My dear Madam,
    Commodore Stone will take care of you. Do not be alarmed, there is in truth no cause for it.

Ever your faithful servant
Nelson.

At the palace, preparations were complete. Embarkation arrangements were made and signed by Caracciolo:

First Embarkation
    The King
    The Queen
    Prince Leopold
    Prince Albert, and nurse
    Three Princesses
    General Acton
    Prince Castelcicala
    Prince Belmonte
    Count Thurn
    The Hereditary Prince
    His Princess
    Their daughter and nurse
    Duke of Gravina

This embarkation should be made at the Molesiglio at eight o'clock and a half in the night.

Second Embarkation
    Dr Ulderica Sanchez   }
    D. Ma.Giuseppa Bartoldy   }   Her Majesteyes
    Madame Chatelain   }
    Da Rosa, e.d. Giuseppa Pucci – The Princesses's

Mlle. Baselli, first	}	The Princess Hereditaryes
The nurse to the child	}	
D. Gius Garano		King's Confessor
D. Michele Troja – Surgeon		
D. Vin. Falco	}	King's Attendants
D. Niccola de Pietro	}	
D. Gius Vitta		Prince's do.
Abbe Labdan }		
Losinese	}	For the young Princes
Eccevina	}	
M. Pernet		Cook
Gaet. Lombardo and Son		Cook
Leop. Caprioli and Son		Ripostieri
John Kenish	}	Servants
Savari Salvante	}	

This second embarkation ought not to take place but two hours after the first – and some other boats besides should be prepared above those necessary for the embarcation of the described persons; in order to receive their Majestyes and Princesses baggage, for the *own* service. The rest and people appointed shall go on board of the Neapolitan ships.

The Two Princesses of France.
These should come from Caserta, and arrive by 11 o'clock or midnight in Naples, in case the weather should not permit to embark themselves at Portici, where it would be much better, but it is feared that a great swell continues there.

The two Princesses have got in their company four or six persons of their retinue.

As can be seen the operation was going to be no light matter. Nelson, in his turn, made clear instructions to his officers.

Most Secret
Three barges and the small cutter of the *Alcmene* armed with cutlasses only, to be at the Victoria at half-past seven o'clock precisely. Only one barge to be at the wharf, the others to lay on their oars at the outside of the rocks – the small barge of the *Vanguard* to be at the wharf. The above boats to be on board the *Alcmene* before seven o'clock, under the direction of Captain Hope. *Grapnells to be in the boats.*

All other boats of the *Vanguard* and *Alcmene* to be armed with cutlasses, and the launches with carronades to assemble on board the *Vanguard*, under direction of Captain Hardy, and to put off from her at half-past eight o'clock *precisely, to row half way towards the Mola Figlio. These boats to have 4 or 6 soldiers in them. In case assistance is wanted by me, false fires will be burnt.*

Nelson

The Alcmene to be ready to slip in the night, if necessary.

After two days' delay caused by a violent storm which not only upset the passengers in the overcrowded ships and tipped the King's Confessor out of his bunk, breaking his arm, but also made communication between ship and ship well-nigh impossible, the fleet sailed for Sicily at 7 p.m. on 23rd December. Nelson had intended to arrange for the destruction of the Neapolitan men-of-war left in the harbour, but the King and Queen, conscious of the value in hard cash of these vessels, objected strongly to such action. To end a deadlock, he ordered such ships as could be got to sea with jury rigging to sail for Messina as soon as they could, and orders to be left ashore for the remainder to be fired on the arrival of the French. H.M.S. *Alcmene* remained to complete this duty. At an early stage on the passage to Palermo Nelson's convoy encountered even worse weather.

The male passengers on board the *Vanguard* had been consigned to the Ward Room while the Admiral's quarters had been prepared for the women and children. Unaffected by the high seas, Mrs Cadogan valiantly ministered to the gentlemen, including the King, who were prostrate with sea-sickness, while Emma was even more occupied with the female members of the Royal Family. The little Prince Albert, aged six, had convulsions and the Duchess of Castelcicala cut her head on Nelson's sideboard. On Christmas Day the weather moderated and Prince Albert seemed to recover and ate a good breakfast, but by 7 p.m. he was very ill again and died in Emma's arms.

During this hectic and uncomfortable voyage she showed her very best qualities. Her innate kindness made her anxious to help as many people as she could in the cramped quarters below decks. She was as undismayed by the alarming motion of the ship as she was by the infectious atmosphere of fear which spread quickly among the passengers, both male and female. In her own description of this nightmarish passage and of the events that led up to it, some allowance must be made for her proneness to exaggerate, but, when this has been done, it does not alter the impression that she acted with bravery in most arduous conditions. Sir William certainly set her no example. According to one of the *Vanguard's* officers: "During the height of the gale, when Lady Hamilton could think of nothing more wherewith to console the desponding Queen, she looked around for Sir William, who was not to be found. At length it was discovered that he had withdrawn to his sleeping-cabin, and was sitting there with a loaded pistol in each hand. In answer to her Ladyship's exclamation of surprise, he calmly told her that he was resolved not to die with the 'guggle-guggle-guggle' of the salt-water in his throat; and therefore he was prepared, as soon as he felt the ship sinking, to shoot himself."

The *Vanguard* anchored inside the Mole at Palermo at 2 a.m. on 26th December, and the distressed Queen and the Princesses were rowed ashore before dawn, accompanied by Nelson himself, who returned to his ship by nine o'clock to assist with the more formal landing of the King, who was loudly acclaimed by his Sicilian subjects. Once ashore, Sir William took to his bed with a bilious fever brought on by cold, fatigue and the other discomforts of the voyage. After two nights as their Majesties' guests in the Colli Palace, the British Ambassador and his wife were allocated a house on the Marino promenade, the Villa Bastioni. The building, which adjoined the beautiful gardens known as the Flora Reale, was designed as a summer residence. In the cold and snowy January weather it did not appeal to the suffering Sir William, especially as it had no fireplaces. After a very few days Emma was sufficiently settled in to have the time to write Greville a long and fairly lurid description of the past weeks.

Palermo, Jan. 7. 1799.

I have onely time to write you one line as Sir William is not sure he can have a moment to spare today to let you know of our arrival here. We cannot enter into detail of our being oblidged to quit dear Naples. If you are aquainted with Lords Grenville or Spencer you will know the particulars from them, know onely the Vanguard Lord Nelson brought ous off with all the Royal familly & we arrived here on Christmas day at night after having been near lost, a tempest that Lord Nelson had never seen for thirty years he has been at sea the like; all our sails torn to peices & all the men ready with their axes to cut away the masts & poor I to attend & keep up the spirits of the Queen, the princess Royall, 3 young princesses, a baby six weeks old & 2 young princes Leopold & Albert, the last, 6 years old, my favourite, taken with convulsions in the midst of the storm & at 7 in the evening of christmas day expired in my arms, not a soul to help me, as the few women her Majesty brought on board were incapable of helping her or the poor Royal children. The King & prince were below in the ward room with Castelcicala, Belmonte, Grovina, Acton & Sir William, my mother their assisting them, all their attendants being so frighten'd & on their knees praying. The King says my mother is an angel. I have been for twelve nights without once closing my eyes, for 6 nights before the embarkation I sat up at my own house receving all the Jewells, money & effects of the Royall familly & from thence conveying them on board the Vanguard, living in fear of being torn to peices by the tumultous mob who suspected our departure, but Sir Wm. & I being beloved in the Country saved ous. On the 21st. at ten at night, Lord Nelson, Sir Wm. mother & self went out to pay a visit, sent all our servants a way & ordered them in 2 hours to come with the coach & order's supper at home. When they were gone, we set off, walked to our boat & after 2 hours got to the Vanguard. Lord N. then went   with armed boats to a secret passage adjoining to the pallace, got up the dark staircase that goes in to the Queens room & with a dark lantern, cutlasses, pistol etc. etc. brought off every soul, ten in number to the Vanguard at twelve a clock. If we had remained to the next day we should have all been imprisoned, but we remained 2 days in the bay to treat with the Neapolitans but alas with such vile traitors what can you do.

It is not a month since Mack went out with forty thousand men & shamefully to tell those forty thousand have been frightened & beat by about six, eight or ten at the most, nor cou'd the brave unhappy Mack make them fight all the officers bought by the French & all the army naturally corrupt. The gallant Mack is now at Capua fighting it out to the last & I believe coming with the remains of his vile army in to Calabria to protect Sicily, but thank God we have got our brave Lord Nelson, the King & Queen & the Sicilians adore, next to worship him & so they ought for we shou'd not have had this Island but for his glorious victory. He is called here nostro liberatore nostro salvatore.

We have left every thing at Naples but the vases & best pictures, 3 houses elegantly furnished, all our horses & 6 or 7 carriages I think is enough for the vile French for we cou'd not get our things off not to betray the Royal familly & as we were in councel we were sworn to secrecy, so we are the worst off; all the other ministers have saved all by staying some days after us. Nothing can equal the manner we have been receved here, *but dear, dear Naples*; we now dare not shew our love for that place for this country is jelous of the other. We cannot at present proffit of our leave of absence for we cannot leave the Royal familly in their distress. Sir William however says in the Spring we shall leave this as Lord St Vincent as order'd the ships to carry us down to Gibraltar. God onely knows what yet is to become of us, we are worn out, I am with anxiety & fatige, Sir Wm. as had 3 days a billious attack, but is not well. My dear adorable Queen whom I love better *than any person in the world*, is allso unwell, *we weep together* & now that is our onely comfort. Sir William & the King are philosophers, nothing affects them thank God, & we are scolded even for showing proper sensibility. God bless you my dear Sir. Excuse this scrawl & believe me, ever your most oblidged & gratefull

Emma Hamilton

I had a letter yesterday from Graham at Minorca. He is very well. I never saw him but we are in correspondence. God bless you; give our loves to the Col.

Life at Palermo was both busy and uncomfortable to start with. The very first official ceremony, and in wretched wet weather, was the funeral of the little Prince. The gloomy Colli Palace was insufficiently furnished, but nevertheless a reception was given for the local nobility almost at once. It was managed with efficiency, but it entailed a hasty note from the Queen to Emma apologetically asking her to arrange for getting the cases out of the *Vanguard's* hold, which contained all the Royal Family's Court dress.

On 1st January, 1799, the Queen wrote, "There is death in my heart, but in order not to give offence I have to be present at all this. The weather is so perishingly cold and it snows continually, so that all the streets and roofs are white, which is very extraordinary for Palermo. I have never been so cold in my life. Not a window or door can be closed, and there is not a fireplace or carpet in our rooms... ."

According to the journal of Cornelia Knight, who had reached Palermo with her mother, though not in the *Vanguard*, "We were, in all, about two thousand persons who had left Naples at that time." She and her mother seem to have been more fortunate in the matter of accommodation ashore than they were afloat, for later in the year she records in her diary: "At length we took apartments on the Marino, a magnificent promenade of considerable length. It consisted of a row of good houses, some of them really handsome buildings, a wide road for carriages, and along the sea-shore a terrace for foot passengers, with statues of the kings of Sicily at regular intervals. The Marino led to a beautiful garden named the Flora Reale, for in Sicilly all gardens are called Flora, and in the summer time bands of music used to play there for the entertainment of the company. The garden belonged to the king, and near it was a very pretty villa, which Sir William Hamilton occupied until he moved to a larger one near the Mole."

On 6th January, Sir William wrote to Greville to ask what he knew of the events in Naples since they had left. This was before the *Colossus*, with his treasures on board, was wrecked off the Scilly Isles. In the course of time some of his belongings were salvaged:

You have certainly the means of getting every intelligence of the singular events that have rapidly taken place in the kingdom of Naples, and from my last dispatch to Lord Grenville you will hear of the King & Queen of Naples and all their Royal Family having been obliged to take refuge on board the Vanguard, and by the contrivance and assistance of Lord Nelson and I are safely lodged in their Palace here with a treasure in jewells and money of not less than two and a half millions sterling. Emma has had a very principal part in this delicate business, as she is and has been for several years the real and only confidential friend of the Queen of Naples... .

After the initial festivities and receptions, the tempo of life at Palermo slowed. Sir William moved to a larger house, the Palazzo Palagonia, as Miss Knight said, near the Mole, and Nelson shared expenses with him, living there too when he was ashore. As the life at Court settled down to a routine, Emma found herself in an excellent position to increase the scope of her entertaining. She was beginning to get a taste for gambling. Like so many women in her position, she discovered that there is a delicious thrill in cards when one does not have to earn the money one plays with. In her case, Nelson was happy to supply it, and she was already starting to gain momentum on her downward path.

Naples was soon occupied by the French under General Championnet. There had been sporadic fighting and resistance by the lazzaroni, but this was quickly quelled and a form of government headed by pro-French Neapolitans was set up. It was idealistic and ineffective, and it went by the grandiose name of the Parthenopean Republic.

Gloom descended on Palermo and there were riots because of the high price of provisions. The Queen was in the depths of despair:

Palermo is in full ferment and I expect grave events. Having neither troops nor arms, lacking everything, I am ready for anything and quite desperate. Here the priests are completely corrupted, the people savage, the nobility more than uncertain and of questionable loyalty. The people and clergy might let us leave if we promised to agree to the

126

establishment of a republic. But the nobility would oppose our departure because then they would be ruined, and they dread the democratization of the country. They would prefer to rise and put themselves at the head of the movement and have us massacred, ourselves and all Neapolitans. The dangers we run here are immense and real. You may imagine what I suffer. Before forty days revolution will have broken out here. It will be appalling and terribly violent. My daughters are all ill. As for my daughter-in-law (the Princess Royal), she is dying of consumption.

The Queen's worst fears proved to be unfounded, nor did King Ferdinand share her worries – he was more concerned with organising a little hunting.

It was early in April that Nelson received amongst his mail from England a letter from his friend, Alexander Davison, written in February. It contained an ominous passage which suggested that Lady Nelson was not too happy with the news she had heard of her husband. "Lady Nelson", it read, "this moment calls, and is with my wife. She bids me say, that unless you return home in a few months, she will join the Standard at Naples. Excuse a woman's tender feelings – they are too acute to be expressed."

Nelson wrote to Fanny guardedly.

Palermo. April 10, 1799.

My dear Fanny,

Yesterday brought me your letters of December; they had been stopped in Italy, and now came by way of Venice. I had three days ago received two of February 4th and 11th. You must not think it possible for me to write even to you as much as I used to do. In truth, I have such quantities of writing public letters, that my private correspondence has been, and must continue to be, greatly neglected.

You would by February have seen how unpleasant it would have been had you followed *any* advice, which carried you from England to a wandering sailor. I could, if you had come, *only* have struck my flag, and carried you back again, for it would have been impossible to have set up an establishment at either Naples or Palermo. Nothing but the situation of affairs in this country has kept me from England; and if I have the happiness of seeing their Sicilian Majesties safe on their throne again, it is probable I shall yet be home in the summer. Good Sir William, Lady Hamilton, and myself, are the mainsprings of the machine, which manage what is going on in this country. We are all bound to England when we can quit our posts with propriety... .

Nelson was kept busy, as on 12th May the news reached him at Palermo, that Admiral Bruix had managed to sail from Brest in April and to enter the Mediterranean with a sizeable fleet. He recalled Troubridge, who with four ships was attacking Naples, and requested two more ships from Ball who was blockading Malta. During the last weeks of the month he carried out a search for the French. He returned on 29th May and on 8th June shifted his flag to the *Foudroyant*, under the command of Captain Hardy. On 13th June he set out for Naples with Neapolitan troops in charge of the Hereditary Prince, but returned again on receiving a signal from Lord Keith with further information about Admiral Bruix. For four or five days he cruised off Sicily to give protection should the French make an assault on the island. When they did not appear, he returned to Palermo.

Events on the mainland now looked more promising. Cardinal Fabrizio Ruffo, whom Nelson disliked and referred to as a "swelled-up priest", was a man of no little initiative and daring, even if his allegiance was sometimes doubted by the Royal Family. He had left Palermo, when all was depression and gloom, and had landed on the coast of Calabria with a few followers, including an ex-bandit, Michele Pezza, more generally known as "Fra Diavolo". The Cardinal's vivid personality and ruthless bravery appealed to the local peasantry who flocked to his standard and as he moved towards Naples his army of supporters grew, and he succeeded in forcing his way into the city.

Nelson sailed from Palermo in the *Foudroyant*, with the Hamiltons on board, having been given every authority by King Ferdinand to act as his representative for the recapture of Naples. On his arrival, he found that Ruffo, who had been besieging the forts commanding the town, had made terms with the defenders, who were to be allowed to leave their fortifications and stay in Naples or be returned to France if they chose. The Cardinal's idea in offering easy terms was to complete the capture of the city as quickly as possible, for, according to reports at the time, it seemed as likely that a French fleet would sail into the Bay as it did that an English one would. Nelson, however, had very different ideas, and from his position of superiority to Ruffo conferred on him by the King, countermanded the terms of truce and forced the defenders of the castles of Nuovo and Ovo to capitulate unconditionally. There was an unpleasant interview on board the *Foudroyant* between Nelson and Ruffo at which Emma and Sir William were present as interpreters, and which resulted in a disgruntled Ruffo becoming inactive and uncooperative. Captain Foote of the *Seahorse*, who had been left in Naples Bay under the Cardinal's orders when Troubridge returned to Palermo, received, rather unfairly, his admiral's unstinted displeasure on the subject of his falling in with Ruffo's plans. Nelson was undoubtedly in an unpleasant mood. He had no sympathy for rebels of any kind and he made it quite clear that he was prepared to give no quarter. Emma, who could be counted on to echo her hero's opinions, is reputed to have said, as the *Foudroyant* sailed into Naples, "Haul down that flag of truce. No truce with the rebels."

The feelings of the Queen are expressed in the letter she wrote to Emma on 25th June. It read:

I have received your dear letters from on board, undated, as well as those of Sir William to the General (Acton). I am sending the same ship back at once, and I wish I could give it wings to reach you sooner. The General writes the King's wishes, and the King himself writes a note in his own hand for the dear Admiral. Conforming in all things to their will, I can do no less than tell you our own sentiment. From the 17th of this month until the 21st the Cardinal has not written to us. He has written very casually to the General, but not a single line to us. He says little of the negotiations, nothing of military operations and mentions very cursorily those he has appointed, many of whom are guilty, suspect and inadmissable. These are the foundations, according to the King and myself, which we submit to the excellent judgement, heart and mind of our dear Admiral Nelson.

The rebels can receive no more help from the French either by land or sea. Consequently they are lost and at the mercy of the King, offended, betrayed but clement. He offered them a first pardon, and instead of accepting it they defended themselves desperately. The commandant of the Ovo Castle replied verbally, and with the greatest insolence, to the written intimation of the English Captain [Foote] and drove away his vessel. During the armistice they made a sortie by night and captured our batteries. It is therefore impossible for me to deal tenderly with this rebellious rabble. The sight of the valiant English squadron forms my hope. The garrison of Sant' Elmo must retire, escorted to Marseilles or Toulon, without permission to remove anything. The rebels must lay down their arms and leave at the King's discretion. Then, to my way of thinking, we must make an example of the leading representatives, and the others will be deported... . Note will be taken of these, and among them will be included the municipality, chiefs of brigades, members of clubs, and the most rabid scribblers. No soldier who has served them will be admitted into our army. Finally there must be an exact, prompt, just severity. The same apply to the women who have distinguished themselves during the revolution, and that without pity... .

The Cardinal must not appoint any official without proposing him beforehand. The sedili, the source of all our ills, the first real assembly of rebels, who ruined the kingdom and dethroned the King, must be for ever abolished, also the privileges and jurisdiction of the barons, to deliver from bondage a faithful people who have restored the King to his throne, from which the treachery, felony, and criminal indifference of the nobles had driven him. This may not be popular, but it is absolutely necessary; without it the King would not govern six months in peace. After having done so much for him, the people will expect his justice to uplift them. Finally, dear Milady, I recommend Lord Nelson to treat Naples as if it were a rebellious city in Ireland which had behaved in such a manner. We must have no regard for numbers: several thousands of villains less will make France the poorer, and we shall be better off. They deserve to be dropped in Africa or the Crimea. To throw them into France would be a charity. They ought to be branded so that nobody could be deceived by them. Thus I recommend to you, dear Milady, the greatest firmness, force, vigour and rigour. Our reputation and future tranquillity are concerned, and the loyal people desire it.

With such communications arriving, personally addressed to her from the Queen, it is not surprising that Emma should make no attempt to ameliorate Nelson's harsh contempt for the rebels. Much criticism has been levelled at the admiral's behaviour on this occasion, both at the time and subsequently, but, viewed dispassionately, his measures may have been stern although it does not seem that he acted outside his authority. The event that caused the greatest controversy was the execution of Admiral Caracciolo. The admiral, who had left Palermo with the King's permission to return to Naples in order to try to safeguard his property there, had gone over to the enemy and had in fact attacked English ships and those of the Royal Neapolitan Navy, including his own ex-flagship. When Naples was retaken, he realised that his life was in jeopardy and fled, disguised as a peasant. He was betrayed by one of his servants and hauled out from his hiding-place in a well. He was brought on board the *Foudroyant* and Nelson handed him over to a court-martial made up of Neapolitan officers under Count Thurn an Austrian in the Neapolitan service. The result was a foregone conclusion and he was condemned to death. Certain pathetic descriptions of the scene make him out to be an old man, but he was no more than forty-seven, and although his trial was a very summary affair, his despicable treachery could hardly recommend, in the heat of the moment, anything but the severest penalty. He was hanged, at five o'clock the same day, from the yard-arm of his own ship, the *Minerva*, where his body remained until cut down at sunset. Emma has been accused of taking pleasure in the wretched admiral's death and of being rowed round the *Minerva* to gloat on his fate. It certainly appears that she made herself scarce when Lieutenant Parkinson, to whose charge Caracciolo was committed, wished to invoke her assistance in trying to persuade Nelson to allow his prisoner to be shot and thus avoid the added disgrace of hanging. Whether Emma was at dinner at the time of the execution, as some say, or whether she was in one of the ship's boats or on the *Foudroyant's* deck is a matter for conjecture, but it would not be out of character if she relished the fact that an enemy of the Queen, to whom she was so devoted, had met his death.

On 10th July 1799, the King and Acton entered the Bay of Naples in the Neapolitan frigate, *Sirene*. Troubridge was busy bombarding the fortress of Sant' Elmo, which still held out but which had just hoisted the white flag. On sighting the King's ship, the defenders re-hoisted the French flag out of defiance. However, having transferred to the *Foudroyant*, Ferdinand watched the castle through a telescope and was delighted when he saw the tricolour and flagstaff blown down and a white flag appear once more. Sant' Elmo surrendered next day, but it was four weeks before the King went ashore.

Doubtless with the idea of pleasing Emma, Nelson found the time to write to Mrs Cadogan, whom he addressed as "Signora Madre". Dated on board the *Foudroyant*, Naples, 17th July 1799:

I cannot longer resist the pleasure it will give me to write you a line, especially as I can tell you that Sir William is grown very much better since his embarkation. Our dear Lady is also, I can assure you, perfectly well; but has her time so much taken up with excuses from rebels, Jacobins, and fools, that she is every day most heartily tired. Our conversation is, as often as we are liberated from these teazers, of you and our other friends in the house at Palermo; and I hope we shall very soon return to see you. Till then recollect that we are restoring happiness to the kingdom of Naples, and doing good to millions. Remember me kindly to Graeffer and the children. Tell them I hope they are much improved in their dancing, and particularly in *French*, as I hear you have taken a new master for them. Believe me we all long to see you, and we will go and dine at the Colli from a dinner of your ordering for us. Captain Troubridge goes against Capua to-morrow, and I am sure he will very soon take it. Mr White goes with him as a volunteer. Harryman is made a Colonel, and he now hopes Lady K. will have no objection to his connection in her family – in short, the poor man is almost mad with anger. God bless you, my dear Madam, and believe me, etc.

In fairly close succession Greville received three of Emma's newsletters.

Foudroyant, Bay of Naples. July 14 1799.

Dear Sir,
Lieut. Parkinson will deliver this to you; he carried a letter to the King from our King. We have placed him on his Throne again. Parkinson is a worthy good man; he will tell you our situation here for I have no time to write having so much to do, but you will be pleased to find we have done all in our power & succeeded for the Royal family & this Kingdom, but Parkinson will inform you. God bless you & believe me ever yours, etc.

E. Hamilton.

I came with a particular commission from the Queen to the Royalists & all is as we *wish'd*. S. Elmo surrender'd yesterday.

On board the Foudroyant, July 19th 1799.
Bay of Naples

Dear Sir,
We have an oppertunity of sending to England & I cannot let pass this good opertunity without thanking you for your kind remembrance in Sir William's letter. Everything goes on wel here, we have got Naples, all the forts & tonight our troops go to Capua. His Majesty is with us on board were he holds his Councils & leves every day. General Acton & Castelcicala with one gentleman of the bed chamber attend his Majesty. Sir Wm. & Lord Nelson with Acton are the Kings Counsellers & you may be assured that the future government will be most just & solid. The King has bought his experience most dearly, but at least he knows his friends from his enimies, he allso knows the defects of his former government & is determined to remedy them for he has great good sense & his misfortunes have made him steady & look in to himself. The Queen is not come, she sent me as her deputy for I am very popular, speak the Neapolitan Language & consider'd with Sir W. the friend of the people. The Queen was waiting at Palermo & she was determined as their had been a great out cry against her not to risk coming with the King for if it had not succeeded his arrival & not been well receved she wou'd not have been the blame nor be in the way. We arrived before the King 14

132

days & I had privatly seen all the Loyal party & having the head of the Laseronys, an old friend, he came in the night of our arrival. He told me he had 90 thousand Laseronis ready at the holding up of his finger, but onely twenty with arms. Lord Nelson to whom I enterpreted got a large supply of arms for the rest & they were deposited with this man. In the mean time Calabrease were commiting murders, the bombs we sent in to St Elmo were returned & the citty in confusion. I sent for this Pali, the head of the Laser's & told him in great confidence that the King wou'd be soon at Naples & that all we required of him was to keep the citty quiet for ten days from that moment. We give him onely one hundred of our marine troops, he with these brave men kept all the town in order & he brought the heads of all his 90 thousand round the ship on the King's arrival, & he is to have promotion. I have thro him made the Queens party & the people at large have prayd for her to come back & she is now very popular. I send her every night a messenger to Palermo & she gives me the orders the same. I have given audiences to those of her party & settled matters between the nobility & her Majesty. She is not to see on her arrival any of her former evil counsellers, nor the women of fashion alltho Ladys of the bedchamber formerly her friends & companions & who did her dishonner by their desolute life. *All, all* is changed, she has been very unfortunate but she is a great woman & has sense enough to proffit of her past unhappiness & will make for the future *amende honorable* for the past. In short, if I can judge it may turn out fortunate that the Neapolitans have had a dose of Republicanism but what a glory to our good King, to our Country, to ourselves that we, our brave fleet, our great Nelson has had the happiness of restoring the King to his throne, to the Neapolitans their much loved King & being the instrument of giving a future good, solid & just government to the Neapolitans. The measures the King is taking are all to be approved of, the guilty are punished & the faithfull are rewarded. I have not been on shore but once; the King gave us leave to go as far as St Elmo's to see the effect of the bombs. I saw at a distance our despoil'd house in town & Villa Emma that have been plunder d & Sir Will s new appartment, a bomb burst in it but it made me so low-spirited I dont desire to go again. We shall as soon as the government is fix'd return to Palermo & bring back the Royal familly for I foresee not any permanent government tell that event takes place nor wou'd it be politick after the hospitality the King & Queen receved at Palermo to carry them of in a hurry, so you see their is great management required. I am quite worn out for I am enterpreter to Lord Nelson, the King, Queen & altogether feil quite shatter'd but as things go on well that keeps me up. We dine now every day with the King at 12 a clock, dinner is over by one, his Majesty goes to sleep & we sit down to write in this heat & on board you may guess what we suffer. My mother is at Palermo, but I have an English lady with me who is of use to me in writing & helping to keep papers & things in order. We have given the King all the upper cabbins, all but one room that we write in & receve the ladies who come to the King. Sir Wm. & I have an appartment below in the ward room & as to Lord Nelson he is here & there & every were, I never saw such a zeal & activity in my life as in this wonderfull man. My dearest Sir Wm., thank God, is well & of the greatest use now to the King. We hope Capua will fall in a few days & then we shall be able to return to Palermo. On Sunday last we had prayers on board, the King assisted & was much pleased with the order, decency & good behaviour of the men, the officers, etc. etc. Pray write to me. God bless you, my dear Sir & believe me ever yours most sincerely

Emma Hamilton.

P.S. It wou'd be a charity to send me some things for in saving all for my royal & dear friend I lost my little all; never mind.

Foudroyant, August 5, 1799.
Bay of Naples

As Sir Wm. wrote to you to day my dear Sir, I will onely say that the Kingdom of Naples is clear. Gaeta & Capua have capitulated & we sail to night for Palermo having been now seven weeks & every thing gone to our wishes. We return with a Kingdom to present to my much loved Queen. I have allso been so happy to succeed in all my comissions & every thing I was charged with. The King is in great spirits. I have receved all the Ladies for him & he calls me his grande Maitresse. I was never taking him at his word but as I have had seven long years service at court I am waiting to get quiet. I am not ambitious of more honners, il est bonne d'etre chez le Roi, mais mieux d'etre chez soit. We have had the King on board a month & I have never been able to go once on shore, *do you not call that slavery*. I believe we shall come here in the Spring. It is necessary, for our pockets & bodys want bracing. Captain Oswald will give you this, he has been indefatigable under Troubridge & goes home to be made post. God bless you & believe me my dear Greville (tis not a crime to call you so) your sincere & affectionate

Emma Hamilton.

My mother is at Palermo longing to see her Emma. You cannot think how she is loved & respected by all. She has adopted a mode of living that is charming, she as a good appartment in our house, allways lives

134

with us, dines, etc. etc. onely when she does not like it, for example, great dinners she herself refuses & as allways a friend to dine with her & La Signora Madre dell' Ambasciatrice is known all over Palermo the same as she was at Naples. The Queen has been very kind to her in my absence & went to see her & told her she ought to be proud of her glorious & energick daughter that has done so much in these last suffering months. Their is great preperations *for our return*, the Queen comes out with all Palermo to meet us, a landing place is made, balls, suppers, illuminations all ready, the Queen has prepared my cloaths, in short, if I have fag'd I am more than repaid. I tell you this that you may see I am not unworthy of having been once in some degree your elevé. God bless you.

Swollen-headed though Emma was fast becoming, it is pleasant to see signs in these letters to Greville of her genuine feelings for him and her recognition of his kindness to her in the past.

The final days of victory in Naples coincided with the anniversary of the Battle of the Nile, and celebrations were organised on board the *Foudroyant*. Nelson described the festivities on 1st August to Lady Nelson in a letter three days afterwards.

To Lady Nelson, Round Wood, Ipswich, Suffolk.
Naples. August 4, 1799.

My dear Fanny,
A few days ago brought me your letter of May 6th from Clifton, but since then I see by the papers you have been in London. I am glad you went to court on the King's birthday. By the next I have no doubt but the world will be at peace and if Lord Keith had fallen in with the French fleet we should have had it by this time. Thank God all goes well in Italy and the kingdom of Naples is liberated from thieves and murderers, but still it has so overthrown the fabric of a regular government that much time and great care is necessary to keep the country quiet. Their Majesties have confidence in my councils which they know to be disinterested and are fixed in the belief that whatever I undertake is sure of success and indeed this is general to the Kingdom. However flattering this may be, it has its alloys for if anything was to go wrong my popularity would be over.
The first of August was celebrated here with as much respect as our situation would admit. The King dined with me and when his Majesty drank my health a royal salute of 21 guns was fired from all H.S.M.'s ships of war and from all the castles. In the evening there was a general

illumination. Amongst others a large vessel was fitted out like a Roman galley. On the oars were fixed lamps and in the centre was erected a rostral column with my name, at the stern elevated were two angels supporting my picture. In short the beauty of the thing was beyond my powers of description. More than 2000 variegated lamps were fixed round the vessel, an orchestra was fitted up and filled with the very best musicians and singers. The piece of music was in a great measure my praises, describing their distress, but Nelson comes, the invincible Nelson and we are safe and happy again. Thus you must not make you think me vain so far very far from it and I relate it more from gratitude than vanity.

I return to Palermo with the King tomorrow and what may then be my movements it is impossible for me to say. As to the co-operation of Turks and Russian fleets I see none of them.

May God bless you all. Pray say what is true that I really *steal* time to write this letter, and my hand is ready to drop, and as to my eyes I cannot see half what I write. My dear father must forgive my not writing so often as I ought and so must my brothers and friends but ever believe me your affectionate

Nelson.

The King's arrival in Palermo, on board the *Foudroyant*, was acclaimed with great enthusiasm. The Queen and her children came aboard to dine, and the whole party was later received ashore by the city dignitaries, dressed in togas. A twenty-one-gun salute was fired as they set foot on the newly erected landing stage, covered with decorations, and they were driven off to attend a thanksgiving service at the cathedral. Fireworks and illuminations followed and in the words of the Queen, "Palermo was drunk but not disorderly". Emma was embraced by Maria Carolina and given a diamond necklace from which hung a miniature of her dear Queen bearing the words, "Eterna gratitudine". Sir William received the King's portrait set in jewels. When they were back on shore, Emma was given further evidence of her Majesty's generosity in the form of two coach loads of dresses to make up for the finery she had lost in Naples. The Hamiltons, between them, are reputed to have received, in all, gifts valued in the region of £6,000. Nelson was persuaded to accept the Sicilian Duchy of Brontë, which was supposed to be worth £3,000 a year (though in actual fact he never received a penny from it), after much formal hesitation, being implored by Emma, at the Queen's instigation, attitudinising on her knees. The King is supposed to have clinched the matter by saying, "Lord Nelson, do you wish that your name alone should pass with honour to posterity and that I, Ferdinand Bourbon, should appear ungrateful?" Nelson's officers all received presents, Cardinal Ruffo and his brothers came in for pensions and estates and even Fra Diavolo and the guerrilla leaders were rewarded.

The festivities were rounded off with an evening *fête champêtre* during which the nine-year-old Prince Leopold, dressed as a midshipman, entered a Temple of Fame containing the life-size effigies in wax of Nelson, Emma and Sir William, removed the laurels surrounding the brow of the waxen hero of the Nile and placed it on the living one. Songs were sung in the admiral's honour and a firework set-piece represented the blowing up of *L'Orient*.

Rather naturally Emma was the recipient of many letters begging favours and was doubtless flattered into feeling herself a person of the greatest importance. She also heard from Lady Elizabeth Foster, who wished her to put in a word to help forward a friend's romance. Writing from Devonshire House (18th August 1799) she said:

I have kept my bed these last few days, which prevents my writing above a line to thank you for your kind letter & to congratulate you on the happy change of affairs at Naples. Have the goodness to offer my sincerest congratulations to their Majestys on this occasion; nobody can rejoice more sincerely than I do, & amidst the general joy could not you, dear Lady Hamilton, add to the number of happy my friend, Miss Ashburner, & let her be a bride at last? I really believe Perconte to be a worthy man, & that he would make her happy. Adieu, dear Lady Hamilton. The D^{ss}D. desires her best comp^{ts} to you, &c, with mine to Sir William Hamilton, I am, etc.

The social whirl, accompanied as it was by the relaxation of tension now that the Naples episode was over, had the unfortunate effect of taking Nelson's attentions from naval affairs and focusing them more and more upon Emma and on life in close company with her ashore.

It has been said, and there is some justification for such a supposition, that had Nelson been concerned solely with operations in the Mediterranean, of which he was now in command, his zeal for searching the seas for the French might easily have resulted in the capture of Napoleon on his return from Egypt. That, however, was not to be, and it suited his present amorous mood to consider as most important the instructions that part of his duty lay in co-operating with England's Neapolitan allies. He spent much time ashore and his evenings were for the most part taken up with attending Emma while she gambled happily at cards. Having paid a five-day visit to Minorca in October, he remained until the following January (1800) at Palermo. Scandal about his behaviour with the wife of the British Ambassador spread rapidly, not only in Sicily but in England too. Lord Keith remarked in a letter to his sister that Nelson was "cutting the most absurd figure possible for folly and vanity". Sir John Moore, who made a short visit to Palermo at this time, was appalled by what he found: "There is much less amusement here than I expected," he said. "I have seen no handsome women, and the kind of life I am obliged to lead is quite tiresome." His opinion of the Queen was anything but flattering. "The Queen is generally called clever; she is active, meddling and intriguing. She has assumed so much of the character of a man as to make her unamiable as a woman. The late Empress Catherine of Russia is perhaps her model. She has a lover, but with this difference – that Catherine rewarded her lover with titles and riches, but was not governed by him. The Queen of Naples has placed hers in an employment for which he has not capacity, is influenced by him, and as he is a Frenchman [an émigré named Monsieur de St Clair whom she had appointed to the staff of the Sicilian troops] it is more than suspected that she is betrayed by him. But the truth is that she is not clever, but in intrigue. She is a violent wicked woman." Sir John then crossed out "woman" and substituted "bitch". In order not to be unfair to the Queen, perhaps a comment should be added here from the journal of Cornelia Knight who wrote: "The Queen, who has been accused of so much vindictive cruelty, was, to my certain knowledge, the cause of many pardons being granted. And there was one lady in particular whom she saved, who was her declared enemy, and at the head of a revolutionary association."

Sir John Moore himself, at a later date, expressed a more considered opinion of the Queen, saying: "She is not herself a wicked or bad woman, rather the reverse, but she is guided very much by those about her, and unfortunately she shows little discretion in the choices she makes. If she could see, as other people do, the things her counsellors make her do, she would disapprove of them as much as anybody, for they are in general quite contrary to her principles. Her misfortune is to dabble in publick affairs, for which she has not capacity. In private life she would have been a clever entertaining woman, violent in her passions, but upon the whole kind and good."

"Nelson", to continue Sir John's earlier comments, "is covered with stars, ribbons and medals, more like a Prince of an Opera than the Conqueror of the Nile. It is really melancholy to see a brave and good man, who has deserved well of his country, cutting so pitiful a figure."

Troubridge felt so strongly about the situation that he courageously addressed a note to his admiral, saying: "Pardon me, my Lord, it is my sincere esteem for you that makes me mention it. I know you can have no pleasure sitting up all night at cards; why then sacrifice your health, comfort, purse, ease, everything to the customs of a country where your stay cannot be long. Your lordship is a stranger to half that happens and the talk it occasions. If you knew what your friends feel for you, I am sure you would cut out all the nocturnal parties. The gambling of the people of Palermo is publicly talked of every where. I beseech your lordship leave off. I wish my pen could tell you my feelings, I am sure you would oblige me. Lady Hamilton's character will suffer; nothing can prevent people from talking. A gambling woman, in the eyes of an Englishman, is lost." He had also written to Emma, as this paragraph from a further letter suggests.

"I am duly favoured with your Ladyship's letter of the 8th inst. & feel most completely happy at your promise to play no more. Be assur'd I have not written to you from any impertinent interference, but from a wish to warn you of the ideas that were going about, which you could not hear of, as no person can be indifferent to the construction put on things which may appear to your Ladyship innocent, and I make no doubt, done with the best intention – still your enemies will, and do give things a different colouring… ."

As a result of ships passing to and fro between Palermo and Gibraltar, the Rock was chattering hard about Emma's behaviour. Staying there, on their way to Sicily, Lord and Lady Elgin heard the rumours and decided to have as little to do with the Hamiltons at the Palazzo Palagonia as they conveniently could. Lord Elgin found Nelson full of zest and enthusiasm on naval matters though his wife commented that "they say that there never was a man turned so vainglorious (that's the phrase) in the world as Lord N." She considered that Emma was pleasant, looked handsome and sang well, but she added that, "My Father would say, 'There is a fine woman for you, good flesh and blood.' She is indeed a Whapper."

Emma had no thought for the morrow: she ate, drank and gambled to excess, going to bed in the early hours of the morning, caring nothing for the scandal with which she was helping to surround her Hero of the Nile. Her rocket-like path of achievement and success which had reached its highest point when she married was now dipping steeply downwards. The situation was prevented from getting even more out of hand by the return to Palermo, on 20th January, of the *Foudroyant* with Lord Keith on board. Nelson's conceit was sharply curbed by finding himself now only second-in-command and, furthermore, by the remarks which his superior saw fit to address to him. Luck was with him, nevertheless, for when, nine days later, he was ordered to sea with

Keith, the fleet, consisting *of Foudroyant, Northumberland, Audacious* and *Success,* fell in with a French squadron, one of which was *Le Généreux,* and Nelson was able to capture this survivor from Aboukir Bay.

After the engagement, Lord Keith sailed on towards Egypt, leaving Nelson to blockade Malta and pointing out to him that Syracuse, Augusta or Messina were more suitable bases than Palermo. Nelson sailed straight back to Palermo and the Hamiltons. As the *Foudroyant* was needed for duty off Malta, he transferred his flag to a transport and sent back the ship-of-the-line with Captain Berry in command. Back on shore once again, he found that his latest success was eclipsed by what Palermo society considered a greater sensation. Sir John Acton, at the age of sixty-four, had married, by special dispensation, his niece, who was not quite fourteen.

Once more Emma wrote to Greville, rather preening herself that she had been awarded the decoration of Dame Petite Croix of Malta for her personal services to the Maltese. Her own ideas of the assistance she had rendered in this respect may be a little exaggerated. Captain Ball was made Commandeur Grande Croix for his very real services in blockading the island and one may reasonably suppose that Emma's order was given more by way of a compliment to Sir William and, as everyone now knew what was going on, to Nelson as well. Her letter also breaks the news of their return to England.

25th Feb. 1800.

Dear Sir,

I recd. your letter by Mr Campbell. He is lodged with us. We find him a pleasant man; and shall write fully by him. He will tell you a little how we go on, as to our domestic happiness. We are more united and comfortable than ever, in spite of the infamous Jacobin papers, jealous of Lord Nelson's glory, and Sir William's and mine. But we do not mind them. Lord N. is a truly virtuous and great man; and because we have been fagging and ruining our health, and sacrificing every comfort in the cause of loyalty, our private characters are to be stabbed in the dark. First, it was said, Sir W. and Lord N. fought; then, that we played, and lost. First, Sir W. and Lord N. live like brothers; next, Lord N. never plays: and this I give you my word of honour. So I beg you will contradict any of these vile reports. Not that Sir W. and Lord N. mind it; and I get scolded by the Queen and all of them for having suffered one day's uneasiness.

Our fleet is off Malta; Lord Nelson has taken Le Genereux, and was after the frigates; so the attempt to relieve Malta has failed.

I have had a letter from the Emperor of Russia, with the Cross of Malta. Sir William has sent his Imperial Majesty's letter to lord Grenville, to get me permission to wear it. I have rendered some services to the poor Maltese. I got them ten thousand pounds, and sent them corn when they were in distress. The deputies have been lodged at my house; I have been their Ambassadress, so his M. has rewarded me. If the King will give me leave to wear it abroad, it is of use to me. The Q-n is having the order set in diamonds for me; but the one the Emperor sent is gold. I tell you this little history of it that you may be au fait. Ball has it also, but I am the first Englishwoman that ever had it. Sir W. is pleased, so *I am happy*. We are coming home; and I am miserable to leave my dearest friend, the Q-. She cannot be consoled. We have sworn to be back in six months; and I will not quit her till Sir William binds himself to come back. However, I shall have a comfort in seeing some of my old friends; and you in particular. We have also many things to settle. I think I can situate the person you mention about the Court, as a Camerist to some of the R.F-y, if her education *is good*. It is a comfortable situation *for life*; so I will bring her out. The Q. has promised me. Let this remain entre nous.... .

In view of Greville's past concern for the fate of Emma Carew, it is quite possible that the reference to situating "the person you mention" is intended to allude to her. If that was the case, nothing came of it.

By 24th April, *Foudroyant* was back in harbour, having assisted in the capture of the last major ship that had escaped from the Nile, the *Guillaume Tell*. Feeling that he should make a move of some sort, Nelson decided upon a visit to Malta. He decided too that pleasure should be combined with duty and invited the party from the Palazzo Palagonia, which now included Miss Knight who had been entrusted to the care of Sir William on the death of her mother. Cornelia was a little hesitant about the invitation, but when she was told that a visit to Syracuse would be included in the trip, she agreed to go aboard the *Foudroyant*. Contrary winds slowed the passage to Syracuse and Emma's birthday (26th April) was celebrated at sea. Toasts were drunk, Emma probably played the instrument at which she had been admired, in Naples Bay, by Midshipman Parsons, "bending her graceful form over a superb harp, on the *Foudroyant's* quarter-deck, every day after dinner", and Miss Knight composed a song for the occasion, dedicated "To a lady who is leaving Sicily with great reluctance". It began:

"Come, cheer up, fair Delia, forget all they grief,
For thy ship-mates are brave, and a Hero's their chief."

141

Two days were spent sightseeing in Syracuse, and then *Foudroyant* set course for Malta and joined the blockading force there on the evening of 3rd May. During the night the ship dragged her anchor, bringing her within range of the shore batteries. It was decided to move her at dawn, but as soon as their target became visible the batteries opened fire. Nelson was furious at this mismanagement of his pleasure trip and his temper was not improved when Emma, brave to the point of showing off, refused to go below.

After nine days at Malta, *Foudroyant* sailed for Palermo. Nelson had been subject to some slight heart-attacks and was far from well, while Emma let it be known that she had a fever, causing her hero to give orders for quietness in the ship. Cornelia Knight noted that Emma seemed low-spirited on the voyage back, though what she did not know was that Emma had just realised that she was going to have a child by Nelson – a very sobering thought. Sir William was not in the best of health either, and his condition was not improved by being knocked down on a companion ladder by a bustling Midshipman Parsons, who met him "tottering down with all the caution of age". The British Ambassador's relief was waiting in Palermo. The Hon. Arthur Paget had been sent out by Lord Grenville to take over from Sir William. The move was most unpopular with the Queen, who quickly realised that dealings with the British Government would now be more difficult, as indeed Lord Grenville intended they should be, and she saw to it that Paget was made to feel as unwelcome as possible. Sir William and Emma were depressed at the idea of leaving, although Sir William had, in fact, applied for permission to go home some two years before, saying that if leave could not be granted, he would be prepared to retire.

Once back at Palermo, all arrangements were made for returning to England and Sir William gave a farewell party which conveniently happened to coincide with the birthday of George III. The Queen of Naples had decided to put off taking leave of the Hamiltons by travelling with them as far as Vienna, taking with her her three un-married daughters, her younger son and a suite of some fifty persons. From Nelson's point of view the arrangements were chaotic. He had originally hoped to be allowed to take the Hamiltons, Mrs Cadogan and Miss Knight home with him in the *Foudroyant*, which was badly in need of a refit; but this he was not permitted to do.

Time was pressing. Napoleon had crossed the Alps and the French Army was moving down the Italian peninsula. An overland journey was determined upon and on 10th June the *Foudroyant* with its large cargo of passengers sailed for Leghorn. On arrival five days later, in the most inclement weather, the Queen went ashore, having presented

Nelson with a miniature of her husband, Sir William, and the captain with diamond-encrusted snuff-boxes, and Emma with another diamond necklace, this time set with ciphers of her children's names intertwined with locks of their hair. More bother ensued. The French had been victorious at Marengo, their troops were getting uncomfortably near Leghorn and the Queen of Naples began to get flustered. She decided she wanted to return to Palermo.

Lord Keith had just arrived from the capture of Genoa and was not in the mood to be trifled with. He promptly ordered the *Foudroyant* off to Minorca for repairs, leaving Nelson to transfer to the *Alexander*. He informed the First Lord of the Admiralty that he had been "bored by Lord Nelson for permission to take the Queen to Palermo, and prince and princesses to all parts of the globe". He announced that if Nelson wished to go home by sea with Sir William and his party, they could travel as passengers in the *Seahorse*, a frigate, or go by troopship from Malta. Feeling exasperated, and with some justification, he ended up by saying that Lady Hamilton had had command of the Fleet long enough.

It was therefore announced that the journey home would be made by land. Nelson disapproved, Sir William felt that in his poor state of health he would not survive the rigours of the road, and poor Cornelia Knight was appalled at the idea. Emma had decided that she could not bear the idea of going by sea and that she wanted to visit the different Courts of Germany, cost what it might.

Back in Palermo, Mr Charles Lock was writing in a letter home, "*She is now gone, thank my stars!*" Meanwhile, a resigned Cornelia wrote in her journal, "The die is cast and go we must."

Chapter 8

The Journey Home

THE FIRST PART of the overland journey to England is vividly described by Cornelia Knight in a letter to Captain Sir Edward Berry which she wrote at various stages along the route. She confirms the fact that Emma was ruthlessly having her own way, and her description of the coach accident makes one feel that Nelson was lacking in gallantry in his eagerness to be with Emma, when he left the elderly Mrs Cadogan and the rather naïve Cornelia, albeit in her early forties, to face what might easily have been a most dangerous situation. Only Sir William, ill as he was, expressed concern at having to abandon them. What, one wonders, were Captain Berry's thoughts when he read this letter:

Leghorn, July 2, 1800.

Dear Sir,

The very great, indeed, I may say, fraternal care you had the goodness to take of me while I was on board the *Foudroyant*, and the very sincere esteem I shall always have for Sir Edward Berry, induces me to trouble you with these few lines, as you will be desirous to hear of Lord Nelson, and the plan proposed for the party. The Queen wishes, if possible, to prosecute her journey. Lady Hamilton cannot bear the thought of going by sea; and, therefore, nothing but impracticability will prevent our going to Vienna. Lord Nelson is well, and keeps up his spirits amazingly. Sir William appears broken, distressed, and harassed.

July 16th. It is, at length, decided that we go by land; and I feel all the dangers and difficulties to which we shall be exposed. Think of our embarking on board small Austrian vessels at Ancona, for Trieste, as part of a land journey! to avoid the danger of being on board an English

144

man-of-war, where everything is commodious, and equally well arranged for defence and comfort; but the die is cast, and go we must. Lord Nelson is going on an expedition he disapproves, and against his own convictions, because he has promised the Queen, and that others advise her. I pity the Queen. Prince Belmonte directs the march; and Lady Hamilton, though she does not like him, seconds his proposals, because she hates the sea, and wishes to visit the different Courts in Germany, Sir William says he shall die by the way, and he looks so ill, that I should not be surprised if he did. I am astonished that the Queen, who is a sensible woman, should consent to run so great a risk; but I can assure you that neither she nor the Princesses forget their great obligations to you. If I am not detained in a French prison, or do not die upon the road, you shall hear from me again.

Ancona July 24th, 1800

As I find delays succeed each other, and England still recedes from us, I will not omit at least informing you of our adventures. We left Leghorn the day after I wrote to you by Mr Tyson, and owing more to good fortune than to prudence, arrived in twenty-six hours at Florence, after passing within *two miles* of the French advanced posts. After a short stay, we proceeded on our way to this place. At Castel San Giovanni, the coach, in which were Lord Nelson and Sir William and Lady Hamilton, was overturned; Sir William and Lady Hamilton were hurt, but not dangerously. The wheel was repaired, but broke again at Arezzo – the Queen two days' journey before them, and news of the French army advancing rapidly, it was therefore decided that they should proceed, and Mrs Cadogan and I remained with the broken carriage, as it was of less consequence we should be left behind, or taken, than they. We were obliged to stay three days to get the coach repaired; and, providentially Arezzo was the place, as it is the most loyal city in Tuscany; and every care, attention, and kindness that humanity can dictate, and cordiality and good manners practise, were employed in our favour.... Just as we were going to set off, we received accounts of the French being very near the road where we had to pass, and of its being also infested with Neapolitan deserters; but at the same moment arrived a party of Austrians, and the officers gave us two soldiers as a guard. We travelled night and day; the roads are almost destroyed, and the misery of the inhabitants is beyond description. At length, however, we arrived at Ancona, and found that the Queen had given up the idea of going in the *Bellona*, an Austrian frigate, fitted up with silk hangings, carpets, and eighty beds for her reception, and now meant to go with a Russian squadron of three frigates and a brig. I believe she judged rightly; for there had been a mutiny on board the *Bellona*, and, for the sake of accommodation, she had reduced her guns to twenty-four, while the French, in possession of the coast, arm trabaccoli and other light vessels that could easily surround and take her. This Russian squadron is commanded by Count Voinovitsch, a Dalmatian, who, having seen his people ill-treated, and their colours destroyed by the Germans last year at the siege of Ancona, made a vow never to come ashore, and keeps it religiously, for he has not returned the Queen's visit. I fancy we shall sail tomorrow night or the next morning. Mrs Cadogan and I are to be on board one of the frigates, commanded by an old man named Messer, a native of England, who once served under Lord Howe, and has an excellent reputation. The rest of the party go with the Queen, and say they shall be very uncomfortable. Lord Nelson talks often of the *Foudroyant*, whatever is done to turn off the conversation; and last night he was talking with Captain Messer of the manoeuvres he intended to make in case he accepted of another command. In short, I perceive that his thoughts turn towards England, and I hope and believe he will be happy there. The Queen and her daughters have been very kind to me, especially when I was ill; and poor Sir William suffered much when he left me at Arezzo. The Queen speaks of you often, and always with the highest esteem. Our party is very helpless; and though it is their own fault that they have brought themselves into these difficulties, I cannot help pitying them, and have the comfort to be of some use to them. Lord Nelson has been received with acclamations in all the towns of the Pope's States. Success attend you. Where shall *we* be on the 1st of August? The Queen asked me for the christian and surname of all the captains of the Nile. I am ashamed of the length of this letter, but it is pleasant to forget oneself for some moments, and renew a quarter-deck conversation. Our cots are ready, and the carriages on board, or I should not have had spirits to write so much.

Trieste, August 9th, 1800

As I know you will be anxious to hear how Lord Nelson proceeds on his journey, and as new delays continually occur, I will not refuse an opportunity offered me by Mr Anderson, the Vice-Consul. Perhaps I am a little interested in the affair; for, as I have small comfort in my present situation, my thoughts willingly recur to the Mediterranean, where there were always resources to be found. I told you we were become humble enough to rejoice at a Russian squadron conveying us across the Adriatic; but had we sailed, as was first intended, in the imperial frigate, we should have been taken by eight trabaccoli, which the French armed on purpose at Pisaro. Sir William and Lady Hamilton and Lord Nelson give a miserable account of their sufferings on board the Commodore's ship (Count Voinovitsch). He was ill in his cot; but his First Lieutenant, a Neapolitan, named Capaci, was, it seems, the most insolent and ignorant of beings. Think what Lord Nelson must have felt! He says a gale of wind would have sunk the ship. I, with Mrs Cadogan, came in another ship, commanded, as I believe I told you, by an Englishman, a Captain Messer, a plain, good man, who behaved with distinguished bravery last year at the siege of Ancona, and who was kind and attentive beyond description... . Poor Sir William Hamilton has been so ill that the physicians had almost given him up: he is now better, and I hope we shall be able to set off tomorrow night for Vienna. The Queen and thirty-four of her suite have had fevers: you can form no idea of the *helplessness* of the party. How we shall proceed on our long journey is to me a problem; but we shall certainly get on as fast as we can; for the very precarious state of Sir William's health has convinced everybody that it is necessary he should arrange his affairs... . Poor Lord Nelson, whose only comfort was in talking of ships and harbours with Captain Messer, has had a bad cold, but is almost well, and, I think, anxious to be in England. He is followed by thousands when he goes out, and for the illumination that is to take place this evening, there are many "Viva Nelsons!" prepared. He seems affected whenever he speaks of *you*, and often sighs out, "Where is the *Foudroyant*?"

When the party arrived in Vienna, Nelson and the Hamiltons went to call on Lord Minto,[26] the British Ambassador, who was living at St Veit a little way out of the town, or as Nelson described it "from Vienna about Roehampton distance from London". The house, which had once been a monastery, was a magnificent one and had most attractive and well laid out gardens. Nelson knew Lord Minto well and was grateful to him for his assistance in the matter of the awards that had been made to him for his services to his country. Lady Minto was delighted to see their old friend and was of the opinion that he had not altered in the least, although she expressed her disappointment about "Lady Hamilton and all that", and said: "He is devoted to *Emma*, thinks her quite an *angel*, and talks of her as such to her face and behind her back, and she leads him about like a keeper with a bear. She must sit by him at dinner to cut his meat, and he carries her pocket-handkerchief."

Lord Minto officially presented Lord Nelson and Sir William Hamilton to their Imperial Majesties, while Lady Minto did the same for Emma.

Although England and the English were not very popular with the Austrians at that particular moment in history, Nelson's recent exploits had a glamour for the Viennese which transcended political feeling. Whenever he left the house in which the party was staying, there were crowds of onlookers and on his arrival at the theatre the audience rose to its feet and applauded. This sort of excitement, as Pettigrew remarks, "proved as detrimental to Sir William's health as it was beneficial in recruiting that of Lord Nelson". Sir William had, in fact, had a bad time on the journey, as Lord Minto explained in a letter to Lord Keith:

Vienna, August 30, 1800.

Lord Nelson arrived here with Sir W. and Lady Hamilton a few days after the Queen of Naples having been detained at Trieste some time by Sir William's illness. Sir W. has had a relapse here; and altho' he has recovered a little yet he is so feeble and so much reduced that I cannot see how it is possible for him to reach England alive. Lord Nelson has been received here by all ranks with the admiration which his great actions deserve, and nothwithstanding the disadvantage under which he presents himself at present to the public eye. They talk of proceeding in a few days towards England; and I who am a lover of naval merit and indeed a sincere friend of the man, hope we shall again hear of him on his proper element... .

The stay in Vienna was a long one. The "Tria Juncta in Uno", as Emma liked to refer to the three of them because of the motto on the Order worn by both Nelson and Sir William, were invited here, there and everywhere. The Empress entertained them at the Schönbrunn palace; they stayed for four days with Prince Esterhazy; they visited the Queen of Naples (though not so very frequently) and on three consecutive days there was a firework display, a ball and a banquet. Four concerts were arranged and the old Oberkapellmeister of the Esterhazy's, Franz Josef Haydn, accompanied Emma when she sang his Nelson Aria, the words of which had been composed at short notice by Cornelia Knight. In the general gaiety and excitement, Emma's manners seem to have suffered, for, while Haydn was conducting some orchestral pieces, she went into another room to play Faro, helping Nelson with his hand of cards, and winning, so it is said, between £300 and £400. Haydn, however, either did not know of, or did not resent, her behaviour – or Nelson's for that matter – and was fussing round her as soon as he found himself free. Count Bathany was responsible for a day of aquatic sport and demonstrations on the

Danube, and the banker, Arnstein, pleased Emma with his attentions and entertainments.

On 19th September, the party visited the Minto residence at St Veit a second time and soon the Queen of Naples was off to take a cure at Baden. There was naturally a sentimental leave-taking, during which the Queen said that she would petition the British Government to reappoint Sir William to the Court of Naples. In a farewell letter to Emma she said that for herself her attachment would terminate but with her existence, and added, "To you I shall never change." Not surprisingly, perhaps, this declaration of devotion to "dear, dear Emma" was not to withstand the passing of time, accompanied as it was by the decline in Emma's importance.

Before they left Vienna, Nelson wrote to his prize-agent and friend, Davison, asking him to find him a house in London, "Not too large, yet one fit for my situation, to be hired by the month." He followed this up with a letter to Lady Nelson, saying that he would be home by mid-October and that he hoped that by then he would find her installed in whatever house Davison had managed to procure for him. Alexander Davison, it should be explained, had met Nelson in Quebec in 1782. After the Battle of the Nile he had been appointed as agent for the sale of the admiral's prizes. He had made a fortune as a government contractor, but as a business man his methods were open to question. Davison was proud of his association with Nelson, to the extent of erecting, after Trafalgar, a monument on his Swarland Park estate "in commemoration of private friendship", and never betrayed the trust that Nelson placed in him.

Prague was reached late in the evening of 27th September and they found the Hotel Rothes Haus, where they were to stay, illuminated in their honour (and, Cornelia Knight noted, charged on the bill). During the time they spent in this city they were entertained by Maria Carolina's nephew, the Archduke Charles, who gave them a dinner on Nelson's birthday.

The next port of call was Dresden, which they reached by water. Here they put up at the Hotel de Pologne and immediately notified Mr Hugh Elliot, the British Minister. The Elector and Electress, great sticklers for etiquette and decorum – so much so that Court Balls had been discontinued because of the sad state of Europe – did not view their arrival with enthusiasm. Emma's notoriety had evidently preceded her.

A young Irish widow, Mrs Melesina St George, who was visiting the Elliots, did not approve of what she called "the Nelson party". She recorded their visit in her journal with a cynical wit, but her scathing comments have an unpleasant ring of truth about them. It is an interesting point that even under this heavy fire of criticism, Emma's "Attitudes" come in for nothing but praise.

October 3rd 1800

Dined at Mr Elliot's with the Nelson party. It is plain that Lord Nelson thinks of nothing but Lady Hamilton, who is totally occupied by the same object. She is bold, forward, coarse, assuming, and vain. Her figure is colossal, but, excepting her feet, which are hideous, well shaped. Her bones are large, and she is exceedingly *embonpoint*. She resembles the bust of Ariadne; the shape of all her features is fine, as is the form of her head, and particularly her ears; her teeth are a little irregular, but tolerably white; her eyes light blue, with a brown spot in one, which, though a defect, takes nothing away from her beauty or expression. Her eyebrows and hair are dark, and her complexion coarse. Her expression is strongly marked, variable, and interesting; her movements in common life ungraceful; her voice loud, yet not disagreeable. Lord Nelson is a little man, without any dignity; who, I suppose, must resemble what Suwarrow was in his youth, as he is like all the pictures I have seen of that General. Lady Hamilton takes possession of him, and he is a willing captive, the most submissive and devoted I have seen. Sir William is old, infirm, all admiration of his wife, and never spoke to-day but to applaud her. Miss Cornelia Knight seems the decided flatterer of the two, and never opens her mouth but to show forth their praise; and Mrs Cadogan, Lady Hamilton's mother, is – what one might expect. After dinner we had several songs in honour of Lord Nelson, written by Miss Knight, and sung by Lady Hamilton. She puffs the incense full in his face; but he receives it with pleasure, and snuffs it up very cordially. The songs all ended, in the sailor's way, with "Hip, hip, hip, hurra", and a bumper with the last drop on the nail, a ceremony I had never heard of or seen before.

October 4th 1800

In a note about a visit to the Opera, Mrs St George includes the comment that Nelson and Emma "were wrapped up in each other's conversation during the chief part of the evening".

October 7th 1800

"Breakfasted with Lady Hamilton, and saw her represent in succession the best statues and paintings extant. She assumes their attitude, expression, and drapery with great facility, swiftness, and accuracy. Several Indian shawls, a chair, some antique vases, a wreath of roses, a tambourine, and a few children are her whole apparatus. She stands at one end of the room with a strong light to her left, and every other window closed. Her hair (which by-the-bye is never clean) is short, dressed like an antique, and her gown a simple calico chemise, very easy, with loose sleeves to the wrist. She disposes the shawls so as to form Grecian, Turkish, and other drapery, as well as a variety of turbans. Her arrangement of the turbans is absolute sleight-of-hand, she does it so quickly, so easily, and so well. It is a beautiful performance, amusing to the most ignorant, and highly interesting to lovers of art. The chief of her imitations are from the antique. Each representation lasts about ten minutes. It is remarkable that, though coarse and ungraceful in common life, she becomes highly graceful, and even beautiful, during this performance. It is also singular that, in spite of the accuracy of her imitation of the finest ancient draperies, her usual dress is tasteless, vulgar, loaded, and unbecoming. She has borrowed several of my gowns, and much admires my dress, which cannot flatter, as her own is so frightful. Her waist is absolutely between her shoulders. After showing her attitudes, she sang, and I accompanied. Her voice is good, and very strong, but she is frequently out of tune; her expression strongly marked and various; but she has no shake, no flexibility, and no sweetness. She acts her songs, which I think the last degree of bad taste. All imperfect imitations are disagreeable, and to represent passion with the eyes fixed on a book and the person confined to a spot, must always be a poor piece of acting *manque*. She continues her demonstrations of friendship, pays me many compliments both when I am absent and present, and said many fine things about my accompanying her at sight. Still she does not gain upon me. I think her bold, daring, vain even to folly, and stamped with the manners of her first situation much more strongly than one would suppose, after having represented Majesty, and lived in good company fifteen years. Her ruling passions seem to me vanity, avarice, and love for the pleasures of the table. She shows a great avidity for presents, and has actually obtained some at Dresden by the common artifice of admiring and longing."

October 8th 1800

"... the Electress will not receive Lady Hamilton on account of her former dissolute life. She wished to go to Court, on which a pretext was made to avoid receiving company last Sunday, and I understand there will be no Court while she stays. Lord Nelson, understanding the Elector did not wish to see her, said to Mr Elliot, "Sir, if there is any difficulty of that sort, Lady Hamilton will knock the Elector down, and ───── me, I'll knock him down too!"

October 9th 1800

[The occasion of the Elliots' farewell party, during which Emma repeated her Attitudes "with great effect".] ... All the company, except their party and myself, went away before dinner; after which Lady Hamilton, who declared she was passionately fond of champagne, took such a portion of it as astonished me. Lord Nelson was not behindhand, called more vociferously than usual for songs in his own praise, and after many bumpers proposed the Queen of Naples, adding, "She is my Queen; she is Queen to the backbone." Poor Mr Elliot, who was anxious the party should not expose themselves more than they had done already, and wished to get over the last day as well as he had done the rest, endeavoured to stop the effusion of champagne, and effected it with some difficulty; but not till the Lord and Lady, or, as he calls them, Antony and Moll Cleopatra, were pretty far gone. I was so tired, I returned home soon after dinner, but not till Cleopatra had talked to me a great deal of her doubts whether the Queen would receive her, adding "I care little about it. I had much rather she would settle half Sir William's pension on me". After I went, Mr Elliot told me she acted Nina intolerably ill, and danced the Tarantola. During her acting Lord Nelson expressed his admiration by the Irish sound of astonished applause, which no written character can imitate, and by crying every now and then "Mrs Siddons be ─────". Lady Hamilton expressed great anxiety to go to Court, and Mrs Elliot assured her it would not amuse her, and that the Elector never gave dinners or suppers. "What!" cried she, "no guttling?" Sir William also this evening performed feats of activity, hopping round the room on his backbone, his arms, legs, star, and ribbon, all flying about in the air."

October 10th 1800

Mr Elliot saw them on board to-day. He heard by chance from a King's Messenger that a frigate waited for them at Hamburg, and ventured to announce it formally. He says: – "The moment they were on board, there was an end of the fine arts, of the attitudes, of the acting, the dancing, and the singing. Lady Hamilton's maid began to scold in French about some provisions which had been forgot, in language quite impossible to repeat, using certain French words, which were never spoken but by *men* of the lowest class, and roaring them out from one boat to another. Lady Hamilton began bawling for an Irish stew, and her old mother set about washing the potatoes, which she did as cleverly as possible. They were exactly like Hogarth's actresses dressing in the barn." In the evening I went to congratulate the Elliots on their deliverance, and found them very sensible of it. Mr. Elliot would not allow his wife to speak above her breath, and said every now and then, "Now don't let us laugh to-night; let us all speak in our turn; and be very, very quiet."

The journey to Hamburg took eleven days and was not a very comfortable one. They stayed overnight at inns on or near the river, and these they found poorly furnished, with hard chairs and sanded floors; the food, too, was poor both in quality and quantity.

They were put out on arrival to find that the information about the frigate had been incorrect and that no ship awaited them. Nelson therefore wrote to request one and they settled down to enjoy the welcome that the city had organised for them. The English merchants provided a Grand Gala consisting of a dinner, a concert, a supper and a ball, while the Baron de Breteuil gave a breakfast at which all the guests were titled *émigrés*. General Dumouriez, who had defeated the Austrians at Jemappes in 1792, but who had subsequently refused to serve under Napoleon, came and joined the party. He was now in very reduced circumstances and was trying to make a living by writing. Nelson felt compassion for this shabbily dressed brother-in-arms and managed with much tact and even more generosity to find an excuse to give him £100.

Even the nice-minded Cornelia Knight was becoming uncomfortably aware that the behaviour of Nelson and Emma was not quite *comme il faut*. As she expressed it, she was "uneasy on many accounts". However, she felt a little better when she went on a shopping expedition with the admiral and helped him to choose some very fine lace to trim a Court dress for Lady Nelson and a black lace cloak for someone else. Walter Sichel mentions a little episode which certainly seems to suggest that Nelson's insatiable appetite for praise sometimes prevented him from realising that he was having his leg pulled. It appears that a local wine merchant pressed him to accept half a dozen bottles of hock as a token of esteem. In accepting, with Emma's encouragement, this tribute, one wonders what Nelson was thinking of, for the vintage was 1625, and, after the passing of 175 years, the wine would have been, to say the least, undrinkable.

On 31st October, (six weeks after the time Lady Nelson had been led to expect her husband's return home) no vessel had arrived in Hamburg in response to Nelson's written request, and so the party lowered their standards of travel and took the mail-packet, *King George*, from Cuxhaven to Yarmouth. To make matters worse, they had an extremely rough crossing.

Chapter 9

London

THE CROSSING of the North Sea, retarded as it was by the stormy weather, took the best part of six days, and the "Nelson party" did not land at Yarmouth until 6th November. The citizens felt rather strongly that the Admiralty had let their national hero down by failing to send a ship to bring him home, and were therefore determined to redress what they considered a slight by giving him the warmest welcome they could.

It was raining when the party arrived, but the bells of the town were ringing and a stout band of volunteers was ready to replace the horses and to draw Nelson's carriage up to the "Wrestler's Arms", where an infantry band struck up as the admiral, with Emma unsuitably clad in a muslin dress bordered with a design of oak leaves and laurel incorporating the words "Nelson" and "Brontë", came out on to the balcony and stood in the drizzling rain. Nelson was presented with the freedom of the city by the Mayor and Corporation and, at his request, a service of thanksgiving for his safe return was arranged in the church, where, on his arrival, the organist, according to Miss Knight, struck up "See the Conquering Hero comes".

In spite of writing to Fanny from Palermo, saying that he expected her to be in London for his arrival, Nelson seemed to think she would still be at Round Wood (their house near Ipswich), and posted a letter in Yarmouth heralding his coming. It read:

Nov, 6th, 1800,

My dear Fanny,
 We are this moment arriv'd and the post only allows me to say that we shall set off tomorrow noon, and be with you on Saturday, to dinner. I have only had time to open one of your letters, my visits are so

numerous. May God bless you and my Dear Father, and believe me ever, your affectionate
Brontë Nelson of the Nile.

Sir and Lady Hamilton beg their best regards, and will accept your offer of a bed. Mrs Cadogan and Miss Knight with all the servants, will proceed to Colchester.

I beg my Dear Father to be assured of my Duty and every tender feeling of a son.

Next morning when they left Yarmouth, a mounted escort of the local Volunteers accompanied them as far as the county boundary and they were greeted with enthusiastic cheering from the crowded streets of the towns and villages as they passed on their way. The detour to Round Wood was an anti-climax. The carriage, with Nelson, Sir William and Emma in it, drew up at the house only to receive the information that Lady Nelson was in Town staying at No. 64 Upper Seymour Street, Portman Square, and that Nelson's father, the Rev. Edmund Nelson, had left early that morning to join her. It is likely that the admiral was more irritated than disappointed by the news, especially if he remembered that Fanny was simply obeying his own previous instructions, and the more so as he had expressed to Davison his dislike of the Portman Square neighbourhood. As the carriage drove away from the house in which he had never stayed, lightning flickered in the sky, theatrically and ominously. As if to continue this dramatic effect, the worst storm for nearly a hundred years broke over London when the travellers, who had taken the journey in easy stages, still had two more hours on the road to complete.

With the thunder still rumbling, Nelson met his wife and father in the foyer of Nerot's Hotel (17 King Street, St James's – a site subsequently occupied by the St James's Theatre) at 3 p.m. on Sunday, 9th November 1800. The Saturday papers had heralded the homecoming of Lord Nelson. One had actually gone so far as to quote the song Cornelia Knight composed for Emma's birthday on board the *Foudroyant* and had made no bones about changing the words "fair Delia" for "fair Emma". Whether or not Lady Nelson had read this particular paper, she was by now well aware of the rumours that were going about and her reception of her husband was distinctly cool; the fact that he was in full uniform with two medals and two stars failed to impress her. Poor Fanny Nelson must have realised as soon as she saw Emma that if her husband was infatuated by this type of womanhood, her day was done. For the sake of appearances, and also because Fanny was devoted to her ageing father-in-law, she held herself in check for the dinner to which the five of them sat down at five o'clock. It is doubtful whether Emma would have been affected by the strained atmosphere, but Sir William must have been very conscious of it even if the full implications of his wife's reserved manner had not yet dawned on Nelson. Charles Greville had called earlier and had presumably left a note of welcome for his uncle, while the Duke of Queensberry paid a short visit on Sir William about ten minutes after the initial introductions had been made. At 7.30 p.m. Nelson was off to report to the First Lord of the Admiralty and soon after, to avoid, perhaps, having to spend the rest of the evening with the Hamiltons, Fanny left Nerot's Hotel on a visit to Lady Spencer, though, as she was the First Lord's wife, it seems a little pointed that Fanny did not take the opportunity of sharing her husband's coach.

Mrs Cadogan and Cornelia Knight had gone straight to an hotel in Albemarle Street. "In the evening," writes Miss Knight, "Sir Thomas Troubridge called upon me. He was at the point of starting for Torbay, being appointed captain of the Channel fleet, under Lord St Vincent. He advised me to go to my friend Mrs Nepean, whose husband was Secretary to the Admiralty, and who, on the following day, made me take possession of a room in her house till her children came home for the holidays. Sir William and Lady Hamilton also left the hotel to occupy a house in Grosvenor Square (No. 22), which had been lent to them by Mr Beckford, whose wife, Lady Margaret, had been a relative of Sir William." While the general populace was full of enthusiasm for the hero of the hour, the upper strata of society were not so favourably impressed. Lord St Vincent, on Nelson's first evening in town, wrote to Sir Evan Nepean: "It is evident from Lord Nelson's letter to you on his landing, that he is doubtful of the propriety of his conduct. I have no doubt he is pledged to getting Lady H. received at St James's, and everywhere, and that he will get into much *brouillerie* about it... ."

The Nelsons soon moved into the house that Davison had taken for them. It was No. 17 Dover Street, a large house that had been taken for a year. Although they were now apart from the Hamiltons, the separation was only a matter of a few streets, and without any need on Nelson's or Emma's part for engineering meetings it was natural that the two couples should find themselves frequently in each other's company. The newspapers kept the curiosity of their readers well fed. They reported that Sir William visited Lord Grenville at the Foreign Office on the Monday (7th November) and that Nelson called at the Admiralty and then at the Navy Office. One reporter volunteered the information that the admiral, accompanied by Davison, went to a shop in Holborn to buy a dog for Lady Hamilton. It was a large and rather wild animal and in a matter of weeks the unfortunate creature was again in the news. Wearing a silver collar bearing its name, "Nileus", it was reported as lost, stolen or strayed.

On the same day as he bought Nileus, Nelson spent some time in the apartments of the Duke of Clarence watching the procession of peers to the House of Lords, and in the evening he was present at the Lord Mayor's banquet, where he was presented with a jewelled sword worth some two hundred guineas. After the triumphant success of the evening, which even began by his coach being dragged from Ludgate Hill to the Guildhall by cheering citizens, the levée at St James's Palace next day was a sobering affair. Attending with Sir William, Nelson found himself put in his place by the King, who, after expressing the hope that his health had improved, turned away and spoke to him no more. Lady Elizabeth Foster, who was an admirer and whose son Nelson was later able to get placed in the Navy, wrote kindly that "It is supposed that Nelson was not so well received by the King as was expected, that H.M. disapproved of his having interfered with politics at Naples and that he was influenced to it by Lady Hamilton. Fox and many think that she did not exert that influence on the side of mercy – but I am unwilling to believe this. The Hero of the Nile is as humane as brave and she is a good-natured woman."

Arriving after the levée at Admiralty House for a dinner party given by Lady Spencer, Nelson was in a black mood. It appears that at the end of the meal, Fanny had shelled some walnuts for her husband and pushed them across the table to him in a wine glass. When he roughly pushed the glass aside so that it broke, she burst into tears. When the ladies were on their own, Lady Nelson confided to her hostess "how she was situated".

Even knowing he was so much in the public eye, Nelson seemed to have little thought for the impression he was creating. Having taken a box at Covent Garden for the performance of a piece entitled "The Mouth of the Nile", he was greeted enthusiastically by the audience and then tactlessly sat down with Lady Nelson on his left and Emma in the seat of honour, giving the public something to talk about and making his father and Sir William Hamilton feel very uncomfortable. The *Morning Herald* reported as follows:

Wednesday, November 19, 1800.

Lord and Lady Nelson, Sir William and Lady Hamilton and the Reverend Mr Nelson, the venerable father of the hero of the Nile, were last night present at the last new comedy of "Life" and the musical entertainment of "The Mouth of the Nile".

The noble and gallant Admiral as soon as he presented himself to the audience was received with the most ecstatic and reiterated bursts of applause we ever recollect to have witnessed on any similar occasion. While this generous manifestation of regard on the part of the admiring crowd took place, his Lordship standing up in the front of the box bowed frequently to the applauding company in grateful return; and his venerable father, completely overcome with the interest of the scene, at length gave vent to his paternal feelings by a most plenteous flow of tears. "Rule Britannia" was then called for and sung amidst the general plaudits of the house, after which the performance of the comedy commenced and the whole went off with infinite éclat. At the conclusion of the play Munden sang the last new song of the junior Dibdin, in honour of the splendid achievements of the noble Admiral, which was encored amidst an unprecedented tumult of enthusiastic exultation and applause: his Lordship by a graceful bow returned the flattering compliment. "Rule Britannia" was then again called for and the demand was instantly complied with. In the entertainment of "The Mouth of the Nile" Emery's song recounting the exploits of our several naval heroes was also encored: and the whole of the performance being terminated, his Lordship took his departure amidst the joyous acclamations of a full and splendid audience.

The hero of the Nile was in the front of the second box from the stage on the Prince's side, Lady Hamilton being seated on his right, and Lady Nelson on his left. Sir William Hamilton sat behind his lady, and the Reverend Mr Nelson in the front of the adjoining box.

Lady Nelson appeared in white with a violet satin head dress and a small white feather. Her ladyship's person is of a very pleasing description: her features are handsome and exceedingly interesting, and her general appearance is at once prepossessing and elegant. Lady Hamilton is rather *embonpoint* but her person is nevertheless highly graceful and her face extremely pretty. She wore a blue satin gown and head dress with a fine plume of feathers.

Prince Augustus, the Duchess of Leeds, Lords Chesterfield and Shrewsbury formed also a part of the brilliant circle.

For a short time Lady Nelson did her best to keep up outward appearances. Any hopes that she may have had that their reunion would curb her husband's flagrant behaviour must have vanished within the first twenty-four hours.

On 20th November, Nelson took his seat in the House of Lords, and on the 21st there was a dinner and concert given by the Hamiltons at

Grosvenor Square, to which certain minor royalty had been invited. It would seem that Fanny did not feel up to facing Emma as hostess, for she was indisposed that evening. Two days later, however, she did dine at Grosvenor Square, as Cornelia Knight was there and noted down that "Lord and Lady Nelson were of the party, and the Duke of Sussex and Lady Augusta Murray came in the evening". She went on to say that "Lord Nelson was to make his appearance at the theatre next day, but I declined to go with the party. I afterwards heard that Lady Nelson fainted in the box. Most of my friends were very urgent with me to drop the acquaintance, but, circumstanced as I had been, I feared the charge of ingratitude, though greatly embarrassed as to what to do, for things became very unpleasant. So much was said about the attachment of Lord Nelson to Lady Hamilton, that it made the matter still worse. He felt irritated, and took it up in an unfortunate manner by devoting himself more and more to her, for the purpose of what he called supporting her."

The incident at the theatre took place at Drury Lane. The party in Nelson's box, as well as Lady Nelson, the Hamiltons and the Rev. Edmund Nelson, included Princess Castelcicala, who was very soon to realise that though the Hamiltons were *persona grata* at the Neapolitan Court this was not so at St James's. She therefore followed Cornelia Knight's lead and refused all further invitations to Grosvenor Square. The piece was "Pizarro", a tragedy by Sheridan concerning the Spanish conqueror of Peru.

According to contemporary accounts, when Lady Nelson fainted, Nelson remained watching the play, while Emma and his father helped Fanny from the box and did their best to revive her. *The Morning Herald* tactfully did not comment on the admiral's unfeeling behaviour but stated:

Tuesday, November 25, 1800. Drury Lane.

The play "Pizarro" attracted last night a most splendid assemblage of beauty and fashion. The house was literally crowded in every part, and the performance went off with universal éclat. Kemble in the Peruvian hero never acted better, nor did his great exertions ever produce a more happy effect.

Lord and Lady Nelson, Sir William and Lady Hamilton, formed a part of the brilliant circle. His Lordship on his entrance was received with the most flattering testimonials of public regard; and "Rule Britannia" with an additional verse in favour of the gallant hero of the Nile was sung amidst the universal plaudits of the admiring crowd.

After the play, Dibdin's favourite song of the Navy and Nelson was sung in character by Dignum and deservedly encored: and every opportunity was eagerly seized by the audience to evince the high estimation in which they held the valiant conqueror of Aboukir. The heat, owing to the crowd, was so great that about the end of the third act Lady Nelson fainted away, and was obliged to be carried out of her box. Her Ladyship however soon became sufficiently recovered to resume her seat, and to the great satisfaction of all present remained in the box during the rest of the performance. We understand she has for some days been in a very indifferent state of health.

The play itself had an additional point of interest: the part of Elvira was played by Mrs Powell. After their meeting in 1791, Emma naturally wanted to see Jane act again, and had made sure that the night chosen for the theatre party was one on which her friend was billed in a good part. There is no evidence to show what other meetings there were between them but, as will be seen, they were still in correspondence in 1803.

Just after the unfortunate scene at Drury Lane, Nelson and Fanny drove to Stanmore with Emma and Sir William to visit Lord Abercorn, Sir William's cousin: the Nelsons had been asked to dine, but the Hamiltons were staying the week-end. This is the last recorded occasion on which Lord Nelson and his wife were officially together. An additional suggestion that matters were going from bad to worse is made by Harrison who records that on one occasion Nelson walked the streets of London all night, arriving in the early morning at the Hamiltons' front door to be consoled by Sir William, who suggested that he would do better "to seek that happiness in his professional pursuits when it seemed unlikely he would ever find it at home".

About this time, two very pointed paragraphs appeared in the Press. On 9th December, the public read:

Lady Hamilton has not yet been at Court. The cause is said to be her not having received any answer from her Majesty to the letter of recommendation of which her Ladyship was the bearer from the Queen of Naples.

And on 5th January 1801:

Lady Hamilton has received no answer whatever to the recommendatory letter which the Queen of Naples wrote to our Queen in her favour, although a Great Personage received it at the Levée from Sir W.

H. and was himself the bearer of this courtly epistle to his Royal Consort.

Arrangements for this Christmas of 1800 caused a complete break between Nelson and his wife: William Beckford issued an invitation to the Hamiltons to spend a "mock-Gothic Yuletide" with him at Fonthill. Nelson learnt from Emma that he was asked, but that Fanny was not to be included in the party. He accepted.

The "Tria Juncta in Uno" drove down on a foggy December day, stopping in Salisbury where Nelson was presented with the freedom of the city by the Mayor, to whom he made a generous donation in return, for the benefit of the poor. Accompanied by a mounted detachment of the local volunteers, their band playing *Rule Britannia*, the party was welcomed by Beckford and his friends under the tower of the main entrance to his estate. For three days, the large house-party, kept indoors by the bad weather, enjoyed the splendours of a house built at the cost of £250,000. In the evenings Emma sang, as also did another of William Beckford's visitors – Madame Banti, with whom Emma had sung in Naples. The Banti, born Brigitta Giorgi, had been a street and café singer in Venice. She had been in London, singing at the Pantheon, but although her contract included instruction under Sacchini and Piozzi, she had returned to Italy in 1779, according to Dr Burney, "as ignorant of music as when she left that country". Her gifts, one understands, were all bestowed by nature. However, she was now again in England, and with her husband, became a constant guest of the Hamiltons in London.

On Tuesday, 23rd December, came the real *pièce de résistance*, and the whole party went in carriages from what the *Gentleman's Magazine* referred to as the "mansion house" to the ancient Abbey in the grounds. The entertainment provided by the strange Mr Beckford was certainly unusual. In reading the account of it (*Gentleman's Magazine*, April 1801) it should be borne in mind that Emma was by now eight months pregnant: the high-waisted fashion of the time seems to have enabled her to hide her secret even when doing her "Attitudes".

"The Company being assembled by five o'clock," the report ran, "a number of carriages waited before the mansion house to receive them. The several parties as arranged for each took their places. Lord Nelson was loudly huzzaed by the multitude as he entered the first coach. They all proceeded slowly and in order, as the dusk of the evening was growing into darkness. In about three-quarters of an hour, soon after having entered the first great wall which encloses the Abbey woods, the procession passed a noble Gothic arch. At this point the company were supposed to enter the Abbot's domain, and thence upon a road winding through thick woods of pine and fir, brightly illuminated by innumerable lamps hung in the trees, and by flambeaux moving with the carriages, they proceeded between two divisions of the Fonthill volunteers, accompanied by their band, playing solemn marches, the effect of which was much heightened by the continued roll of drums placed at different distances on the hills. What impression at this dark hour – the blaze of light partly stationary and partly moving, as reflected from the windows of carriages, or gleaming on the military armour, together with the music echoing through the woods – what impression, I say, this *ensemble* of light, sound, and motion must have made on those who could quietly contemplate it all at a distance, may be left to the imagination without any attempt to describe it.

The company, on their arrival at the Abbey, could not fail to be struck with the increasing splendour of lights and their effects, contrasted with the deep shades which fell on the walls, battlements, and turrets of the different groups of the edifice. Some parts of the light struck on the walls and arches of the Great Tower, till it vanished by degrees into an awful gloom at its summit, over which, mounted on a flag of sixty feet, the broad sheet (the Admiral's flag, in compliment to Lord Nelson) of colours could at some moments be discerned by catching lights mysteriously waving in the air. The parties, alighting by orderly succession from their carriages, entered a groined Gothic hall through a double line of soldiers. From thence they were received into the great saloon, called the Cardinal's parlour, furnished with rich tapestries; long curtains of purple damask hung before the arched windows; ebony tables; chairs studded with ivory, of various but antique fashion; the whole room in the noblest style of monastic ornament, and illuminated by lights in silver sconces. At the moment of entrance they sat down at a long table occupying nearly the whole length of the room (fifty-three feet), to a superb dinner, served in one long line of enormous silver dishes, in the substantial manner of the antient abbeys, unmixed with the refinements of modern cookery. The tables and sideboards glittering with piles of plate and a profusion of candlelights, not to mention a blazing Christmas fire of cedar and the cones of pine, united to increase the splendour, and to improve the *coup d'oeil* of the room.

It is needless to say, the highest satisfaction and good humour prevailed, mingled with sentiments of admiration at the grandeur and originality of the entertainment. It should not be omitted that many of the artists whose works have contributed to the embellishment of the

Abbey, with Mr Wyatt (the designer of Fonthill) and the President of the Royal Academy at their head, formed a part of the company. The gentlemen with the distinguished musical party before mentioned, and some prominent characters of the literary world, formed altogether a combination of talent and genius not often meeting at the same place. Dinner being ended, the company removed upstairs to the other finished apartments of the Abbey. The staircase was lighted by certain mysterious living figures at different intervals, dressed in hooded gowns, and standing with large wax torches in their hands. A magnificent room, hung with yellow damask, and decorated with cabinets of the most precious Japan, received the assembly. It was impossible not to be struck, among other objects, with its credences (or antique buffets), exhibiting much treasure of wrought plate, cups, vases, and ewers of solid gold. It was from this room they passed into the Library, fitted up with the same elaborate taste. The Library opens by a large Gothic screen into the Gallery. This room, which when finished will be more than two hundred and seventy feet long, is to have that length completely fitted up and furnished in the most impressive monastic style. A superb shrine, with a beautiful statue of St Anthony in marble and alabaster, the work of Rossi, placed upon it, with reliquaries studded with brilliants of immense value, the whole illuminated by a display of wax lights on candlesticks and candelabras of massive silver gilt, exhibited a scene at once strikingly splendid and awfully magnificent. The long series of lights on either side resting on stands of ebony enriched with gold, and those on the shrine, all multiplied and reflected in the great oriel opposite, from its spacious squares of plate glass, while the whole reflection narrowed into an endless perspective as it receded from the eye, produced a singular and magic effect. As the company entered the gallery, a solemn music struck the ear from some invisible quarter, as if from behind the screen of scarlet curtains which backed the shrine, or from its canopy above, and suggested ideas of a religious service – ideas which, associated as they were with so many appropriate objects addressed to the eye, recalled the grand chapel scenes and ceremonies of our antient Catholic times.

After the scenic representation, a collation was presented in the Library, consisting of various sorts of confectionery served in gold baskets, with spiced wines, etc., whilst rows of chairs were placed in the great room beyond, which had first received the company above stairs. A large vacant place was left in front of the seats. The assembly no sooner occupied them than Lady Hamilton appeared in the character of Agrippina, bearing the ashes of Germanicus in a golden urn, as she presented them before the Roman people, with the design of exciting them to revenge the death of her husband, who, after having been declared joint Emperor by Tiberius, fell a victim to his envy, and is supposed to have been poisoned by his order, at the head of the forces which he was leading against the rebellious Armenians. Lady Hamilton displayed with truth and energy every gesture, attitude, and expression of countenance which could be conceived in Agrippina herself, best calculated to have moved the passions of the Romans on behalf of their favorite General. The action of her head, of her hands, and arms in the various positions of the urn; in her manner of presenting it before the Romans, or of holding it up to the Gods in the act of supplication, was most classically graceful. Every change of dress, principally of the head, to suit the different situations in which she successively presented herself, was performed instantaneously with the most perfect ease, and without retiring or scarcely turning aside a moment from the spectators. In the last scene of this most beautiful piece of pantomime, she appeared with a young lady of the company, who was to personate a daughter. Her action in this part was so perfectly just and natural, and so pathetically addressed to the spectators as to draw tears from several of the company. It may be questioned whether this scene, without theatrical assistance of other characters and appropriate circumstances, could possibly be represented with more effect. The company, delighted and charmed, broke up at eleven o'clock to sup at the Mansion House. On leaving this strange nocturnal scene of vast buildings and extensive forest, now rendered dimly and partially visible by the declining light of lamps and torches, and the twinkling of a few scattered stars in a clouded sky, the company seemed, as soon as they had passed the sacred boundary of the great wall, as if waking from a dream, or just freed from the influence of some magic spell. And at this moment that I am recapitulating to you in my mind the particulars of the description I have been writing you, I can scarcely help doubting whether the whole of the last evening's entertainment were a reality or only the visionary coinage of fancy.

This flowery description, typical of the reporting of the time, was read by Emma with the greatest pleasure. To enthral an audience when in an advanced state of pregnancy was no little achievement. She was supremely confident of herself, but one wonders whether Nelson was apprehensive. According to Joseph Farington, the guests included several French *émigrés*, a Portuguese nobleman, a few country neighbours and (presumably friends of his) West, Tresham and Smith. His comment on Emma was that "she is bold and unguarded in her manner, is grown fat and drinks freely".

On 26th December, the party broke up, the Hamiltons returning to Grosvenor Square for a short while until the house that Sir William had bought – No. 23 Piccadilly – was ready for them. Nelson went back to 17 Dover Street.

On 1st January (1801) his promotion to Vice-Admiral of the Blue was made official, and he was soon aware that he was to be appointed to the *San Josef*. On the 13th, little more than two months since his arrival at Nerot's Hotel, the break between Lord and Lady Nelson was complete. William Haslewood, an attorney working for Nelson in the matter of prize money, tells one story, while in the Diaries of Joseph Farington, R.A., Sir Thomas Lawrence is quoted as giving another. Taking a middle course between the two, it seems probable that Fanny did become exasperated by her husband's continued references to "dear Lady Hamilton" and did, in fact, burst out with, "I am sick of hearing of dear Lady Hamilton and am resolved that you shall give up either her or me". Whether this happened at the breakfast table, as Haslewood has it, or not, is of little consequence, but in all probability she took to her bed instead of leaving the house straight away. In this event, Lawrence's version of the scene could easily follow on, as he said that in their last interview Lady Nelson was in bed and that she took her husband's hand and asked him if he had ever suspected or heard from anyone anything that rendered her fidelity to him disputable. Nelson replied, "Never", and left the room. On his way to Plymouth to join his ship, he wrote her a note the same night, which read:

Southampton, January 13th 1801.

My dear Fanny,
    We are arrived and heartily tired; and with kindest regards to my father and all the family, believe me, your affectionate,

Nelson

For Emma the field was now clear and she had the undivided attentions of her hero, even if, for the time being, he could not be at her side. On 17th January, amidst much cheering from the fleet, Nelson went aboard the *San Josef* in Plymouth. While the last-minute preparations for sea were being made, so that the ship could join the Commander-in-Chief's flagship in Torbay, he learned from some newspapers which Fanny had sent on to him, that she had left London for Brighton, and that Davison was taking the lease of a fine London house for Lord and Lady Nelson. Writing immediately to Davison, he said, "Let her go to Briton [*sic*] or where she pleases. I care not." He added: "I do not believe that Lady Nelson can have desired any such thing", in reference to the new London house (Shelburne House) and commented, "I am not, thank God, forced to live in it." He was now writing to Emma daily and sometimes even more than once a day. It was a crucial time, as Emma's child was due at any moment. His eye was troubling him and he was low in health. His doctor had told him that he needed rest, that his eye should be bathed every hour and that he should wear a shade, but he did not let this interfere with his correspondence with Emma. No doubt he would dearly have liked to have been in London at such a critical time and he must have felt distracted at the thought of his duties which kept him so far away. However, on joining Lord St Vincent in Torbay on 1st February, he found that he was to be transferred temporarily to the *St George* for service in the Baltic under Sir Hyde Parker. This meant putting in to Portsmouth, and from here Nelson intended to request three days' leave "on private affairs". Before he left Torbay he received the letter for which he had been waiting. He was now the father of a daughter, to be called Horatia, born on 28th January.

Emma, at 23 Piccadilly, had been confined to her room for three days "with a very bad cold". Mrs Cadogan, who knew all about her indisposition, looked after her and kept the closely guarded secret. Sir William, now ailing and elderly, was not supposed to know what was taking place under his very roof. It is generally accepted, however, that he was well aware of the facts, and indeed it is difficult to understand how he could have been ignorant, but for the sake of peace and quiet, because he wished for nothing but Emma's happiness, and because he liked Nelson, it suited him very well to know nothing.

Emma's normally generous proportions and remarkable constitution helped her in her deception. On 1st February, three days after the happy event, she was not only up and about but in full evening dress attending a Grand Concert at the Duke of Norfolk's house in St James's Square. The occasion was reported in the papers, some of them giving the unwittingly naïve information that the guests included Sir Harry Fetherstonhaugh and the Hon. Charles Greville.

The child was removed from No. 23 Piccadilly as soon as possible – concealed, so the story goes, in a muff – and taken by hackney carriage to a Mrs Gibson who lived at 9 Little Titchfield Street, Marylebone. This good lady was a widow who had a malformed daughter of her own and was happy to earn extra money by taking care of a baby that she judged to be not more than eight days old.

Nelson's letters to Emma were now full of a new father's enthusiasm and to cover the possibility of these incriminating missives being opened or wrongly delivered by the postal authorities, he resorted to a rather poor and ill-kept-up subterfuge. A "Mr Thomson" (sometimes spelt Thompson) was invented who was supposed to be a shipmate of Nelson. The fictitious Mrs Thomson and her new-born child were assumed to be under the protection of Lady Hamilton, while Sir William was translated into an uncle. The letters which follow are written in this vein except on the occasions when a messenger was available and safe delivery could be guaranteed. Nelson's jealousy was strongly aroused at this time by the suggestion that the Prince Regent was interested in meeting Emma, and as will be noted, his fury produced language which hardly befitted an admiral.

(Addressed to Mrs Thomson)
No date (8 Feb. 1801)

Mr Davison will deliver this letter and its enclosure. He is very good and kind to me, and perhaps I can never repay the great and heavy obligation I owe him; but if it pleases God that I should retire into the country, I should not want a carriage, for I can walk, and my affairs would soon arrange themselves. I do not think I ever was so miserable as this moment. I own I sometimes fear that you will not be so true to me as I am to you, yet I cannot, will not believe you can be false. No, I judge you by myself; I hope to be dead before that should happen, but it will not. Forgive me, Emma, oh, forgive your own dear, disinterested Nelson. Tell Davison how sensible I am of his goodness; he knows my attachment to you, and I suspect he admires you himself. I cannot express my feelings. May God send me happiness. I have a letter from Sir William; he speaks of the Regency as certain, and then probably he thinks you will sell better – horrid thought. Only believe me for ever your, etc.

(With superscription to Mrs Thomson)
No date. (1801)

Your dear friend, my dear and truly beloved Mr T, is almost distracted; he wishes there was peace, or that if your uncle would die, he would instantly then come and marry you, for he doats on nothing but you and his child; and, as it is my godchild, I desire you will take great care of it. He has implicit faith in your fidelity, even in conversation with those he dislikes, and that you will be faithful in greater things he has no doubt. May God bless you both & send you a happy meeting is the wish of yours, etc.

(With superscription to Mrs Thomson, to the care of Lady Hamilton) No date.

Your most dear friend desires me to say that he sincerely feels for you, and that if your uncle is so hard hearted as to oblige you to quit his house, that he will instantly quit all the world and its greatness to live with you a domestic, quite life. Lady Hamilton will always give you good advice, and you will always find an affectionate friend in your, etc. Love to my godchild.

(Addressed to Emma)
St George. February 19th 1801.

Forgive my letter wrote and sent last night, perhaps my head was a little affected. No wonder, it was such an unexpected, such a knockdown blow, such a death. But I will not go on, for I shall get out of my senses again. Will you sing for the fellow, *The Prince, unable to Conceal His Pain, etc*? No, you will not. I will say no more for fear of my head. It was so good of you to send to thank Mr Nisbet for his not asking you to meet the fellow, as he knew his vile intent, and yet, the same morning to let him come and dine with you *enfamille!* – but I know it was not my Emma; Sir William always asks all partys to dinner. I forgive you. Forgive, I beseech, your old and dear friend! Tell me all, every word, that passes. He will propose if you – no, you will not try; he is Sir Wm's guest.

Thursday. – I have just got your letter, and I live again. DO NOT let the lyar come. I never saw him but once, the 4th day after I came to London, and he never mentioned your name. May God Blast him! Be firm! Go and dine with Mrs Denis on Sunday. Do not, I beseech you, risk being at home. Does Sir William want you to be a whore to the rascal? Forgive all my letter; you will see what I feel, and have felt. I have eat not a morsel, except a little rice, since yesterday morning, and till I know how this matter is gone off. But I feel confident of your resolution and thank you 1,000,000 of times. I write you a letter, which may be said as coming from me if you like, I will endeavour to word it properly. Did you sit alone with the villain for a moment? No, *I will not believe it!* Oh, God! oh, God! keep my sences. Do not let the rascal in. Tell the Duke that you will never go to his house. Mr G must be a scoundrel; he treated you once ill enough, & cannot love you, or he would sooner die. Ever for ever, aye for ever, your, etc.

I have this moment got my orders to put myself under Sir Hyde Parker's orders, and suppose I shall be ordered to Portsmouth tomorrow or next day, & then I will try & get to London for 3 days. (May

Heaven bless us! but do not let that fellow dine with you. Don't write here after you receive this, I shall be gone. You can, in Sir Wm's name, write a note to Sir H. Parker, asking if the St George is ordered to Spithead. If so, write to Portsmouth desiring my letters to be left at the Post Office till the ship's arrival. *Forgive every cross word, I now live.*

(Addressed to Emma)
St George. Thursday night (Feb. 19th 1801)

Here I am, fixed in my new habitation, which it is my firm intention never to sleep out of, except from dire necessity, till the campaign is over, except when I may get three days' leave to go to London to settle many of my private affairs, and I hardly think it will be refused me. Your good sense, judgment, and proper firmness, must endear you to all your friends, and to none more than your old & firm friend, Nelson. You must have shown that you are above all temptation, and not to be drawn into the paths of dishonour for to gratify any pride or to gain any riches. How Sir William can associate with a person of a character so diametrically opposite to his own, but I do not choose, as this letter goes through many hands, to enter more at large on this subject, I glory in your conduct and in your inestimable friendship, and good Sir William, when he reflects, must admire your virtuous & proper conduct. I wish you were my sister, that I might instantly give you half my fortune for your glorious conduct. Be firm! Your cause is that of honor against infamy. May the Heavens bless you, and let no consideration suffer you to alter your virtuous and sensible resolution. Pardon all this from an old and interested friend. You know I would not in Sir William's case have gone to Court without my wife, and such a wife, never to be matched. It is true you would grace a Court better as a Queen than a visitor.

(11 o'clock, Friday) I have this moment my orders to go to Portsmouth, and expect to be there to-morrow noon. (I again, my dear friend, entreat both you and Sir William not to suffer the Prince to dine, or even visit. 'Tis what no real modest person would suffer, and Sir William ought to know that his views *are dishonourable*. May God bless you and make you firm in resisting this vile attempt on your character, and with best regards to Sir William, believe me ever your most sincere and affectionate friend, etc.

You can, my dear friend, write a line on Sunday evening. It can be made up as a small parcel, and then I shall get it on Monday morning, although there is no regular post. It will make me so happy to be assured that the fellow did not even see you on Sunday. The Portsmouth mail coach setts out either from the Golden Cross, Charing Cross, or

Gloucester Coffee House, Piccadilly, anybody can tell you the direction as underneath. Heavens bless you, my own, only dear friend! I write on this side that you may tear off the half sheet in case you choose to read any part of it. [The half-sheet has not been torn off] Pray give the enclosed to our dear friend. Your letters are just come. Heavens bless you! Do not let the villain into your house. Dine out on Sunday. Sir William will find out the Prince does not come to dine with him.)

(Superscription "Mrs Thomson", to the care of Lady Hamilton)
No date.

Your friend is at my elbow, and enjoins me to assure you that his love for you and your child is, if possible, greater than ever, and that he calls God to witness that he will marry you as soon as possible, and that it will be his delight to call you his own. He desires you will adhere to Lady H's good advice and, like her, keep those impertinent men at a proper distance. He behaves, I can assure you, incomparably well, and loves you as much as man ever loved woman, and do you, my dear, believe me ever your dear friend.

(Addressed to Emma)
St George, Torbay. February 19th 1801.

I have received your most affectionate letter, and I feel very much for the unpleasant situation the Prince, or rather Sir William, has unknowingly placed you, for if he knew as much of the P's character as the world does, he would rather let the lowest wretch that walks the streets dine at his table than that unprincipled lyar. I have heard it reported that he has said he would make you his mistress. Sir William never can admit him into his house, nor can any friend advise him to it unless they are determined on your hitherto unimpeached character being ruined. *No* modest woman would suffer it. He is permitted to visit only houses of notorious ill fame. For heaven's sake let Sir William pause before he damns your good name. Mr Greville I take to be a man of strict honour, and he knows what I say of the Prince to be true. If *I have not mistaken* my man, which I shall be truly sorry to have done, I will answer with my head that Mr Greville would go down on his knees and beg Sir William to save your unspotted honour, for although I know you would send him to the Devil were he to propose such a thing to you, yet all the world have their eyes upon you, and your character, my amiable friend, is as much lost as if you was guilty. Let Sir William consult any man of honor, and with readiness they will join me in opinion. Let Sir William write the Prince and say that you ought not to receive him, and beg him never to come to the house – it is what I would do, I give you my word of honour. I am sure the Duke of Queensberry would agree with me. I have, my dear friend, perhaps, given too full an opinion, but you know, when I do give an opinion, it is generally to be understood, and, hitherto, seldom wrong. Make my affectionate regards to Sir William, and entreat him not to suffer such bad company into his house, and do you and him ever believe me your most attached and affectionate friend, etc.

(Addressed to Mrs Thomson, to the care of Lady Hamilton)

Off Portland, 10 o'clock, Friday, February 20th (1801)

... If you think that Lady Hamilton or any one else open your letters tell me where to direct them, & then your friend may write himself. Ever your affectionate N.B. Kiss my godchild for me; her father sends his blessing to you and it.

No date. (23 Feb. 1801)

To the Care of Lady Hamilton.
My dear Mrs T, poor Thompson seems to have forgot all his ill health, and all his mortifications and sorrows, in the thought that he will soon bury them all in your dear, dear bosom; he seems almost beside himself. I hope you have always minded what Lady H^n has said to you, for she is a pattern of attach^t to her love. I daresay twins will again be the fruit of your & his meeting. The thought is too much to bear. Have the dear thatched cottage ready to receive him, & I will answer that he would not give it up for a queen and a palace. Kiss dear H. for me. etc.

Nelson's remark in this last letter about twins being *again* the fruit of their meeting has been taken by some people to infer that Horatia was the survivor of twins. However, this would be crediting Emma with even greater physical stamina, although one supposes it would not have been impossible. The remark, on the other hand, could equally well have been some private joke between the two of them.

Having been granted leave of absence by Lord St Vincent, Nelson left Portsmouth on the evening of Monday, 23rd February, and drove through the night in a carriage which reached London and No. 23 Piccadilly by 7 a.m. King George III had been taken seriously ill and perhaps because of this the attention of the Press was diverted from lesser happenings, and Nelson's visit escaped unwanted publicity. As his house in Dover Street was shut up, he stayed at Lothian's Hotel, in Albemarle Street, to be as near Emma as possible. Commitments, official on his part and social on hers, made it difficult for them to slip away for long enough to visit Mrs Gibson and to see their child. Nevertheless, sometime during the three days that objective was secretly and satisfactorily accomplished.

Back again in the Admiral's cabin of the *St George*, Nelson was soon at the writing desk. In a note headed "Sat. noon" he wrote passionately, "Would to God I had dined alone with you. *What a desert* [*sic*] *we would have had.* The time will come, and believe me, that I am, for ever, for ever, your own". In a further letter written the same day, it was:

"Now, my own dear wife, for such you are in my eyes and in the face of heaven, I can give full scope to my feelings.... You know, my dearest Emma, that there is nothing in this world that I would not do for us to live together, and to have our dear little child with us. I firmly believe that this campaign will give us peace, and then we will set off for Brontë.... Nothing but an event happening to him could prevent my going, and I am sure you will think so, for unless all matters accord it would bring 100 tongues and slanderous reports if I separated from her (which I would do with pleasure the moment we can be united; I want to see her no more), therefore we must manage till we can quit this country or your uncle dies. I love, I never did love anyone else. I never had a dear pledge of love till you gave me one, and you, thank God, never gave one to anyone else. I think before March is out you will either see us back, or so victorious we shall insure a glorious issue to our toils. Think what my Emma will feel at seeing return safe, perhaps with a little more fame, her own dear loving Nelson. You, my beloved Emma, and my Country, are the two dearest objects of my fond heart – a heart susceptible and true.... My longing for you, both person and conversation, you may readily imagine. What must be my sensations at the idea of sleeping with you! it setts me on fire, even the thoughts, much more would the reality. I am sure my love & desires are all to you, and if any woman naked were to come to me, even as I am this moment from thinking of you, I hope it might rot off if I would touch her even with my hand. No, my heart, person, and mind is in perfect union of love towards my own dear, beloved Emma – the *real bosom* friend of her, all hers, all Emma's, etc.

Feeling his responsibilities for Emma and her child, Nelson drafted out a codicil to his will which he had witnessed on board.

Dated March 6th 1801.

Whereas the R^t Honble Sir William Hamilton K.B., is in my debt the following sums, viz., nine hundred & twenty seven pounds lent him at Palermo, in January 1799; also the sum of two hundred and fifty five pounds lent him between July and November 1800; also one thousand and ninety-four pounds, being one-half of our expenses from Leghorn to London in 1800, making in the whole the sum of two thousand two hundred and seventy-six pounds. I give this debt aforementioned in trust to Thomas Ryder, Esq. of Lincoln's Inn, and to Alexander Davison, Esq. of St James's Square, for the use & benefit of Emma Hamilton, to be disposed of as she may direct, and I likewise request that my friends, Thomas Ryder, Esq. & Alexander Davison, Esq. will execute the office of executors, to my will made fifth March 1801, and that they will each accept of one hundred pounds to buy a ring; and it is my directions that the sum necessary to pay Lady Nelson the sum of one thousand pounds a year (which I calculate will be twenty thousand pounds) be at her death equally divided as directed by will. Given on board his Majesty's ship, Saint George at sea March sixth one thousand eight hundred and one.

Nelson & Bronte.

I declare this a codicil to my last will and testament,

March 6th 1801.

(witnessed by T.M. Hardy Capt. of H.M.S. St George & Frederick Thesiger Capt R.N.)

Nelson continued to write to Emma even while the *St George* was sailing round to Yarmouth. In a letter headed "10 o'clock, March 6th, at night (1801)" he made a reference to Greville: "Sir Wm has a treasure, and does he want to throw it away? That other chap did throw away the most precious jewel that God Almighty ever sent on this earth." Two days before this he had written a letter to Fanny that she referred to as her "letter of dismissal". According to Oliver Warner, he even went so far as to send a copy to Emma. It said:

St George, March 4, 1801.

Josiah is to have another ship and to go abroad if the Thalia cannot soon be got ready. I have done *all* for him and he may again as he has often done before wish me to break my neck, and be abetted in it by his friends who are likewise my enemies, but I have done my duty as an

174

honest generous man and I neither want or wish for any body to care what become of me, whether I return or am left in the Baltic, seeing I have done all in my power for you. And if dead you will find I have done the same, therefore my only wish is to be left to myself and wishing you every happiness, believe that I am your affectionate Nelson and Brontë.

Finally, he informed Emma that "I have directed all my letters to be returned to No. 23 Piccadilly, so take care they get into your possession". As far as Emma was concerned it was now a matter of waiting to hear the outcome of Nelson's present exploit. He had disappeared, both metaphorically and literally, into a fog which spread across the North Sea. He was to be away from England until 1st July and during that time his initiative had overridden Sir Hyde Parker's cautious tactics and had resulted in the defeat of the Danish fleet at Copenhagen – the occasion of the famous gesture of the telescope to the blind eye. Sweden and Denmark were linked by treaty with Russia, and the Czar had now turned against England.

The Czar was murdered on 24th March and the Danes, when the news came through after the battle, were pleased to be able to come to terms with the English, with whom they were prepared to be friendly. Nelson hoped to be able to return home by travelling overland to Hamburg, but, before he was able to do so, Sir Hyde Parker was recalled by the Admiralty, and he found that duty demanded he should sail into the Baltic in order to silence the Russian fleet. The Swedes, met at sea, were willing to temporise and Nelson's voyage to Reval resolved itself into one of peaceful negotiations.

As and when it was possible for letters to get through, Nelson and Emma had corresponded. Hers to him were destroyed as Nelson had written in March: "I burn all your dear letters. It is right for your sake and I wish you would burn all mine – they can do no good, and will do us both harm, for any seizure of them, or the dropping even one of them, would fill the mouths of the world sooner than we intend."

With the satisfaction of Copenhagen gloriously behind him, Nelson gave thought to clearing the decks, so to speak, for his return to Emma.

He wrote to Davison:

St George , April 23rd 1801.

My dear Davison,

You will, at a proper time, and before my arrival in England, signify to Lady N. that I expect, and for which I have made such a very liberal allowance to her, to be left to myself, and without any inquiries from her; for sooner than live the unhappy life I did when I last came to England, I would stay abroad for ever. My mind is as fixed as fate; therefore you will send my determination in any way you judge proper; and believe me ever your obliged and faithful friend, Nelson and Brontë.

Rather tactlessly, as many of his junior officers felt embarrassed by his liaison with Emma, Nelson arranged a party on board the *St George* on Sunday, 26th April, to celebrate what he called, in his invitation to his friend Fremantle, "the Birthday of Santa Emma." Sir Hyde Parker was present and the toast was drunk in champagne.

Although he put his "Santa Emma" on such a pedestal, Nelson was extraordinarily jealous of her to the point of mistrust when he was not with her. Emma may have been flattered by his frenzy at the idea of her succumbing to possible advances by the Prince Regent. She would have been quite within her rights to be offended at the slur on her loyalty and devotion. He may never have realised it himself, but something at the back of Nelson's mind told him that she was not quite the *belle dame sans rapproche* that he would like everyone to think her. He did not trust her in Greville's company any more than in the Prince Regent's, although for some reason he had no qualms about the Duke of Queensberry. He expressed his feelings about her being with Greville in a letter written a week before her birthday in which he said: "I hope you will not be gone into Wales, for that would afflict me very much. What signifies the dirty acres to you? and Sir William and Mr Greville will not consult you on the granting new leases. I want a real friend to comfort me, and I know none so sincere and affectionate as yourself." He had never had such doubts of poor Fanny, but with Emma it was not quite the same.

About this time Mrs Cadogan had travelled north to visit friends and was taking the opportunity to call and see how Emma Carew was developing. She wrote to her daughter:

Chester, April 16th 1801.

I have to inform you that I arrived in Chester yesterday, and am happy to say that I left all friends in Hawarden very well. I mean to stop in Chester 2 days, and then to go to Liverpool and to stop there two or three days, and then I mean to proceed on my journey to Manchester. I beg you will send me Mrs Blackburn's directions, and send me every particular how I am to proceed about the little girl. The next letter you send you must direct to me at Jno. Moore, Moore Street, Liverpool. My sister Kidd and all her family sends their kind love to you, and they are all very well. Give my kind love to Sir William, and accept the same yourself from your loving and aff^te mother, etc.

Sarah sends her love to her mother, and sisters, and brothers, and to you, which, I am happy to say, we are both well.

Nelson arrived back in England on 1st July. He landed once again at Yarmouth, acclaimed by the population and the Press alike. Before setting off for London in a decorated post-chaise whose six postilions were dressed as sailors, he visited the Naval Hospital, chatted with the wounded and, with characteristic generosity, presented each nurse with a guinea.

Emma had celebrated the news of victory, when it reached 23 Piccadilly on 15th April, by dancing a Tarantella and tiring out Sir William, now seventy-one, a Neapolitan duke, her maid and finally the black servant, Fatima, whom Nelson had given her after the Battle of the Nile. She now made arrangements for her battle-worn hero to spend a little time out of London to recuperate. The first few days were passed at Burford Bridge, at the foot of Box Hill, and then the scene was changed to the Bush Inn at Shepperton, where Nelson and Sir William amused themselves by fishing in the Thames. The party was quite large though informal, consisting of the Rev. William Nelson, for whom Nelson was trying to obtain preferment, his wife and daughter, Captain Edward Parker and one or two other young officers of Nelson's entourage, with, of course, servants, including the black Fatima. The Duke of Queensberry and Lord William Gordon had also been asked, but had declined.

The pleasure of idling by the river was spoilt to some degree by undercurrents. While the Press rhapsodied over Nelson's achievements, the ruthless, clever and unkind caricatures by Gillray, "Dido in Despair" and "Cognoscenti contemplating the Beauties of the Antique" were being sniggered at in London. More serious things were being talked of too. Buonaparte was busy massing troops and ships along the French coast in preparation for an invasion of England. The news had been in the wind when he arrived and Nelson knew that there could only be a short respite before he would be needed again. His personal feelings were stirred when he received this letter, in a familiar handwriting:

My Dear Husband,
I cannot be silent in the general joy throughout the Kingdom. I must express My thankfulness and happiness it hath pleased God to spare

your life. All greet you with every testimony of gratitude and praise. This Victory is said to surpass Aboukir. What my feelings are, your own good heart will tell you. Let me beg, nay intreat you to believe no Wife ever felt greater affection for a Husband than I do, and to the best of my knowledge I have invariably done everything you desire. If I have omitted anything, I am sorry for it.

On receiving a letter from Our Father, written in a melancholy and distressing manner, I offered to go to him, if I could in the least contribute to ease his mind. By return of post he desired to see me immediately, but I was to stop a few days in Town to see for a House. I will do everything in my power to alleviate the many infirmities which bow him down. What can I do more to convince you that I am truly,

Your Affectionate Wife,

Frances H. Nelson.

If this made him feel guilty, it also caused Emma to question whether he was going back on his word to her, and for a while their happiness was clouded. The holiday terminated on 20th July, when he received word that he was required at Whitehall. He was to be given command of a special squadron of small ships stationed in the Downs and would be responsible for the protection of the coast between Orfordness and Beachy Head. He left Lothian's Hotel at four in the morning on the 27th and went to Sheerness. In a day or two he moved on to Faversham, reassuring the volunteers and Sea Fencibles with his presence: finally, he arrived at Deal. On 1st August, the anniversary of the Nile, he was at sea in the *Medusa*, making towards Boulogne to reconnoitre the enemy coast. He made two sorties of this nature without any particular success, except that they convinced him that Napoleon's invasion threat was no longer a serious one. "The craft which I have seen I do not think it possible to *row* to England; and sail they cannot", was his opinion.

During their recent time together, he had been making plans with Emma to buy a house in which Horatia could be brought up and which would be his home whenever he was ashore. Emma, who was still in London, had been looking for a suitable place, and had reported a find. Nelson's answer, written on board the *Medusa*, "off Boulogne", on 4th August, said:

Buy the house at Turnham Green, I can pay for it. How can you be angry with me? I do not deserve it. Conscious of that, I think no more of your reproaches. Respecting the seal, it is your pleasure that I have it; you said, "She has no right to it", none has a right to me but yourself. I took it as you desired & now to be abused. But I forgive you, though my heart is almost broken. Damn that Christie, how negligent he has been, for ever your, etc.

I have not a moment. 10,000 kisses were due.

Another mention of the house is made in a further letter.

August 15th, 1801.

My dearest Emma,

From my heart I wish you could find me out a good comfortable house, I should hope to be able to purchase it. At this moment I can only command £3000; as to asking Sir William, I could not do it. I would sooner beg. Is the house at Chiswick furnished? If not, you may fairly calculate at £2000 for furniture; but if I can pay as you say, little by little, we could accomplish it. Be careful how you trust Mr.——. All must be settled by a lawyer. It is better to pay £100 than to be involved in law.

After that, no more is heard of the house in the neighbourhood of Chiswick and Turnham Green. Soon the Hamiltons left their London house to go and stay for a fortnight in Deal so that they would be on hand when Nelson was free from his duties. The following excerpts from letters give a picture of the events leading up to the purchase of Merton Place.

Nelson to Emma

... I grieve, my dear Emma, to hear you are unwell. Would I could do anything to comfort you; try and get well. We shall all meet at Naples or Sicily one of these days. I thank Castelcicala for his aff^{te} note, and send him an answer.... .

Nelson to Messrs. Marsh, Page & Creed   September 15th 1801.

I believe I have wrote before sufficient for you to pay to the order Messrs. Booth & Haslewood, six thousand pounds, in part payment of my purchase of a little farm at Merton. I shall also want money for to purchase several articles....

Nelson to "Mrs Thomson" c/o Lady Hamilton
No date (end of Sept. 1801)

I came on board, but no Emma. No, no, my heart will break. I am in silent distraction. The four pictures of Lady H^n are hung up, but alas! I have lost the original. But we part only to meet very soon again; it must be, it shall be (Turn over)

My dearest wife, how can I bear our separation? Good God, what a change! I am so low that I cannot hold up my head.... .

Nelson to Emma
Amazon   September 21st 1801

Noon. I have this moment your kind line from Rochester. I grieve at your accident. I am obliged to send my letters now, for I doubt if a boat can go at 3 o'clock.

Greville to Sir William
September 27th 1801

I see by the papers you and L^{y}H. are returned to Town. I hope you left Ld Nelson in good health; I make no doubt but your visit was comfort to him. I intended to have wrote to you at Deal, and to have sollicited some news.... .

Nelson to Emma
Amazon   September 28th 1801.

... Pray write me when I am to direct my letters to Merton; is it a post town, or are the letters sent from the General Post Office? I wish I could see the place, but I fear that is impossible at present (and if I could you would not, perhaps, think it right for me to come now Sir William is away.) I entreat I may never hear about the expenses again. If you live in Piccadilly or Merton it makes no difference, and if I was to live at Merton I must keep a table, and nothing can cost me one-sixth part of what it does at present, for this I cannot stand, however honorable it may be.... .

Nelson to Emma
Amazon, Dungeness   October 2nd 1801

I am sorry the lawyers should have been the cause of keeping you one moment from Merton, and I hope you will for ever love Merton – since nothing shall be wanting on my part. From me you shall have every thing you want. I trust, my dear friend, to your economy, for I have need of it.... .

Nelson to Emma
Amazon　October 5th 1801

... I am vexed but not surprized, my dear Emma, at that fellow's wanting you for his mistress, but I know your virtue too well to be the ——of any rank stinking king's evil; the meanness of the titled pimps does not surprize me in these degenerate days. I suppose he will try to get at Merton, as it lays in the road, I believe, to Brighton; but I am sure you will never let them into the premises... .

Nelson to Emma
Amazon　October 7th 1801

I have just got your letter of yesterday, and am very angry with Mr Haslewood for not having got you into possession of Merton, for I was in hopes you would have arranged everything before Sir William came home... .

You are to be, recollect, Lady Paramount of all the territories and waters of Merton, and we are all to be your guests, and to obey all lawful commands. What have you done about the turnip field, duck field, etc? Am I to have them? ...

Chapter 10

Merton

MERTON PLACE became officially Nelson's property on 18th September 1801. He had bought it, furnished, for £9,000, and was supposed to take possession on 10th October, but the owner, a Mr Greaves, seems to have been a little reluctant to move out, causing a few days' delay. As Sir William had been away seeing to his properties in Milford Haven, calling on his family at Warwick Castle and visiting Newmarket, Emma had been kept busy attending to the various legal requirements, which she seems to have done quite competently. The solicitor, Haslewood, worried her rather, towards the end, by becoming, Emma thought, rather rude to Mr Greaves. One of her letters to the lawyers, however, shows that she herself was not prepared to put up with any nonsense.

6th October 1801.

As in the agreement Mrs Greves is to give up her house to Lord Nelson the tenth of October, which is Saturday I do not understand why milords Lawyers cannot settle every thing as the title Deeds are good. Their is nothing more required it is of the greatest consequence that Tuesday or Wednesday milords people shou'd go down & many things are ready order'd to be sent from Portsmouth Deal & other places to Merton their are (coming) now 2 green house plants waiting to be sent & the painters waiting to begin (*why not then conclude*) Lord Nelson now not in very good health may be in town every moment why not let him have his house. Can the difference be so great between this & Saturday for that day he MUST have it *according to* AGREEMENT. We are all on Honner no person wishes to out reach the other tis of no consequence to Mrs Greves to give it up 3 days before the time & it is of Consequence to milord to have the house put in order. Let me beg then for the last time that this affair that is to be fixed for certain on Saturday may be

182

done & settled by Wednesday as Lord Nelsons *Letters* of *this Day* are very pressing to get in to his house & as his Lordship says that terms are agreed on that the tenth possession is to be given why not 3 days sooner as it is of real inconvenience to have his various furniture & other things thrown about let me beg of you then Dear Sir to let the affair be settled directly & you will oblidge your Humble Servant,

E. Hamilton.

On his return, Sir William wrote to Nelson to let him know that they had moved in.

Merton, Oct 16th 1801.

We have now inhabited your Lord$^{p's}$ premises some days, & I can now speak with some certainty. I have lived with our dear Emma several years. I know her merit, have a great opinion of the head & heart that God Almighty has been pleased to give her; but a seaman alone could have given a fine woman full power to chuse & fit up a residence for him without seeing it himself. You are in luck, for in my conscience I verily believe that a place so suitable to your views could not have been found, & at so cheap a rate, for if you stay away 3 days longer I do not think you can have any wish but you will find it compleated here, & then the bargain was fortunately struck 3 days before an idea of peace got abroad. Now every estate in this neighbourhood has increased in value, and you might get a thousand pounds tomorrow for your bargain. The proximity to the capital, and the perfect retirement of this place, are, for your Lordship, two points beyond estimation; but the house is so comfortable, the furniture clean & good, & I never saw so many conveniences united in so small a compass. You have nothing but to come and enjoy immediately; you have a good mile of pleasant dry walk around your own farm. It would make you laugh to see Emma & her mother fitting up pig-sties and hen-coops, & already the Canal is enlivened with ducks, & the cock is strutting with his hens about the walks. Your L^{ds} plan as to stocking the Canal with fish is exactly mine. I will answer for it, that in a few months you may command a good dish of fish at a moment's warning. Every fish, if of any size, has been taken away, even after the bargain was made, for there are many *Troubridges* in this world, but Nelsons are rare. I think it quite impossible that they can keep you at Deal more than 3 or 4 days longer; it would be *ridiculous*. This neighbourhood is anxiously expecting your L$^{dp's}$ arrival, and you cannot be off of some particular attention that will be shewn you, of which all the world know that you have merited above all others... .

183

At dawn on Friday, 23rd October, Nelson arrived at Merton in a post-chaise, having driven through the night from Deal. The house cannot have looked its best at this early hour, but Nelson saw it in the sentimental light of the home he had been longing for. He had been dreaming of the pleasure he would have from it ever since he knew that it was his. It was going to be a sort of pastoral paradise in which life would flow as evenly as did the little river Wandle through the grounds. He even thought, quite erroneously, that his Emma would be content to lead a quieter life in this country retreat, managing the household with great economy.

The arrangement with Sir William was that he should be responsible for half the expenses of Merton whenever he and Emma were staying there. Nelson, however, insisted that everything in the place should be his, and that Sir William was to bring nothing there from his house in Piccadilly. It is understandable that Nelson should want his dream-house to be his very own to share with Emma, but a letter that he wrote to her from Deal, while it shows him revelling in the anticipated pleasures of house-ownership, also suggests that he had a slightly guilty feeling that servants' tittle-tattle might get back to Sir William's ears:

Sept. 29th (1801)

I send by the coach a little parcel containing the keys of the plate chest and the case of the tea-urn, and there is a case of Colebrook Dale breakfast set, and some other things. Will you have your picture carried to Merton? I should wish it, and mine of the Battle of the Nile. I think you had better *not* have Sir William's books, or anything but what is my own. I have sent in the parcel by the coach this day, two salt cellars and two ladles, which will make four of each, as two are in the chest. You will also find spoons and forks sufficient for the present. If sheets are wanting for the beds, will you order some and let me have the bill. I also think that not a servant of Sir William's, I mean the cook, should be in the house; but I leave this and all other matters to your good management. Would to God I could come and take up my abode there, and if such a thing should happen that I go abroad, I can, under my hand, lend you the house, that no person can molest you; not that I have at present any idea of going anywhere but to Merton.

In spite of the fact that Nelson was more than prepared to bear the entire expense of Merton Place, Sir William stuck rigidly to his promise to bear half the cost while residing there. Having a house of his own to keep up, he could well have done without this further drain on his pocket, but he clearly saw that the arrangement would counter, to a certain extent, reflections on the character of his Emma and comments on his own benignly foolish position. Seeing that Emma, Mrs Cadogan and himself made up three-quarters of the residents at Merton Place, he was getting off lightly with 50 per cent, of the bills. Nelson, perhaps, saw things in a different light.

The residents of Merton were delighted to welcome the national hero who had come to live amongst them. They had put up some sort of a triumphal arch near the gates of the house, and on the evening of the admiral's arrival there were "illuminations". In a small community such a demonstration can hardly have been more than a show of candles in the windows of the houses and perhaps a bonfire in some prominent spot, but the gesture would have been fully appreciated by Nelson whose idea it was to identify himself as much as possible with Merton. "To be sure," he said, "we shall employ the tradespeople of our village in preference to any others, in what we want for common use, and give them every encouragement to be kind and attentive to us." As far as neighbouring landowners were concerned, however, he felt that it would be best if the residents of Merton Place kept themselves to themselves. "No person can take amiss our not visiting. The answer from me will always be very civil thanks, but that I wish to live retired." In one respect his views were both naïve, in respect of his behaviour with Emma, and a trifle condescending towards the villagers. Before his arrival he had asked, "Have we a nice church at Merton? We will set an example of goodness to the under-parishioners."

The Rev. William Lancaster, vicar of the Church of St Mary the Virgin, the parish church of Merton, either did not see or did not want to see any imperfections in the new members of his flock. A great admirer of Lord Nelson, he soon changed the name of the school he ran at Eagle House, Wimbledon, to "Nelson House", and he and his family became very friendly with the admiral who, in his turn, showed much generosity both to the church and to the vicar's family.

Merton Place was hardly the "little farm" that Nelson referred to in his letters. It stood in seventy acres of land which was divided into two almost equal parts by the road that is now Merton High Street, but the two parts were later joined by a brick-built subway under the road. The northern portion consisted of shrubberies and gardens, while the house itself stood on the southern part, surrounded by lawns and having an offshoot of the river Wandle, described sometimes as a canal, sometimes as a moat (and christened "The Nile" by Emma), forming an ornamental water and spanned by a delicately constructed Italianate bridge.

The house had been built at the end of the seventeenth or the beginning of the eighteenth century on what had been the estate of Merton Priory, ruins of which were to be seen in the grounds. The house, when Nelson bought it, consisted of one wing and an annexe, but was later enlarged, under Emma's auspices, into a double-fronted building facing east. On either side of the large entrance hall was a dining-room (south side) and a drawing-room (north side). Behind the drawing-room lay a breakfast-room facing north, and facing west behind this, the library. The south wing behind the drawing-room contained pantries and servants' quarters. In 1805, further additions were proposed, including an entirely new kitchen to be built on to the south wing. The main drawing-room was upstairs and there were five large bedrooms, each with a dressing-room and a water closet. Eight servants' rooms were in the other wing.

The Rev. William G. Bartlett, in his *History of Wimbledon* (1865), gives some additional details of the house and grounds, which he obtained from Thomas Saker, "the carpenter and factotum about Merton Place". Saker was then about eighty-four years of age. In his opinion, the house was roomy, but not magnificent. Glass doors in front and a long passage with glass doors opening into the lawn behind, and even plate-glass reflecting doors to some of the principal rooms, allowed plenty of light to penetrate into the house. The grounds were studded with shady trees and some fine specimens of yews. By the shrubbery near the Quicks, on a small mound, sometimes called the Quarter Deck, a rustic seat was placed from which an extensive view was obtained of the fresh unbroken country stretching out to Wimbledon Hill and Wandsworth.

On the first Sunday after Nelson's arrival, the party from Merton Place attended morning service at the parish church. His little niece, Charlotte, daughter of his elder brother William, had been fetched from school for the week-end and gained general approval for her pretty manners by her thoughtful attentions to her uncle and to Sir William, now in his seventies. During the first weeks there was a good deal of coming and going between Merton and London, "exactly one hour's drive from Hyde Park or the Bridge". Nelson had naval business to attend to, which in his poor state of health tired him out and worried Emma. Sir William visited No. 23 Piccadilly, taking Emma with him, and went on from there to auction rooms and the British Museum. Up in town, Emma visited the shops, and in particular that of Messrs. Webb whom she commissioned at short notice to make the necessary alterations to Nelson's peer's robe now that he had become a viscount. Presumably without Sir William's knowledge, although she used the Piccadilly house, Emma organised a meeting between father and ten-month-old daughter. To this end she wrote a note to No. 9 Little Titchfield Street:

Dear Mrs Gibson,
Will you come to Piccadilly with Miss Thomson on Monday at 10 o'clock, not later? I hope my dear god-child is well.

Ever yrs.
E. Hamilton.

As the weeks passed, the tempo of life slackened. The days were getting shorter and colder, and Nelson found it pleasant to be able to spend his time entirely at Merton Place. He had much writing to do in his new library. There were applications from old shipmates who asked his assistance in obtaining appointments, in securing pensions for disabilities, or even for help in financial difficulties. There was the involved business of trying to get the Government to act regarding decorations for the action at Copenhagen, and there was the practical necessity of arranging, through Davison, for the sale of some of the presents he had been given after the Battle of the Nile in order to help to pay the money owing on the house. As these trinkets failed to raise sufficient funds, some India Stock had to be sold as well. Although he was busily occupied, Emma was pleased to be able to report to his sister-in-law that his health was improving.

The Nelson family, as was perhaps only natural, sided with their own relation and blatantly cold-shouldered Lady Nelson. The only member remaining on good terms with both husband and wife was Nelson's old father. Fanny now had a house in Somerset Street, Portman Square, and the Rev. Edmund Nelson was going to spend some of the winter with her there, as he usually passed the cold months with his daughter-in-law away from his Norfolk home.

In answer to a letter from his father, which he received at Deal, Nelson wrote a reply which he forwarded to Emma for her to see and to send on. She did more than she was asked, currying favour with Mrs William Nelson by sending her a copy of part of it:

Merton Place. Saturday, (October 17, 1801.)

My dearest Friend,
I had letters yesterday from our dear Lord. He has sent me a letter open for me to read and put in the post which I have done this day but I send you an extract.

"My dear Father, – I have received your letter and of which you must be sensible I cannot like for as you seem by your conduct to put me in the wrong it is no wonder that they who do not know me and my disposition should. But Nelson soars above them all and time will do that justice to my private character which she has to my public one. I that have given her (ie. Lady Nelson and Josiah), with her falsity and his £2000 a year and £4000 in money and which she calls a poor pittance, and with all that to abandon her son bad as he is and going about defaming me. May God's vengeance strike me dead if I would abandon my children. If he wants reformation, who should reclaim him but the mother? I could say much more but will not out of respect to you, my dear Father, but you know her, therefore I finish,

On the 23rd I shall be at Merton with Sir William and Lady Hamilton and them with myself shall be happy, most happy to see you, my dear beloved father, that is your home. My brother and sister, the dear children will soon be with us and happy shall we all be, but more so if you will come. Plenty of room for you and your servant, Abram's brother will live with us. Allen's wife is the dairy maid.

Ever my dear father's dutiful son, N. and B.

This is an extract what do you think of it? When you and Mr Nelson has read it, pray burn it. I would have sent you the letter but am obliged to send it to day. God bless you. In a hurry. Sir William is gone to fetch Charlotte. Viganoni comes so she will have 3 lessons. 2 today and perhaps 2 tomorrow. Sir William is quite charmed with her. She will have her Italian lesson and French from Oliver. She shall be early at school on Monday morning and as milord is to arrive on Friday at dinner, she shall be here to receive him and go back to school on Monday early.

Emma Hamilton.

As a result of the invitation, the Rev. Edmund Nelson came and spent ten days at Merton in November, being the first guest, apart from the young Charlotte, to whom Emma was to act as hostess in the new house. Three of his grandchildren were there at the same time: the twin daughters of Mr and Mrs Bolton, Jemima-Susanna and Catherine, and the Rev. and Mrs William Nelson's Charlotte. No doubt the old man was pleased to have the children around him, but he was worried by the split in the family, commenting, "My part is very distressing." However, he was somewhat relieved to hear that the breach was to be carried no further, and he seems to have been pleased by Emma's attentions and kindness. From Merton he went on to Bath.

Just before Christmas, Fanny wrote again to her husband and although one would have thought that a polite negative reply would not have been out of place, her letter was returned to her, marked "Opened by mistake by Lord Nelson, but not read", and signed "A. Davison". Not read? She had written:

16 Somerset St.

My dear Husband,

It is some time since I have written to you; the silence you have imposed is more than My affection will allow me and in this instance I hope you will forgive me in not obeying you. One thing I omitted in My letter of July, which I now have to offer for your accommodation, a comfortable warm House. Do, my Dear Husband, let us live together. I can never be happy till such an event takes place. I assure you again I have but one wish in the world, To please you. Let everything be buried in oblivion; it will pass away like a dream. I can only now intreat you to believe I am, most sincerely and affectionately,

Your wife,
Frances H. Nelson.

A letter posted on 14th December (1801) shows that Emma was doing all she could to conjure up the sort of "Paradise Merton" that Nelson had dreamed about.

My dear Mrs Gibson,

If you will take a post-chaise tomorrow, Tuesday, and set off at half-past ten o'clock, and bring my god-daughter and your little girl with you, I shall be glad to see you. Tell them to drive you to Merton, and the best way you can come is over Clapham Common. Hire the chaise for the day. You can go back at three o'clock. *Do not fail.*

Ever yours sincerely
E. Hamilton.

If the Nelson-Hamilton menage was shunned by the *haut ton* this was far from the case with the immediate neighbours of Merton Place – the Goldsmids, who lived at Morden Hall. Abraham Goldsmid, a partner in the firm of Mocatta and Goldsmid, bullion brokers in the City, was an extremely wealthy man. He was kind-hearted and generous as well as rich, and he, his wife and his daughters were delighted to entertain such a famous neighbour as Lord Nelson. Parties on the most lavish scale were given and Emma needed little encouragement to join the talented Miss Goldsmids in singing and playing to the company. The Goldsmids were a large, closely knit Jewish family. Abraham had three brothers, George, Benjamin and Asher, and four sisters, Goley, Esther, Polly and Sarah. All the brothers were in business in the City and all were wealthy. It would have been Abraham and Benjamin that Emma knew best, for they were nearest to Merton, Benjamin having bought himself a large establishment at Roehampton, which even included a private synagogue.

Such, then, were the neighbours and intimate friends of the household at Merton Place.

By now Emma was beginning to revel in the pleasures of complete control of a large house. She had been the mistress of Edgware Row – and very thankful to be so, at the time – but her every movement had been made under the careful supervision of Charles Greville; at Naples she had enjoyed a degree of extravagance, but had been limited by the conventions of society and the etiquette of the Court. Here, at Merton, she could do exactly as she pleased, and neither Sir William nor Nelson curtailed the money she spent. The fact that she was not accepted at Court did not seriously worry her any more than did the disapproval of London society. She was happy enough to play the lady bountiful to Nelson's relations, to visitors from town and to certain of the local residents, notably the many Goldsmids. The good-hearted side of her nature was satisfied by pleasing others, as was her conceit, by being praised herself, but what she so sadly lacked was a sense of proportion. Her ideas of entertaining gradually became more and more lavish, and her experiences of the extravagances the homes of the Goldsmids did nothing to moderate the tendency. As the weeks went by, the bills mounted and the number of guests increased.

Sir William was not at all pleased with the way things were going. As he told his nephew, Charles, in a letter he wrote to him on 24th January from Merton Place:

... It is but reasonable, after having fagged all my life, that my last days should pass off comfortably & quietly. Nothing at present disturbs me but my debt, and the nonsence I am obliged to submit to here to avoid coming to an explosion, which wou'd be attended with many disagreeable effects, and would totally destroy the comfort of the best man and the best friend I have in the world. However, I am determined that my quiet shall not be disturbed, let the nonsensicall world go on as it will. I have now fully opened my mind to you, my d^r Chs. Yours, etc.

A month or two later, stronger disapproval was to be expressed by Lord Minto, who stayed the week-end at Merton and then wrote the following to his wife in Scotland:

The whole establishment and way of life is such as to make me angry, as well as melancholy; but I cannot alter it, and I do not think myself obliged or at liberty to quarrel with him for his weakness, though nothing shall ever induce me to give the smallest countenance to Lady Hamilton. She looks ultimately to the chance of marriage, as Sir W. will not be long in her way, and she probably indulges a hope that she may survive Lady Nelson; in the meanwhile she and Sir William and the whole set of them are living with him at his expense. She is in high looks, but more immense than ever. She goes on cramming Nelson with trowelfuls of flattery, which he goes on taking as quietly as a child does pap. The love she makes to him is not only ridiculous, but disgusting: not only the rooms, but the whole house, staircase and all, are covered with nothing but pictures of her and him, of all sizes and sorts, and representations of his naval actions, coats of arms, pieces of plate in his honour, the flagstaff of L'Orient, etc. – an excess of vanity which counteracts its own purpose. If it was Lady H's house there might be a pretence for it; to make his own a mere looking-glass to view himself all day is bad taste. Braham, the celebrated Jew singer, performed with Lady H. She is horrid, but he entertained me in spite of her. Lord Nelson explained to me a little the sort of blame which had been imputed to Sir Hyde Parker for Copenhagen.

In March, the Peace of Amiens was signed, conferring a temporary lull to naval affairs, and seemingly giving Nelson the time to sit for two more portraits, one by Sir William Beechey (half-length – £36 13s.) and one by Hoppner (this wonderful picture is in the Royal Collection).

Emma's birthday (26th April) was not quite so festive as it might have been, for a letter had arrived two days earlier from George Matcham at Bath to say that Nelson's father was very ill. Admittedly travelling was quite an undertaking in those days, but even so there was rather a hypocritical tone to the letter that Nelson wrote to his brother-in-law on the day of Emma's celebration. "Had my father expressed a wish to see me," he said, "unwell as I am, I should have flown to Bath, but I believe it would be too late; however, should it be otherwise, and he wishes to see me, no consideration shall detain me for a moment." His father died that day and when the news came to Merton it was passed on to Nelson's elder brother, William, who felt hurt at not being informed sooner, but who nevertheless undertook to make all the necessary arrangements for the funeral and the subsequent interment at the church at Burnham Thorpe of which the Rev. Edmund Nelson had been rector. Nelson made himself responsible for the expenses and went so far as to forgo his appearance at the Academy Banquet. Emma, however, who was a model of filial devotion, felt badly about her beloved's almost callous behaviour and tried to smooth things over for him by writing to "Dr" William (who was now a Doctor of Divinity and had reminded her that he should be so addressed) to explain that Nelson was very unwell and might quite possibly have to have a surgical operation.

Her birthday had its bright side too, for during the day three carriages left Merton Place taking a party to the parish church for the christening of Emma's black maid, "Fatima Emma Charlotte Nelson Hamilton" who was duly entered in the parish register as "a negress, about 20 years of age, under the protection of the Right Hon. Lady Hamilton".

The next big event, and one which would obviously have appealed greatly to Emma's love of excitement, was the journey that Nelson and Sir William decided to make, partly to visit Sir William's estates near Milford Haven and partly as a sort of triumphal tour for Nelson. This took place at the end of July 1802. The William Nelsons and their son were staying at Merton Place and accompanied the party, as also did two menservants, Francatello and Gaetano. Mrs Cadogan stayed behind to look after the house while they were away.

Driving through Hounslow, Maidenhead and Benson, they arrived in Oxford on 21st July where they met George and Catherine Matcham and their son at "The Angel" in the High Street, where the whole party dined and spent the night. Next day, apart from sightseeing, there was a formal presentation of the freedom of the city to Nelson and on the day following, a Friday, a full congregation of the university conferred on Lord Nelson and Sir William Hamilton honorary degrees of Doctor of Civil Law. The Rev. Dr Nelson was not forgotten either, for he received a degree of Doctor of Divinity of Oxford corresponding to the one he already held at Cambridge.

The next call was to be at Blenheim Palace, and with this in view the carriages drove to Woodstock for the night. In the morning the travellers drove up to the palace and sent in their compliments to the Duke of Marlborough. Their expectations of a warm welcome were short-lived, for they were informed, in due course, that a cold luncheon would be provided for them in the grounds, but that the Duke would not be making his appearance. While Sir William's long diplomatic experience enabled him to shrug off the apparent affront, Emma became incensed, and, it is to be feared, a little unladylike in her comments. Nelson declined the refreshments and ordered the carriages to drive on to Burford. Had the "Tria Juncta in Uno" been a little more worldly wise, they would have known that a scandal concerning a member of the Marlborough family and the wife of an M.P. had been in all the papers the previous year, and it was not surprising therefore that the Duke should seek to avoid a meeting that could give rise to further comment from the Press. By the time horses had been changed at Troymill and the travellers had reached Gloucester they had smoothed their ruffled feathers. Here, after viewing the cathedral, the Matchams made their farewells and returned home to Bath. On the next stage of the journey the air of triumph was regained. At Ross there was a boat, suitably garlanded with laurel, waiting to row the hero and his friends up the Wye to Monmouth. Accompanied by a concourse of river craft and with much cheering from the banks, their slow progress gave the Mayor and Alderman of Monmouth time to hustle into their robes and to be ready at the town quay to welcome their visitors. The inspired firing, as the procession came in sight of Hadnock Reach, of four four-pounder guns from a Naval Temple, which had been patriotically erected on a hill called the Kymin near the town, acted as both salute and warning gun. Giving a promise to pass through the town again on their way back from Wales, Nelson and his party continued on their travels. Their route ran through Abergavenny and Brecon, where they turned south to Merthyr Tydfil. Nelson's detailed accounts for the whole journey (Appendix, p. 283) make fascinating reading and throw much light on the expenses and arrangements necessary for a long trip at the beginning of the nineteenth century. Even an amount of 3s. for greasing the carriages is mentioned.

Returning again to Brecon, the carriages turned west and passed through Trecastle and Llandovery on the way to Carmarthen. At this town Emma's love of theatricals was indulged by a visit to the play-house where a ventriloquist made a hit with the company, for Nelson notes him down as receiving a guinea all to himself. Making an early start next morning, Milford Haven was reached by nightfall. Here they were met by Charles Greville and they settled down to a longish stay. Trips were made into the countryside, the foundation stone of a new church was laid, and a fair, a rowing match and a cattle show were duly attended.

Between Milford and Pembroke, the journey was broken in order to spend a night at Ridgeway, the family home of Captain Foley, who had accompanied the party from Milford Haven. Just a week earlier, he had married Lady Lucy Fitzgerald and had bought Abermarlais Park, near Llandovery, which was being made ready for occupation. Lady Lucy did not fancy having to entertain Emma and made no bones about opposing her husband's wishes at this early stage of their married life. However, her brother-in-law and her husband were able to persuade her between them and a repetition of the Blenheim episode was avoided. The lanterns which illuminated the drive to the house reflected a gayer welcome than did the inner feelings of the new bride.

Pembroke and Tenby marked the first stages of the long and round-about return journey, which ran through Swansea, Cardiff, Newport and Chepstow before Monmouth was again reached. "Lord Nelson's tourists", as the party had been referred to by a provincial journalist, arrived at the Beaufort Inn, Monmouth, on the evening of 18th August. At nine o'clock next morning, the two coaches made their way up the steep road to the Naval Temple on the Kymin where a breakfast was provided. In the evening there was a grand Corporation Banquet at which Nelson made a suitable speech and Emma sang. To quote a reporter, "Lady Hamilton charmed the company with several songs sung to the tunes of "Rule Britannia" and "God save the King". Her repertoire may have been limited by having no music with her, and the company simply "charmed" by her vivid personality rather than by the somewhat unoriginal airs.

When Monmouth was left behind and the carriages had appeared once again in Ross, they headed for a long detour to the north, including in their itinerary Hereford, Leominster, Ludlow, Worcester and Birmingham. At Worcester time was taken up by visiting Chamberlain's porcelain factory where Nelson ordered a dessert service which was to be decorated with his coat of arms and insignia. Birmingham was the last of the major stops and apart from the aldermanic ceremonies which, by now, must have become a trifle monotonous to the travellers, they visited the theatre to see a production of "The Merry Wives of Windsor". No possible tribute to the admiral was omitted, even the actor, Blissett, who took the role of Falstaff, declaiming the line, "Before the best Lord in the land, I swear it!" straight at the Nelson-Hamilton box.

The journey had taken far longer than had originally been intended. A tour that was supposed to have been completed in three weeks was to take exactly double that time. The last stretch, from Birmingham to Merton, followed a very straight line. Sir William, at his age, must have found the long hours on the road tiring, but this did not prevent extra miles being traversed to include a visit to his nephew at Warwick Castle before making for Coventry, Towcester, Dunstable, St Albans, Watford and Brentford. A further eleven miles brought the party back home to Merton Place on Sunday, 5th September 1802.

Nelson's health was vastly improved by the air and the relaxation from any naval business during the tour. Emma had enjoyed herself immensely and told Davison, "We have had a most charming Tour, which will Burst *some* of *Them*." To Mrs Matcham she was more restrained. "Oh, how our Hero has been received! I wish you could come to hear all our Story – most enteresting." The expenses of the trip, shared equally between Nelson and Sir William, were £481 3s. 10d.

Possibly Emma's old skin infection had broken out again and it was felt that some sea-bathing would do it good, as it had done before, but whatever the reason, soon after they returned to Merton, Sir William and Emma went to stay in Ramsgate. The *ménage à trois*, and a very one-sided affair in Emma's case, was beginning to get on her nerves. Sir William's masterly forbearance, too, was wearing thin, and it may be that he felt that a short holiday away from Merton Place and its owner would have a good effect upon all concerned. Carola Oman, in her life of Nelson, mentions that Emma's irritability was increased by the fact that it had been arranged that Mrs Gibson should take Horatia for a seaside holiday to Margate at this time, and Emma then discovered that she had lost their address.

It looks very much as if Emma sulked and stormed during the stay at Ramsgate and stayed in her room, sending Sir William a note rather than speak to him. It was worded:

As I see it is a pain to you to remain here, let me beg of you to fix your time for going. Weather I dye in Piccadilly or any other spot in England, 'tis the same to me; but I remember the time when you wish'd for tranquility, but now all visiting and bustle is your liking. However, I will do what you please, being ever your affectionate & obedient, ect.

Sir William wrote his answer on the back of the same piece of paper:

I neither love bustle nor great company, but I like some employment and diversion. I have but a very short time to live, and every moment is precious to me. I am in no hurry, and am exceedingly glad to give every satisfaction to our best friend, our dear Lord Nelson. The question, then, is what we can best do that all may be perfectly satisfied. Sea bathing is usefull to your health: I see it is, and wish you to continue it a little longer; but I must confess that I regret, whilst the season is favourable, that I cannot enjoy my favourite amusement of quiet fishing. I care not a pin for the great world, and am attached to no one so much as to you.

Having read her husband's comments, Emma wrote on the paper: "I go when you tell me the coach is ready." Sir William returned it again with the words:

"This is not a fair answer to a fair confession of mine."

After their return from Ramsgate relations between Emma and Sir William were still strained. Now aged seventy-three and not in the best of health, the old diplomat felt that this uncomfortable relationship must be settled one way or the other, and, taking his pen, wrote the following:

I have passed the last 40 years of my life in the hurry & bustle that must necessarily be attendant on a publick character. I am arrived at the age when some repose is really necessary, & I promised myself a quiet home, & altho' I was sensible, & said so when I married, that I shou'd be superannuated when my wife wou'd be in her full beauty and vigour of youth. That time is arrived, and we must make the best of it for the comfort of both parties. Unfortunately our tastes as to the manner of living are very different. I by no means wish to live in solitary retreat, but to have seldom less than 12 or 14 at table & those varying continually, is coming back to what was become so irksome to me in Italy during the latter years of my residence in that country. I have no connections out of my own family. I have no complaint to make, but I feel that the whole attention of my wife is given to L^{d}N. and his interest at Merton. I well know the purity of L^{d}N's friendship for Emma and me, and I know how very uncomfortable it wou'd make his L^p, our best friend, if a separation shou'd take place, & am therefore determined to do all in my power to prevent such an extremity, which wou'd be *essentially detrimental* to all parties, but wou'd be more sensibly felt by our dear friend than by us. Provided that our expences in housekeeping do not encrease beyond measure (of which I must own I see some danger), I am willing to go on upon our present footing; but as I cannot expect to live many years, every moment to me is precious, & I hope I may be allow'd sometimes to be my own master, & pass my time according to my own inclination, either by going my fishing parties on the Thames or by going to attend the Museum, R. Society, the Tuesday Club, & Auctions of pictures. I mean to have a light chariot or post chaise by the month, that I may make use of it in London and run backwards and forwards to Merton or to Shepperton, etc. This is my plan, & we might go on very well, but I am fully determined not to have more of the very silly altercations that happen but too often between us and embitter the present moments exceedingly. If realy one cannot live comfortably together, a *wise* and well *concerted separation* is preferable; but I think, considering the probability of my not troubling any party long in this world, the best for us all wou'd be to bear those ills we have rather than flie to those we know not of. I have fairly stated what I have on my mind. There is no time for nonsense or trifling. I know and admire your talents & many excellent qualities, but I am not blind to your defects, & confess having many myself; therefore let us bear and forbear for God's sake.

Emma now realised the dangerous breakers that were ahead and decided to alter her course. Nothing more is heard that suggests further marital disagreement. Sir William was content to leave matters as they were and went off on a number of fishing expeditions on the Thames, enjoying the sport and unquestionably the peace of these outings. Nelson must have suspected, even if he was not fully informed by Emma, that "Paradise Merton" was not quite living up to its name, but he, too, had his worries. He knew that if hostilities were resumed, and it seemed likely that they would be, he would be given command of the Mediterranean fleet. The prospect of having to leave Merton and Emma for a further indefinite period at sea must have loomed like a very dark cloud on his horizon. To add to his disquiet, and to Sir William's too, for that matter, the household accounts were extremely high. If Sir William was forgetting his troubles on the river bank, Emma was drowning hers in a whirl of entertaining. There were constant visitors to Merton, some of whom were Nelson's own relations and friends; some, acquaintances that had been made since Nelson and the Hamiltons had returned from Italy. Sir William it would seem preferred to see his own cronies up in town and in quieter surroundings Among those who visited Merton at one time or another were foreign singers like the Banti and her husband, their London counterparts as, for instance, Mrs Lind, Mrs Billington and Mrs Denis, and such personages as the Abbé Campbell, Dr Fisher, Prince Castelcicala and the Queen of Naples' son Prince Leopold. The various members of the Goldsmid family of course drove over quite frequently and then there were visits from Nelson's "band of brothers", Foley, Fremantle, Hood, Hallowell, Ball, Louis, Murray, Bonnett and Sutton. Emma's own friend, the actress Jane Powell, also visited Merton, for a letter that she wrote makes it plain that she had been there at some time:

Southend.

Dear Lady Hamilton,
    I cannot forbear writing a line to inform your Ladyship I am at this place, and to tell you how much your absence is regretted by all ranks of people. Would to Heaven you were here to enliven this at present

dull scene. I have performed one night, and have promised to play six, but unless the houses are better, must decline it. Please to remember me most kindly to your mother and every one at Merton. I am, dear Lady Hamilton, your oblig'd

Jane Powell.

Admiral Troubridge's disapproval of Nelson's conduct was such that he never entered his gates, but Hardy set aside his scruples and admitted, "I stole three hours today to go to Merton. Her Ladyship was quite angry that I could not stay longer."

There were many other visitors and, as Sir William said, there were seldom less than twelve or fourteen places laid for dinner each evening. The guests who came from London would, in most cases, stay the night and return after breakfast the next morning. That the entertaining at Merton was on an extravagant scale can be seen from the housekeeping expenses towards the end of the year 1802, which do not even include items such as servants' wages, wines or coals:

Week ending	October 4th	£66.	7.	1 ½
do.	October 11th	£117	8	2 ½
do.	October 18th	£34	10	4
do.	November 1st	£37	16	10 ½
do.	November 8th	£73	-	2.

In fact, over a long period these accounts averaged £66 per week.

At Christmas-time five of Nelson's nephews and nieces were there and soon after New Year there was a Children's Ball which Emma arranged and rather irresponsibly allowed to continue until 3 a.m. Later in January, Nelson and the Hamiltons stayed for a time at No. 23 Piccadilly and Sir William made his last appearance at Court for Her Majesty's Birthday Drawing Room. Nelson, when he could, paid visits to Horatia at Mrs Gibson's house, taking presents of toys and playing with her by the hour like any adoring papa.

Towards the end of March 1803, Sir William was taken ill. He grew worse and it soon became apparent that he had not long to live. On 6th April, with Emma and Nelson at his bedside, Sir William died. During the sleepless nights attending his sick-bed, Emma may have realised the kindness and care that her husband had had for her, otherwise it would only have been in the attitude of a tragedy queen that she noted down, "April 6th. Unhappy day for the forlorn Emma. Ten minutes past ten, dear, blessed Sir William left me."

Mrs William Nelson came up from Norfolk to be with Emma, and Nelson, in spite of his sister-in-law's presence in the house, decided that propriety decreed that he should not stay under the same roof. It was almost as if he felt that a kind of chaperonage, which had been provided by the figure of Sir William, had suddenly left Emma and himself unprotected. He found lodgings only a few doors away, over a saddler's shop, at No. 19 Piccadilly and from then on only called at No. 23 as a visitor. Emma instructed Mrs Gibson to keep Horatia indoors until after the funeral; an unnecessary precaution it would seem, unless Mrs Gibson had been in the habit of bringing her charge round to the Hamiltons' house during Sir William's illness.

A hatchment, which can now be seen in Merton parish church, depicting Sir William's armorial bearings, was hung outside the Piccadilly residence and, in due course, the coffin was despatched to Pembrokeshire for burial beside the first Lady Hamilton.

It was May before the will was read in the almost empty house. As the furniture was hers, Emma had removed it all to a small house in Clarges Street, which she had taken. The will was quite straightforward. Charles Greville was, as everyone knew, Sir William's heir, and Emma was to receive £300, and an annuity of £800, out of which £100 was earmarked for Mrs Cadogan during her lifetime. A recently made codicil requested Greville to pay Emma's debts, which had been estimated at £700, but of which Sir William had recently paid off £250.

The reference to Nelson in the will has an echo of sarcasm about it. It may have been unintentional, as Sir William had always been a great admirer of his friend's capabilities and daring as an admiral but, at the same time, Nelson's "Merton behaviour" rankled now and then. The words were:

The copy of Madame le Brun's picture of Emma, in enamel, by Bone,[27] I give to my dearest friend, Lord Nelson, Duke of Bronte; a very small token of the great regard I have for his Lordship, the most virtuous, loyal and truly brave character I ever met with; God bless him, and shame fall on those who do not say "Amen".

There is little doubt that at times Emma genuinely mourned her late husband, but at others she busied herself with a tragic outward show, rather suggestive of an "Attitude", and with the practical aspect of continuing her own pleasures, changing her hair style to one referred to as *à la Titus* which was then a fashionable one for widows. She wrote formally to Greville:

Lady Hamilton will be glad to know how long Mr Greville can permit her to remain in the house in Piccadilly, as she must instantly look out for a lodging; and, therefore, it is right for her to know the full extent of time she can remain there. She also begs to know, if he will pay her debts, and what she may depend upon; that she may reduce her expences and establishment immediately.

The answer to this was that Greville would like her out by the end of the month; a request that was not unreasonable, considering that Emma had Merton Place to retire to even if she had not already settled for the house in Clarges Street. The idea of his former mistress "reducing her expences" must have made him smile. However, he felt no resentment at her unfriendliness in addressing him in the third person – he knew Emma too well for that – and, although he was suffering ill-health at the time, he stayed in town to help her with her affairs which included petitioning the Government for the compensation which Sir William had unsuccessfully pleaded as due to him for his services in Naples, and to which Emma added the first of her own pleas for a grant in respect of her own services to the country while the wife of an ambassador. There was nothing in Emma's actions that suggested alarm at the deterioration of her resources. She was at no time a coward. Nevertheless, from the moment of her widowhood, the tide of debt, which was eventually to overcome her, relentlessly started to mount. Nelson, who now knew for certain that he was shortly to take command of the Mediterranean squadron, arranged for an allowance of £100 a month to be paid to Emma for the upkeep of Merton. He considered Greville to be a "shabby fellow" because he deducted the tax from the annuity payable from Sir William's estate, but it is difficult to see his argument that an executor should pay out of his own pocket a yearly tax for which Emma herself was responsible.

Within a few days of Nelson's departure to join H.M.S. *Victory* at Portsmouth, Mrs Gibson received instructions to arrange for the christening of Horatia at Marylebone parish church. She was to pay the officiating clergyman and the clerk double fees, and she was to bring back a signed certificate of baptism. That Mrs Gibson carried out her duty is proved by an entry in the church register of births for 13th May 1803, which does not mention the names of the father and mother, usually recorded on such occasions, but simply states: "Horatia Nelson Thompson B. 29 Oct 1800."[28]

War with France had now been renewed and having received his final orders, Nelson left London at four in the morning on 18th April

1803. He left Emma at 11 Clarges Street, where she was to be busily engaged that day with preparations for a wedding there the same evening between the young Captain William Bolton, R.N., and his first cousin Kitty Bolton. The Duke of Queensberry lent a carriage to take Nelson on the first stage of his journey, which was Kingston, and from here he sent a note back to Emma by one of the Duke's footmen.

Cheer up, my dearest Emma, and be assured that I ever have been, and am, and ever will be, your most affectionate and faithful
Nelson and Bronte.

Nelson was now to be absent from the scene for two years and three months. He sailed from Portsmouth on Friday, 20th May 1803, having sent Emma a farewell letter by messenger, and in five days' time he was in the Bay of Biscay with "nothing to be seen, but the sky and water".

Emma's financial position was commented upon by Lord Minto who informed a correspondent that she was "worse off than I imagined". He also went on to say that "She talked very freely of her situation with Nelson, and the construction the world may have put upon it, but protested that her attachment was perfectly pure which I can believe, though I declare it is of no consequence whether it is so or not". Soon after being left on her own, Emma called on Madame Vigée-Le Brun, wearing deep mourning and enveloped in a huge black veil. Madame Le Brun recorded cynically, "I found this Andromache huge for she had become dreadfully stout. She said to me, with tears in her eyes, that she was deeply to be pitied; that she had lost in Sir William a friend and father, and that she would never be able to console herself. I admit that her grief made little impression on me, for I could see she was acting a part. How little I deceived myself was shown a few minutes later when, having seen some pieces of music on my piano, she began to sing one of the airs which she found there." At a party that Madame Le Brun gave a little later on, she noticed that Emma was drinking astonishing amounts of porter without seeming to be in any way affected, and decided that habit could be the only explanation.

Emma was writing numerous letters to Nelson, but none was to reach him until the end of July when H.M.S. *Phoebe* brought some mail from Naples. Nelson then learned that Emma was going to visit his relations in Norfolk, that she intended to go to Southend for some bathing and that during the winter she would be at Merton with Horatia.

He wrote back as often as opportunity offered, and the following examples give some idea of the topics discussed:

201

Victory, under Majorca , January 13th, 1804.

My own dear beloved Emma,

I received, on the 9th your letters of September 29th, October 2, 7, 10, 12, 17th, November 5th, 8th, to the 24th: and I am truly sensible of all your kindness and affectionate regard for me; which, I am sure, is reciprocal, in every respect, from your own Nelson.

If that Lady Bitch knew of that person's coming to her house, it was a trick; but which, I hope, you will not subject yourself to again. But, I do not like it!

However, it is passed; and, we must have confidence in each other: and, my dearest Emma, judging of you by myself, it is not all the world that could seduce me, in thought, word, or deed, from all my soul holds most dear.

Indeed, if I can help it, I never intend to go out of the ship, but to the shore of Portsmouth; and that will be, if it pleases God, before next Christmas. Indeed, I think, long before, if the French will venture to sea.

I send you a letter from the Queen of Naples. They call out, might and main, for our protection; and, God knows, they are sure of me… .

I am glad you are going to Merton; you will live much more comfortable and much cheaper, than in London: and this spring, if you like to have the house altered, you can do it. But, I fancy, you will soon tire of so much dirt, and the inconvenience will be very great the whole summer.

All I request, if you fix to have it done, (is) that Mr Davison's architect, who drew the plan, may have the inspection; and, he must take care that it does not exceed the estimate.

If it is done by contract, you must not *alter*; or a bill is run up, much worse than if we had never contracted. Therefore, I must either buy the materials, and employ respectable workmen, under the architect; or contract.

I rather believe it would be better for me to buy the materials, and put out the building to a workman; but, you must get some good advice.

With respect to the new entrance… .

Victory, March 14th (1804) off Toulon

… I would not have you lay out more than is necessary, at Merton. The rooms, and the new entrance, will take a good deal of money. The entrance by the corner I would have certainly done; a common white gate will do for the present; and one of the cottages, which is in the barn, can be put up, as a temporary lodge. The road can be made to a temporary bridge; for that part of the "Nile", one day, shall be filled up.

Downing's canvas awning will do for a passage. For the winter, the carriage can be put in the barn; and, giving up Mr Bennett's premises, will save fifty pounds a year: and, another year, we can fit up the coach-house and stables, which are in the barn.

The foot-path should be turned. I did shew Mr Haslewood the way I wished it done; and Mr ... will have no objections, if we make it better than ever it has been: and, I also beg, as my dear Horatia is to be at Merton, that a strong netting, about three feet high, may be placed round the Nile, that the little thing may not tumble in; and, you may have ducks again in it. I forget, at what place we saw the netting; and either Mr Perry, or Mr Goldsmid, told us where it was to be bought. I shall be very anxious until I know this is done... .

The expences of the alterations at Merton *you are* not to pay from the income. Let it all be put to a separate account, and I will provide a fund for the payment... .

Victory, April 2nd, 1804.

I have, my Dearest Beloved Emma, been so uneasy for this last month; desiring, most ardently, to hear of your well doing! ...

You may, if you like, tell Mrs G. that I shall certainly settle a small pension on her. It shall not be large, as we may have the pleasure of making her little presents; and, my dearest Emma, I shall not be wanting to every body who has been kind to you, be they servants or gentlefolks... .

Never mind the great Bashaw at the Priory. He be damned! If he was single, and had a mind to marry you, he could only make you a Marchioness: but, as he is situated, and I situated, I can make you a Duchess; and, if it pleases God, that time may arrive! Amen. Amen.

As for your friend Lady H—, she is, in her way, as great a pimp as any of them.

What a set! But, if they manage their own intrigues, is not that enough! I am sure, neither you nor I care what they do; much less, envy them their chere amies.

As for Lord S—, and the other, I care nothing about them; for I have every reason, by my own feelings towards you, to think you care only for your Nelson... .

The reason for Nelson's particular anxiety over Emma's health was the knowledge that she had had another child—his second daughter. From two letters written during March, it is clear that he knew of the child's existence. In one he said:

… Rememberme kindly to the Duke of Hamilton, I respect him very much indeed, and to the good old Duke of Q^y say what you please. I care not for all those nonsensical letters of Mr Monckton or *your* titled offers. I have confidence in your love and affection, and so ought you in the fidelity, love and affection, of ever yours, etc.

P.S. Kiss dear Horatia for me, and the other. I approved of the name you intended. Best regards to Davison, I shall write by Gib^r to him. *What changes!*

and in the other,

… I send you, my beloved Emma, a note, in order that you may, upon your birthday, make some little presents, and if you do not give it all away it will look in bank notes very pretty in your pocket-book. Kiss dear Horatia for me and the other. Call him what you please, if a girl, Emma. Kindest regards to your good mother, affection to Charlotte and all our friends. It now blows a gale of wind… .

The child had been born sometime at the very end of January, and it seems most likely that Emma was at Clarges Street, for a letter written by a Dr Este confirms that she was there on 3rd February. The baby was evidently not healthy, for in a matter of six weeks it was dead.

As soon as he heard the sad news, Nelson wrote:

I opened – opened – found none but December and early January. I was in such an agitation! At last, I found one without a date, which, thank God! told my poor heart that you was recovering, but that dear little Emma was no more! and that Horatia had been so very ill – it all together upset me. But, it was just at bed time, and I had time to reflect, and be thankful to God for sparing you and our dear Horatia. I am sure the loss of one – much more both – would have drove me mad. I was so agitated, as it was, that I was glad it was night, and that I could be by myself.

Emma's feelings on the loss of her baby cannot be estimated. The necessity for secrecy prevented her from indulging in any theatrical show of grief, which she would most certainly have done had circumstances been different, whatever her real feelings. That Nelson's letters to her do not contain passages of consolation is no proof that she did not mourn sincerely in private, as he was fully aware that the mails were untrustworthy and that, every now and then, some fell into the hands of the French. The loss probably heightened his affection for Horatia to whom he dotingly sent an expensive watch. "I send a very neat watch for our god-child", he wrote, "and you will see it is by a good maker, that is, I suppose it will tick for a year instead of a month or two. You will inform her that it is only to be worn when she behaves well and is obedient."

There seems little doubt that he was fonder of Horatia than Emma was. He insisted that she should be vaccinated, or, as he called it, "inoculated with the cow-pox", he refused to bring her a dog for a present because of the risk of hydrophobia and there was his concern over the netting round the Nile. Emma made no move to take Horatia from the care of Mrs Gibson. She preferred to be free to move from Merton to Clarges Street when the mood took her and to make visits to Norfolk and, on occasion, to Southend. "I am not surprised, my dearest Emma," Nelson wrote, "at the enormous expense of the watering place, but, if it has done my own Emma service, it is well laid out."

Little by little things were beginning to go wrong in Emma's world. In May 1804, Alexander Davison who, in his capacity as friend and agent to Nelson, had been most useful, was sentenced to twelve months in the Marshalsea for attempting to rig a parliamentary election at Ilchester in his own favour. Her debts were mounting to a serious degree, having Horatia's upkeep and the house in Clarges Street to account for as well as heavy bills from the Merton tradesmen.

By November, Horatia was still at Little Titchfield Street, although Nelson was pressing Emma in his letters to have her at Merton. In a postscript to a letter written from the Victory on 29th September, he said, "Kiss dear Horatia. I hope she is at Merton *fixed*."

The expense of keeping the child with Mrs Gibson can be judged from a letter that Emma received at this time:

Tuesday November 7th 1804.

Mrs Gibson's duty to Lady Hamilton, and am happy to inform her Ladyship that Miss Thompson is very well, and desires her love & a kiss to her Ladyship and to her God-papa. I have sent the receipt, and there now remains due up to Nov[r] 5th 24 pounds two shillings. Your most humble, etc.

Receipt.

Novr 5th 1804.

RECEIVED of Lady Hamilton the sum of thirty pounds, for lodging and attendance on Miss Thompson.
Received the contents
(signed) Mary Gibson.
£30. -. -.

It would seem that there was some sort of disagreement between Emma and Mrs Gibson judging by the fact that Nelson wrote to his solicitors asking them to arrange a pension of £20 a year to be paid to Mrs Gibson, providing that she promised to make no further attempt to keep or communicate with the child.

For months he had been thinking of the difficulties attending Horatia's transfer to Merton, and he saw quite plainly that the sudden appearance of a three-year-old child in a ménage which was already questionable, whatever he liked to pretend to himself to the contrary, would call for some carefully prepared explanations. There is no doubt that the matter had been one which he had discussed with Emma before he was called away to sea, and most certainly it had been the subject of some of his letters subsequently. His solution to the problem was as naïve and transparent as the "Mr & Mrs Thomson" subterfuge that he had previously resorted to. It was to send Emma a carefully worded letter, which could be shown to all and sundry, that would explain away the whole situation. It is open to doubt whether Emma felt that their friends would be convinced by the letter, when she read it herself:

Victory, August 13th 1804.

I am now going to state a thing to you and to request your kind assistance, which, from my dear Emma's goodness of heart, I am sure of her acquiescence in. Before we left Italy I told you of the extraordinary circumstance of a child being left to my care and protection. On your first coming to England I presented you the child, dear Horatia. You became, to my comfort, attached to it, so did Sir William, thinking her the finest child he had ever seen. She is become of that age when it is necessary to remove her from a mere nurse and to think of educating her. Horatia is by no means destitute of a fortune. My earnest wish is that you would take her to Merton, and if Miss Connor will become her tutoress under your eye, I shall be made truly

206

happy. I will allow Miss Connor any salary you may think proper. I know Charlotte loves the child, and therefore at Merton she will imbibe nothing but virtue, goodness, and elegance of manners, with a good education, to fit her to move in that sphere of life she is destined to move in.

I shall tell you, my dear Emma, more of this matter when I come to England, but I am now anxious for the child's being placed under your protecting wing. Perhaps I ought to have done this before, but I must not, injustice to my charge, defer it for any consideration longer. May God bless you, my dear Emma, and reward you tenfold for all the goodness you have already shewn Horatia, and ever be assured that I am, etc.

It was not until May 1805 that Horatia was, in fact, brought to Merton Place and, as Nelson put it, "fixed". Sarah Connor, who was a cousin of Emma, was duly installed as her governess. She seems to have been a pleasant young woman and gave general satisfaction in the way she carried out her duties.

By the end of 1804 it was felt that Nelson's return could not be long delayed and Mrs Bolton, in one of her letters, gives a general idea of the tempo of Emma's life at this time:

… I think I have lost both my daughters, for I hear nothing from them; if not gone to school, they must write to Miss Poupard & have the last box I sent with birthday things (as they may take hurt and spoil their cloaks sent with them) unpacked. You, my dear friend, are too good to them; I hope they are fully sensible of your kindness. You will soon now have the Doctor and Mrs Nelson with you, perhaps before my Lord comes home; your house will then be full, but I shall come to town to see him *and you too*, for Mrs Matcham will certainly be there, and where they are I can be, so do not take any trouble about me, for be assured tho' we *sleep* not with you, it will be the only time we shall be *asunder*.

My sister says all thoughts of going to Husum are over; she shall be glad to see the money back again, she is enjoying the thoughts of again meeting all together; she says her spirits are never so good as when with her near connexions and *friends*. She says a *certain Lady is at Bath so condescendingly humble* to those who formerly she would not *notice*, all to *be thought amiable*. Susanna is not returned from Swaffham, where she went to the ball last night. Give my kind love to Mrs Cadogan, thank her for her kindness to my girls; they must be ungratefull if they did not love her. Love to Charlotte and Miss Conner. I have sent a brace of hares by this day's coach. God bless you. Ever your, etc.

Whatever faults may be found with Emma's behaviour, and by now there were plenty, including over-indulgence, lack of discretion, vulgarity and a complete incompetence in handling money, she always retained a most praiseworthy and utterly genuine streak of kind-hearted generosity in her nature. Her own relations, whom she might so easily have ignored from the heights to which she had risen, were never forgotten. Writing three years later, when Emma's position had tragically worsened, Mrs Thomas of Hawarden confirmed that the little nursemaid she once employed, had a heart of gold.

"I am truly sorry", she wrote, "that you have so much trouble with your relations, and the ungrateful return your care and generosity meets with, is indeed enough to turn your heart against them. However, ungrateful as they are, your own generous heart cannot see them in want, and it is a pity that your great generosity towards them shou'd be so ill-placed. I don't doubt that you will receive a satisfaction in doing for them, which will reward you here and hereafter."

Alexander Davison, still in the Marshalsea, was doing what he could to further Emma's petition to the Government. The news that he gave her when he wrote on "Sunday Evening, January 6th 1805" was encouraging.

… I had a conversation about yourself, and am sure it will afford you great satisfaction to know how much Lord Melville interests himself in your favour. He tells me he has spoken to Mr Pitt of the propriety of your having a pension settled upon you of £500 per annum, and that he will speak to him again very shortly about it. I asked Lord Melville if I might say as much to you. He immediately said, "Yes, certainly". He spoke very handsomely of you, and of your services in favor of this country when in Naples… .

About three weeks later, Emma wrote back to him a friendly letter that the prisoner would appreciate. Knowing Emma, the promise of a visit would have been quite genuine – as genuine as her desire to meet Sir Evan Nepean who was Secretary to the Admiralty and through whom she hoped to further her quest for a Government pension. She wrote from Clarges Street on 26th January.

I have been very ill, my Dear Sir; and am in bed with a cold, very bad cold indeed! But, the moment I am better, I will call on you.
I am invited to dine with Mr Haslewood to-morrow, but fear I shall not be able to go… .

I write from bed; and you will see I do, by my scrawl.

I send you some of my bad Verses on my soul's Idol.

God bless you! Remember, you will soon be free; and let that cheer you, that you will come out with even more friends than ever. I can only say, I am your ever obliged, and grateful

Emma Hamilton.

I long to see and know Nepean! Why will you not ask me to dine with him *en famille*? [To this Davison has added, "Yes".]

The verses that Emma enclosed certainly did not justify any better adjective than the one she used herself. However, it was fashionable at the time to write poetry even if only to show that one had the leisure to do so. Admittedly, her feelings for Nelson were no secret to Davison, but to send such lines to a man in prison where they might easily be read by others was hardly discreet:

Emma to Nelson.

I think, I have not lost my heart;
Since I, with truth, can swear,
At every moment of my life
I feel my Nelson there!

If, from thine Emma's brest, her heart
Were stolen or flown away;
Where! where! should she my Nelson's love
Record each happy day?

If, from thine Emma's brest, her heart
Were stolen or flown away;
Where! Where! should she engrave, my Love!
Each tender word you say!

Where! Where! should Emma treasure up
Her Nelson's smiles and sighs?
Where mark, with joy, each secret look
Of love, from Nelson's eyes?

Then, do not rob me of my heart
Unless you first forsake it;
And, then, so wretched it would be
Despair alone will take it.

The present prospect of a possible addition of £500 a year cannot have cheered her financial outlook very much. According to an estimate made by Professor J.K. Laughton, her debts now amounted to £7,000. The fact that she was receiving £1,200 a year from Nelson for the upkeep of Merton Place, and £700 a year (less tax) from Sir William's estate, gives some idea of the rate at which Emma was spending money. She had recently spent £18 8s. on lottery tickets. She was now at Merton, now in Clarges Street, and in July she took herself off to Southend for a rest and some sea-bathing. Her mother was left to battle with the housekeeping at Merton. Mrs Cadogan probably had no idea of the enormity of the debts her daughter was so thoughtlessly amassing, for Emma never even confessed them to Nelson when he returned for the last twenty-five days that he was to spend in her company. Immediately before her visit to Southend, Emma was at Clarges Street where she received this letter from her mother:

Merton, July 18th (1805)

I shall be very glad to see you to-morrow, and I think you quite right for going into the country to keep yourself quiet for a while. My dear Emma, Cribb is quite distrest for money, would be glad if you could bring him the £13 he paid, that he paid for the taxes, to pay the mowers. My dear Emma, I have got the baker's and butcher's bills cast up; they come to 1 hundred pounds, seventeen shillings. God Almighty bless you, my dear Emma, and grant us good news from our dear Lord.

My dear Emma, bring me a bottle of ink and a box of wafers.

Sarah Reynolds thanks you for your goodness to invite her to Sadler's Wells.

Much work had been going on at Merton since Nelson went away. A new entrance had been made on the north side of the house, and a new drawing-room, kitchen and some bedrooms had been added. There were now proper stables instead of the ones rented from Mr Bennett, and the brick tunnel now ran under the Merton High Road connecting them to the house. Cribb had been allowed to use twenty men to assist him in laying out the gardens.

Hearing that Nelson was likely to return very soon, Emma hurried back to Merton from Southend. On 20th August (1805), once again at an early hour (this time 6 a.m.), Nelson arrived back home. After the long night drive from Portsmouth he felt specially delighted to be once again in his own house and with Emma, but there was much for him to do, and the days, that were so tragically to be his last at Merton, were for the most part hectic rather than idyllic.

On the very day of his arrival there was an interview with a Danish author who was engaged on writing a history of Denmark. Two years later Mr J.A. Andersen published his *Excursions in England* in which he referred to the visit:

> Merton Place is not a large, but a very elegant structure. In the balconies I observed a number of ladies, who, I understood to be Lord Nelson's relations. Entering the house, I passed through a lobby which contained amongst a variety of paintings and other objets d'art, an excellent marble bust of the illustrious Admiral. Here I met the Rev. Dr. Nelson, the present Earl. I was then ushered into a magnificent apartment where Lady Hamilton sat at a window. I at first scarcely observed his Lordship, he having placed himself immediately at the entrance. The Admiral wore a uniform emblazoned with different Orders of Knighthood. He received me with the utmost condescension. Chairs being provided, he sat down between Lady Hamilton and myself, and having laid my account of the Battle of Copenhagen on his knee, a conversation ensued.

Early next morning Nelson and Emma set out for London. Their carriage stopped at 9.45 a.m. outside the Admiralty, where Nelson got out and then continued to 11 Clarges Street, where Emma was to meet the Misses Bolton who were coming up from Norfolk, and from whence she wrote to invite the Matchams to Merton. By four o'clock Nelson's series of official visits was over. He had found time to order a knife, fork and spoon for Horatia, to be engraved with her name, and also a silver-gilt cup to be inscribed, "To my much-loved Horatia", and now he was heading for Merton again with Emma and his two nieces in the carriage. Back in his own home it was more pandemonium than peace. What with his relations and their offspring staying in the house, the many visitors as well as the formal congratulatory calls from the local residents, Nelson was left no time to devote solely to Emma. Reading between the lines of the various descriptions of the comings and goings at Merton at this time, it does not seem that Emma resented in any way the lack of privacy caused by the visitors and by Nelson's frequent journeys to town to discuss the possible whereabouts of the combined fleets of France and Spain. She welcomed the Boltons, the William Nelsons and the Matchams, and she encouraged Nelson to visit the Rev. Thomas Lancaster's school at Wimbledon where he listened to

211

recitations and requested a half holiday for the boys. The excitement and the entertaining were things she had missed, and she enjoyed being in the centre of it all once again. If she realised, as Nelson did; that his stay must of necessity be a transitory one, her optimism prevented her from thinking seriously of the dangers which might prevent Merton from becoming a permanent paradise later on when the French were beaten.

The conventions, in London, after Sir William's death, were rigidly adhered to, and whenever Nelson stayed in town he put up at Gordon's Hotel, 44 Albemarle Street, rather than resort to 11 Clarges Street and be under Emma's own roof.

Lord Minto, who was at Merton on the first Saturday after Nelson's arrival, recorded his impression of the party then assembled there. He "found Nelson just sitting down to dinner, surrounded by a family party, of his brother, the Dean, Mrs Nelson, their children, and the children of a sister, Lady Hamilton at the head of the table and Mother Cadogan at the bottom. I had a hearty welcome. He looks remarkably well and full of spirits. His conversation is a cordial in these low times. Lady Hamilton has improved and added to the house and the place extremely well and without his knowing she was about it. She is a clever being after all: the passion is as hot as ever."

On the second Sunday, Nelson missed morning service at Merton parish church as he had an important meeting with the Prime Minister in town. At 5 a.m. the next day, 2nd September, he was already up and dressed when a post-chaise drove up to the house bringing Captain the Hon. Henry Blackwood with news that Villeneuve and his fleet were at Cadiz. Captain Blackwood, who had broken his journey for the admiral's benefit, was soon on his way again with his official despatches for the Admiralty. The often told story that Emma selflessly persuaded her downcast lover to go to London and offer his services to his country, is both romantic and inaccurate. Nelson was convinced that such news must come very shortly and as he already had an appointment in London with Lord Minto, was quickly following on Blackwood's heels. That he bade farewell to Emma with the words, "Brave Emma! good Emma! If there were more Emmas there would be more Nelsons", is quite possible as he had made the same sort of remark before, and Emma, to give her her due, made no attempt to detain him.

The upshot of Nelson's visit to the Admiralty was that he was given what amounted to complete command of the fleet and a free hand in selecting his own officers. Time had become an important factor now, and consequently there were even more journeys to and from Merton, consultations and visits.

Beckford arrived at Merton when he found that Nelson could not possibly accept his invitation to Fonthill. The Duke of Clarence came over to dine and Admiral Sir Sidney Smith was a caller.

On his third Sunday at Merton Place, the whole house party went to church in the morning, the young people being invited to Morden Hall for the day by Abraham Goldsmid. George Matcham, junior, now nearly sixteen, made the following comment in his diary: "Went with Horace, Charlotte and Anne to Mr Goldsmid's – Fine house. Saw his sons – After breakfast row'd in the Boat. Horace shew'd his skill. Grounds poor. Very polite. Did not like their dinner; Jewish. The Hall the height of the house, very gaudy; as are all the rooms; but tasteless."

On 10th September, Nelson drove over to Richmond, alone, to see Lord Sidmouth, and in the evening he and Emma were guests in London at the dinner table of the wealthy Mr James Crawford. The next day, the Bolton family returned home to Norfolk. In arranging for Lord Minto to come down from town to dinner, and for some Merton neighbours, the Perrys, to make up the party, Nelson could not allow for the fact that he would suddenly receive a last-minute request, by special messenger, from the Prince of Wales, who had come up from Weymouth especially to see him. Whatever Nelson's feelings for the Prince, the flattering invitation could not be ignored, and so, in a carriage lent by the Duke of Queensberry, Nelson drove to London with Emma, leaving her at Clarges Street while he went to receive the royal good wishes. He also had an interview with Lord Castlereagh, the Secretary for War, and by the time the host and hostess of Merton Place arrived back, their guests had been waiting two hours.

All was now set for the admiral's departure on the morrow and Emma was in a tearful mood as Lord Minto, who sat next to her at dinner noted. According to him, she "could not eat, and hardly drink, and near swooning, and all at table".

Nelson was up early next morning, as was his custom, but even with so few hours remaining, Emma was not to have him to herself. The Matchams were still there, and it was necessary for him to rush up to London again to get his final sailing orders. After dinner, the post-chaise that had been ordered, was heard to arrive. He went up to the room where Horatia, now five, lay asleep and said a prayer by her bedside. Coming downstairs he made his farewells and was driven away into the night – for ever.

During a stop to change horses, he wrote in his diary:

Friday night, at half-past ten, drove from dear, dear Merton, where I left all which I hold dear in this world, to go to serve my king and country. May the great God whom I adore, enable me to fulfill the expectations of my country; and if it is His good pleasure that I should return, my thanks will never cease being offered up to the throne of His mercy. If it is His good Providence to cut short my days upon earth, I bow with the greatest submission, relying that He will protect those so dear to me, that I may leave behind. His will be done. Amen. Amen. Amen.

Chapter 11

After Trafalgar

IT SEEMS RATHER unlikely that Emma ever thought seriously of becoming Nelson's wife. Mr Crawford, with whom they had recently dined, described how she had said to Nelson, "I would wish with all my heart to die in two hours, so I might be your wife for one", but this was no more than lovers' talk, and Emma can have been in no doubt that, short of Lady Nelson's death, there could be no union. Divorce, in those days, required an Act of Parliament, and even so adultery on the part of a husband was not considered sufficient cause.

As an indication of her attitude of mind at this time, she had gone so far as to request the College of Heralds to draw up a coat of arms for her. In reply she received examples of two alternative designs with references to her family name of Lyon, which, when one remembers the honest trade of her father, seem somewhat ludicrous.

... " 'A' represents part of the Arms to the name of *Lyons*", reads the letter, "with the Cross of Malta in chief; the other, marked 'B', is also part of the Arms borne by the name of Lyons, with a Fess charged with cinque foils and the Cross of Malta, in allusion to the Coat of Hamilton and the aforesaid Order."

In early October, Emma, staying with the William Nelsons, wrote her news to Nelson:

Canterbury, October 4th (1805)

My most dear Nelson, I forgot to tell you that Lord Sidmouth's son stab'd himself at Worthing about a month ago – that was what H. Adington aluded to. He is not dead, it is the Clerk of the Pools, the boy you heard of as being too young to have such a place. Lord Douglas as

215

just call'd; he would have given much to have seen you when you was in England; he looks upon you as the sweetest of all human beings. The Dr has invited him to dinner to-morrow. The poor old Duke must have a letter every day from me. I had begun to fret at not having letters from you. I send you a letter of Miss Connor's, for there is much in it about our dear girl, you will like it. I also had one from my mother, who doats on her, she says she could not live without her. What a blessing for her parents to have such a child, so sweet, altho' so young, so amiable! God spare her to them, and be assured, my life, my soul, of your own Emma's fondest affections. You are my all of good. Heavens bless, bless you. Yours only, yours, etc.

Canterbury, October 8th 1805.

My dearest life, we are just come from church, for I am so fond of the Church Service and the Cannons are so civil; we have every day a fine anthem for me. Yesterday, Mr, Mrs, & Miss Harrison, Mrs Bridges, Marquis of Douglas, and General Thornton, and Mr Baker the Member, dined with us. The Dr gave a good dinner, and Mariana dressed the macaroni and curry, so all went off well. Our Julia is very ill yet, but not brought to bed, as she is only seven months. I do not mean to keep Julia after she gets well. I was obliged to send for Mariana down & my mother can ill spare her; she gives me such an amiable account of our dearest Horatia. She now reads very well, & is learning her notes, & French, & Italian, & my mother doats on her. The other day she said at table, "Mrs Candogging, I wonder Julia did not run out of the church when she went to be married, for I should, seeing my squinting husband come in, for, my God! how ugly he is, and how he looks cross-eyed; why, as my lady says, he looks 2 ways for Sunday." Now Julia's husband is the ugliest man you ever saw, but how that little thing cou'd observe him; but she is clever, is she not, Nelson? We go to-morrow for 2 days to Ramsgate to see an old friend, poor Lady Dunmore, who is there, is in great affliction for the loss of her son, Captain John Murry. To-day we dine alone, to eat up the scraps, & drink tea with old Mrs Percy. Charlotte hates Canterbury, it is *so dull*; so it is. My dear girl writes every day in Miss Conner's letter & I am so pleased with her. My heart is broke away from her, but I have now had her so long at Merton that my heart cannot bear to be without her. You will be even fonder of her when you return. She says, "I love my dear, dear, godpapa, but Mrs Gibson told me he kill'd all the people, and I was afraid." Dearest angel she is! Oh, Nelson, how I love her, but how do I idolize you – the dearest husband of my heart, you are all in this world to your Emma. May God send you victory, and home to your *Emma, Horatia, and paradise Merton*, for when you are there it will be paradise. My own Nelson, may God prosper you & preserve you, for the sake of your affectionate, etc.

I hope Sir Edward Berry has joined you by this time, but I now long to have letters from you. Everybody is full of Sir R. Calder's coming home. Captain Staines called yesterday; he is gone to town, as he wishes much to join you. Lord Douglas beg'd me to ask you if you ever met with Turkish tobacco, &, if you did, he wishes you wou'd send him some. Write often; tell me how you are & how the sea agrees with you, weather it is a bad port to blockade, in short, the smallest trifle that concerns you is so very interesting to your *own*, faithful, etc.

My compliments to the Mr Scotts and Mr Ford. Poor Nancy recommends her brother to you. Nancy has nursed me in many an illness, night and day, & you will love her for *that*. Tyson is going to buy a country seat and park for Mrs Tyson, near Woolwich. My compliments to Admiral Louis. God bless you, my own, own Nelson.

These letters were returned unopened to Emma by Captain Hardy. They had arrived too late. The battle of Trafalgar had been fought and on that Monday, 21st October 1805, when Nelson died, the flimsy structure on which Emma had built all her hopes collapsed completely.

The Rev. A.J. Scott, chaplain of H.M.S. *Victory* and devoted friend of Nelson, wrote at once to Mrs Cadogan: "Hasten the very moment you receive this to dear Lady Hamilton, and prepare her for the greatest of misfortunes. I fear even now I am too late, but ever since the fatal victory we have been separated by a gale of wind from the Fleet, and the news may already have reached you." According to the diary of Lady Elizabeth Foster, Emma had, in fact, received the tragic news direct from the Admiralty. Lady Elizabeth came up from Chiswick House to visit her in Clarges Street as soon as the reports of the battle were current.

I found her in bed [she recorded]. She had the appearance of a person stunned and scarcely as yet able to comprehend the certainty of her loss. "What shall I do?" and "How can I exist?" were her first words. She then showed me some letters which were lying on the bed – they were from Lord Nelson of the 1st and 7th – and I think the 13th day of October. The greater part of them had appeared in the Morning Chronicle of today.

In a letter not given to the press he wrote that he thought a battle was inevitable, but if he returned to be smiled upon by her he should be thrice a victor.

Lady H. said she had heard nothing, knew no particulars. I told her as nothing could increase her suffering now, I would tell her what I had heard and read, for she kept repeating she was sure there must be some message to her, some later letters on board the Victory. I asked her if she knew when the Victory came. She said, "Oh, no – I know nothing." I then told her different circumstances. She cried and it seemed to relieve her. I asked her if she thought he had any presentiment of his fate. She said No, not till their parting. That he had come back four different times, and the last time he had kneeled down and holding up his hand had prayed God to bless her. She also told me he had requested her to take the sacrament with him at Merton, "for," he said, "we both stand before our God with pure hearts and affection."

I asked her how she had heard the dreadful news. "I had come to Merton," she said, "my house not being ready, and feeling rather unwell I said I would stay in bed, on account of a rash. Mrs Bolton was sitting by my bedside, when all of a sudden I said, 'I think I hear the Tower guns. Some victory perhaps in Germany, to retrieve the credit lost by Mack'. 'Perhaps', said Mrs Bolton, 'It may be news from my brother'. 'Impossible, surely. There is not time.' In five minutes a carriage drove up to the door. I sent to enquire who was arrived. They brought me word, Mr Whitby, from the Admiralty. Show him in directly, I said. He came in, and with a pale countenance and faint voice said, 'We have gained a great Victory'. 'Never mind your victory', I said, 'My letters – give me my letters' – Capt. Whitby was unable to speak – tears in his eyes and a deathly paleness over his face made me comprehend him. I believe I gave one scream and fell back, and for ten hours after I could neither speak nor shed a tear – days have passed on, and I know not how they end or begin – nor how I am to bear my future existence."

I asked her if his family were kind to her. She said, "No words could say how much so, and how affectionate, and most particularly that dear Boy, Lt Marten (Lt M. Matcham, son of Nelson's sister and brother-in-law). He scarcely leaves me, but tries to make me take some food, or medicine – something to do me good – and with the greatest affection – the present Lord is a strange original, but he'll cry one moment and sing the next."

She said she understood he (Nelson) had left her Merton, that at first she would have given it up to this Lord Nelson but then she thought not. I advised her not by any means.

Emma's despair was inevitable and it is greatly to her credit that within a few days of receiving this shattering blow, she should be concerned for the welfare of others to the extent of getting her mother to write the following to the Rt. Hon. George Rose, Vice-President of the Board of Trade, who had been a great friend and admirer of Nelson's.

9th Novr 1805

Lady Hamiltons most wretched state of Mind prevents her imploring her dear good Mr Rose to solicite Mr Pitt to consider the Family of our great & Glorious Nelson, who so Gallantly died for his Country leaving behind his Favorite Sister with a large Family unprovided for. Her Ladyship is confident you will exert every Nerve for these good People as a Mark of your true & Real attachment to our Lamented Hero. Mr Bolton has & was ever much esteem'd by his Brother in Law & had it pleased the Almighty to have spar'd him to his Family, he meant to have settled them independent; they at this Moment surround her Ladyships Bed bewailing their sad loss & miserable state. Lady Hamilton who's situation is beyond description only prays that you good Sir will do all you can for this Worthy Family it will be the greatest Relief to her Mind, this is written by the Mother of the most to be pitied Lady Hamilton who begs leave to subscribe her self Mr Roses
    Most Obd^t & very Hum^{le} Servt

Mary Cadogan

P.S. If Mr Rose would condecend to acknowledge this it would be a comfort to her just now.

For about three weeks Emma kept to her bed. Lionel Prager Goldsmid recalled in later life his memories of a visit to Lady Hamilton with his family at this time:

I was eight years old and was allowed to accompany my mother and those of the family who made up the party from our House. I was a great favourite of Lady Hamilton's and bathed in tears at times as she talked over his virtues and exhibited the various gifts he had made her on different occasions. I was on the bed to aid in passing the rings, shawls, bracelets, etc, shewn to the company of about 15 persons seated in a semi-circle at the foot of the bed – and as she thought perhaps at moments of her truly lamented Hero and friend, I came in for numerous kisses and her usual remark – thank you my funny boy – or child you must come every day. The very coat in which the dear old Admiral was dressed in the fatal battle and received his death wound was on the outside of the bed – the hole where the bullet passed through stiffened with congealed blood. There was most certainly a very serio comic performance throughout the visit. I was too young to avail myself of any mischievous act – but when orders for departure was given in my hurry I believe I removed too much one of the several shawls too hastily from its position round her Ladyship's shoulders, and she did not appear quite so wholesome in her freedom from stays, etc.

On 8th November 1805, Mrs Creevey wrote to her husband:

The first of my visits this morning was to "my Mistress" … (Mrs Fitzherbert) … I found her alone, and she was excellent – gave me an account of the Prince's grief about Lord N., and then entered into the domestic failings of the latter in a way infinitely creditable to her, and skillful too. She was all for Lady Nelson and against Lady Hamilton, who, she said (hero as he was) overpower'd him and took possession of him quite by force. But she ended in a natural, good way, by saying:- "Poor creature! I am sorry for her now, for I suppose she is in grief."

It was not until 9th January, 1806, that Nelson's body was deposited in its final resting-place in St Paul's Cathedral. The funeral assumed enormous proportions, cost the country £14,698 11s. 6d., and by all accounts was not remarkable either for good taste or for good management. As a sidelight on the momentous occasion, a small paragraph in the Annual Register for 1806, dated 1st January, mentions that, "The four vergers of St Paul's cathedral, who have the exclusive property of the body of the church, are said to make more than a thousand pounds by the daily admissions to see the preparations for the funeral of Lord Nelson; the door-money is taken as at a puppet-shew, and amounted for several days to more than £40 each day!"

Nelson's will, made in 1803, and the seven codicils that went with it, had been read over to the family congregated in Emma's bedroom at Merton some days after the news of his death had reached London. By the terms of it, Emma was left Merton, with the furniture and fittings, and seventy acres of land, plus all the hay belonging to Nelson at Merton and Wimbledon. She was also to have £500 a year from the Brontë estate, and this was to come from the trustees appointed by Nelson, who were William Nelson and William Haslewood.

Dr William Nelson, who now became Earl Nelson of Trafalgar with a government grant of £5,000 a year and a large sum with which to buy an estate, was not a popular figure. Years later *Punch* had some very uncharitable remarks to make. "As for the Earl Admiral's brother," it said, "who inherited the profits of Trafalgar, and bobbed in for the coronet that missed the dead – he was in heart and soul as much allied to the sailor as a barnacle upon the copper of the 'Victory' was a portion of her heart of oak. Nevertheless they took Parson Barnacle and gilded his simoniacal head with a coronet, and he – keeping the even tenor of his way – cheated Lady Hamilton, duly robbing the sailor's child, Nelson's orphan, Horatia. Whereon the Prince of Wales wrote letters of sympathy that, like all such epistles from his royal hand, were by no means worth the ink that blotted the paper."

William was certainly a self-seeking and pompous man and no great credit to the cloth, but his character does not seem to be quite so black as it has been painted by some of Emma's rather biased biographers. She herself accused him of suppressing the eighth codicil that Nelson had written, at the last moment, in a notebook on board the *Victory*. It would appear that William did no such thing. The codicil, which merely, in so many words, bequeathed Emma and Horatia to the nation, had been seen by George Rose, Pitt and even the Prince of Wales, and, furthermore, had no legal bearing on the estate. However, Emma, in her ignorance, chose to view it differently, and openly accused the new Earl of hiding the notebook until he heard, while at dinner in her house, of the generous grant to be made to him by the Government. Whereupon, according to her, he threw the book across to her "with a very coarse expression" and told her that she might now do as she pleased with it. An unpleasant scene followed, of the sort that Emma knew well how to create when she felt that things were not going as she wished; even her doting Nelson had been heard to remark that "she knew how to raise the hell of a dust when she could not get her own way". As a result, relations became very strained between Emma and the Earl. In informing Lady Elizabeth Foster of her grievance over the codicil, Emma's remarks can hardly be called dignified. "And now," she said, "ought I not to be proud? Let them refuse me all reward. I will go with this paper fixed to my breast and beg through the streets of London, and every barrow-woman shall say, 'Nelson bequeathed her to *us*'." Poor foolish Emma! With her world in ruins, she should not, perhaps, be judged too harshly.

While she was staying in Clarges Street, her mother wrote from Merton about the difficulties with which she was bravely endeavouring to contend.

Merton, February 13th (1806)

I will not show them one bill or receipt; I will tell them you have them locked up. Some were as Cribbe (Cribb, it will be remembered, was the gardener at Merton) has sumed it up. I have receipts for thirteen hundred pounds, besides the last forty-two. Mrs Cribbe advises me not to show them till you have seen them. On Saturday I shall send Sarah with them, as Frances comes to town. I had a very canting letter from Haslewood yesterday saying the Earl & him was coming down to-day. God bless you, etc.

P.S. I will write and tell you all to-morrow, if it is too late to-night for the post.

March 29th 1806.

I have enclosed to you Cribb's account he brought me from Hasle-wood the other day. Let me know whether you have a copy of the will or not, as I understand the executers are to pay every expence for six months after his death. Pray write me word wether you have employed a lawyer against Haslewood; let me, in particular, for if you have not I will. I am well informed of the measure the land your house stands upon, and will not allow the pleasure ground that is taken in, that you have a right to take in what part you like of Linton's farm, and leave out what you like of the Wimbledon estate. Write me every particular that I may not be taken unawares. Don't you think if you was to write to Mr Goldsmid and let me know very particularly who I am to aply to. I was in hopes Mr Bolton would have been here at the time. Pray, my dear Emma, let me know wether you have answered Mr Roberts's bill or not, as I shall write to Mr Roberts and Mrs Burt. I should not be surprized if (I) was to see Mr Kidd come up with Mr Hughes, but if he does he never sleeps in the house where I do. I had a letter from poor Mrs Dodsworth yesterday to say she should come to Merton to-day. I am very glad of it, as poor Sarah & me has not the newspapers now, and the weather very wet and dirty one cannot get out. God bless you, etc.

P.S. S. Reynold's love to all.

The kind-hearted Abraham Goldsmid was doing what he could to help Emma out of her financial difficulties. He says himself that he hardly knew what he had written, and, to judge from the following excerpt from his letter, one feels that Emma would have been left in much the same state.

Finsbury Square, April 8th 1806.

… Now for business, & please keep it to yourself and Mr Bolton. I have been, as you suppose, most busily employed respecting the late loan of which, my dear Lady, you have a third of 6000, which is neat am^t 2000, being divided into 3 parts; of course, every person has a third, being after battling about coalition took place, but have never lost sight of Mr Bolton & Mr Matcham. I have seen and conversed with all the parties and pushed all I could. The answer from L^d G was, he meant to give to Mr B. £10,000 at his disposal, & 10,000 to Mr M. for his disposal. My answer was that, as Mr M they might be an apoligy for such a sum, but as to Mrs B I hoped & trusted they would give at least 20,000 ready money, exclusive of a respectable place under Government for Mr B. Mr Vansitart answer was, that he admired my zeal in the promotion the wellfare of the late Ld Nelson family; but they had a deal to contend with, which was the service of the late Duke of Marlborough. My answer was, that I look it much more, and no example whatever, as times stood, required more exertion than the present. My final answer I have not received, but expect, in a week or ten days, to know the result of Lord Grenville; but as to a place for Mr Bolton, he agreed it ought to be done and no doubt, if any confidence is to be placed in ministers – it will be so. I think that Mr B ought to be here in London the latter end of next week at farthest, that I may have him at hand. Yours, etc.

Excuse all faults, as I have not a minute & hardly know what I have written, therefore take the will for the deed.

On Emma's birthday Mrs Cadogan wrote again. She was beginning to feel the strain, but the letter, and especially the note from Emma's cousin, Sarah Reynolds, is touching:

Merton,   April 26th 1806.

I pray God send you many happy returns of this day. I have sent you a gown of Sarah Reynold's making. If I had ten thousand pounds to send you this day, I should have been very happy. I have sent Mariann, as I thought she might be of use to you today. I am all over with bricks and dust and stinking paint, being no-body but our own family. On Saturday you shall have a menesstra verde and one thing roasted. Mariann will tell you how miserable I have been this week
My dear Emma, I owe Mariann 4 months' wages, which is two guines; I had it not to give her, and she want shoes and stockings. If you can, give Sarah Conner thirty shillings to pay her washer-woman, as she is indebted to her for three month's washing; I have got her washing down here. You must send Mariann as soon as you can in the morning.
God bless you, my ever dear Emma, etc.

[Note enclosed from Sarah Reynolds]

I wish you many happy returns of this day. I should have been very happy had it been in my power to have made you a small present on this day, but not having anything but what my dear aunt and you have been so good as to give me. I wish it had been in my power; I should have been very happy, believe me, my dear Lady Hamilton. With gratitude and thank for what you have done for me and my dear father and family. God bless you, dear Lady Hamilton.

Among the many outstanding bills with which Emma was faced were those for the improvements and alterations to Merton Place. In an attempt to obtain assistance from some quarter, she seems to have decided to forget the fracas over the codicil and to write to Earl Nelson. The wording of her letter suggests that she had assistance from some legally minded friend.

Merton, Novr 14, 1806.

My Lord, – Having seen with inexpressible pleasure that every expressed wish of the late Lord Nelson regarding the interests of his Family, when only communicated to the gracious Sovereign in whose service he so gloriously fell, has been instantly and Liberally granted by the generous bounty of our King and Country, I am naturally induced to consider as equally certain that the same mode of conveying his last, humble request in favour of the Infant, Horatia Nelson, his adopted daughter, as well as of myself, will be observed with a proportionate degree of attention. I have therefore to require not only on my own behalf, but as Guardian of the said Infant, by virtue of his late Lordship's will, and the CODICIL particularly expressive of that request, that you will have the goodness immediately to assist me in regularly carrying into effect the evident intention of the Testator whose executor you have *the honour to be.* – I am, etc.

The answer was, under the circumstances, an extraordinarily polite one, although no tangible assistance seems to have resulted.

Canterbury, November 16, 1806.

Dear Lady Hamilton, – No one is more ready and willing to comply with every wish of my late Dear and lamented Brother than myself. With regard to what you allude to in your letter of 14th instant – if you will point out to me what it is you want me to do, either for yourself or the child, I shall be glad to give you every assistance in my power. – We expect to be in town about Xmas, and shall hope to see you at our house.

Lady Nelson has been in daily expectation of hearing from you. She and Charlotte beg to join in best regards and good wishes with your faithful humble servant,

Nelson.

Emma seems to have made no attempt to reduce her expenses at Merton. Nelson's several nieces were still frequent visitors and she entertained lavishly a host of guests amongst whom were Signor Rovedino and Madame Bianchi. The story goes that when the ladies retired from the dining-room, Signor Rovedino acted as host to the gentlemen, dispensing with liberality the best wines from the Merton cellars. On being questioned on the advisability of such extravagance, Emma replied that having Rovedino and Madame Bianchi at Merton was less expensive than taking Horatia to town for singing lessons. That she accepted invitations out as well, can be seen from the last part of a letter she received from Lady Abercorn: "Thursday will answer just as well for us, except being a day longer without the pleasure of your company. When does Madame Bianchi come?

"We hope you will not forget any of your shawls or things for attitudes. Yours, etc."

In April 1807, Mrs Bolton mentions Emma having stayed at No. 136 New Bond Street, so presumably the Clarges Street house had been disposed of or the lease had run out.

"I am glad the Duke [of Queensberry] has said he does not approve of No. 136 for you," wrote Mrs Bolton. "It looks as if he really meant to leave you something to keep up a better establishment. Shall I say the truth, I was very much hurt to see you were obliged whether you liked it or not to mix with their society, indeed, if they had given you up the front drawing room entirely & two bedchambers you might have been more comfortable."

To add to Emma's worries, her mother was taken ill. On 29th April 1807, Mrs Matcham wrote from Bath:

We were very sorry to find by a letter from Lady Charlotte that Mrs Cadogan had been dangerously ill, we hope before this she has been getting strength, as the weather is very fine for invalids; it has been a very unhealthy season in Bath, everybody, young & old, has been complaining.... .

For the remainder of 1807 Emma continued to spend money with the greatest abandon. The loan raised for her by Abraham Goldsmid the previous year could not have lasted her long. On looking through the correspondence she received during the year, one becomes appalled by her recklessness. She was, at the same time, being extremely generous, in particular to the Boltons, but in the long run, it was with other people's money. The following extracts serve to show the pace at which she was living:

from Mrs Bolton, 1st June 1807

... How happy I am I was not at your *grumtulation* dinners. I am rejoiced to hear your affairs are drawing to a crisis, I hope to a good purpose, you may have waited so long as you have done. I hope in God Mr Rose will have the power as well as the will to serve us all...

from Mrs Bolton, 24th June 1807

... I am glad you found out who the tickets were for. I should have been sorry those Berneys & Atkins should have received any favor from you. I am glad Charlotte is going with you. She will find out she will have no such pleasant parties as you can introduce her to. I hope I shall hear from you after the masquarade all news about it... .

from Mr Bolton, Saturday, 24th July 1807.

... Yesterday Mr North, joining us in a party to Vauxhall, mentioned his intention of calling upon your Ladyship before he left town, and has kindly offered to take me down on Wednesday next if your Ladyship should be at home, of which I am to inform him as soon as I receive your answer. I shall certainly come. Knowing that Mrs Cadogan will not be far from Richmond, I shall add no more, reserving everything until we meet, Yours etc... .

from Mr Bolton, Byfleet, August 23rd 1807

... Pray do you like Worthing as much as you did Southend? I suppose Mrs Cadogan is improving now very fast as to her health. Do you find that the bathing is very beneficial both to you & Horatia? ...

from Mrs Bolton, "Sunday noon" (29th November 1807)

Many thanks, my dear Lady, for thinking of such a *little body* as myself in the midst of royalty. Mr Bolton will be much obliged to His

Royal Highness for the tobacco to be sent here; *you must deliver the message in your own name*, we are not in the habit of sending & speaking to such great personages. You delight me by saying Horatia has so much notice taken of her. I hope, when she is introduced at Windsor, George our King will fall in love with her, & give her a good pension out of his privy purse. He ought to have a fellow-feeling, for, like her, he has lost a *great* supporter. I may say this to you, and indeed it is true...

... What a bountiful supply of food you have sent us! I see you are with us for *clothing the naked* & feeding the hungry. I only wish you had fortune equal to your generosity. How does the old Duke *do* this severe weather? ...

from Mrs Bolton, Cranwich, December 8th (1807)

... How favoured you have been by their Royal Highnesses passing so many days with you. I do not wonder their liking Merton & *your* society. Did the Prince of Wales spend more than one day with you? Poor Blindy! had I been in her place I should have kept my room the time they were there – at least the Prince... .

By the beginning of the next year, Emma had moved up to London, probably to Bond Street again. She still moved in fashionable circles, as is evident from a letter of Mrs Matcham's:

March 10th 1808

... I am delighted to hear of your going to all these great parties; London is certainly the place for your constant residence, where you can enjoy the society of your friends, without the immense expence of entertaining their servants, which you are obliged to do in the country. I hope to hear in your next that Mrs Cadogan is quite recover'd, to whom & to all your party we beg to be kindly remember'd, not forgetting my dear Horatia, & accept our sincere good wishes from, my dear Lady Hamilton, your affectionate, etc.

By April, it had become evident that Merton Place would have to be sold, and a valuation of the house was made by "J. Willock" of Golden Square, who submitted this document:

The Particulars of Lady Hamilton's Villa at Merton, in the Parishes of Mitcham and Wimbledon, in the County of Surrey.

The House with the Offices, Lawns, Shrubberies, Canals, Plantations, Farm House, Barns, Stables, Outbuildings, Yards, and Four Inclosures of Land, situate altogether within a Ring Fence, and bounded on the North & West by the Turnpike Road from London to Epsom, and on the East partly by Merton Abbey Lane, in the Parish of Mitcham.
And
the Kitchen Garden, Gardener's House, Plantation, and Three Inclosures of Meadow Land, lying all within a Ring Fence opposite the House, and bounded on the south by the said Turnpike Road, east by the Road from Merton to Wandsworth, west by the Road from Merton Turnpike, and north by a common footpath in the Parish of Wimbledon, which contain altogether seventy-two acres, or thereabout, and are all Freehold.
I have carefully surveyed the above described Premises, and I am of opinion they are worth the sum of

£10,430.

And that the furniture and effects in the
House, Offices, Gardens, and Grounds are
worth the sum of   £2,500.
£12,930.

Emma was now becoming aware of the seriousness of her predicament. The Duke of Queensberry, now eighty-four, but still intrigued by a pretty figure, had Emma's interests at heart and offered to let her have the use of a property of his in Richmond, at a nominal rent. While accepting his generous offer, she was also banking on the probability, in view of "Old Q's" long friendship, and indeed, kinship, with Sir William Hamilton, that he would leave her a considerable sum in his will. Abetted by Mrs Bolton, Emma did all she could to fascinate the old Duke with this mercenary object in view. Her standards were falling very low, and the remarks, on this subject, in Mrs Bolton's letters seem almost depraved.

Sunday morning, (15th May 1808)

... I am glad you treated the old Duke with a sight of you in all your brilliancy. Depend upon it, it will be a thousand *pounds* more in your pocket, for he does love to look at a handsome woman; *still*, depend upon it, your person has more charms for him than all the beauties of the mind. Treat him as often as you can with a sight of you, that's the only way...

Cranwich, "Tuesday", (26th May 1808)

… I was surprized to see by the papers to-day the Duke of Q was in the park – a *flash* before death, or does he never mean to depart this life? Poor old man! he must have outlived all his pleasure except looking at your Ladyship, which I hope he will remember with *gratitude*… .

In July, Emma went on a visit to Norfolk with the idea that, when she returned, she would take up her residence at Richmond. The house which the Duke of Queensberry had made available, was known as "Herring House" and stood in a small cul-de-sac (Herring Court) backing on to the river.

The building itself was hardly smaller than Merton Place though it had no grounds other than a terraced riverside garden. There were eight bedrooms, a dressing-room, box-room and bathroom, four reception rooms, lounge hall, vestibule, billiard-room, the usual offices, and stabling for four horses. The principal bedroom was a generous 20 ft 3 ins by 18 ft, and had a dressing-room (15 ft by 13 ft) communicating with it, making, one would assume, a most convenient suite for Emma and Horatia.

When she took up residence, Emma brought with her a servant of long standing, named Nanny, and a housekeeper, affectionately referred to as "old Dame Francis", whose services she was to retain to the end of her life.

Almost at once, she received a letter from George Rose about Merton and about the last codicil to Nelson's will.

Old Palace Yard. July 21st 1808

I have seen Mr Dawson this morning in consequence of my sending for him, and I find there is now a gentleman from the East Indies about the property at Merton, who is likely to give nearly £13,000 for the house, land & fixtures – exclusive of the furniture, wine, & books, the latter I am sure should be packed up and sent to London. From all that passed with Mr Dawson I am led to hope the sale is likely to take place, and if that should fail, I have advised the place being let as the only possible means of putting an end to the expence, and it would produce some money to you. I would not, however, advise the letting the house except in the case of absolute necessity. I said everything to Mr Dawson that I could to incite him to activity, and I verily believe he will now exert himself.

I had an opportunity of a very quiet conversation with Mr Canning on Sunday last, about the paper written by Lord Nelson just before he went into his last action, which has led to a further communication on the same subject. I repeat, what I think I before said, that there is a perfect disposition in Mr Canning's mind to give effect to that paper, but the difficulties are, I fear, insurmountable. I can most truly assure you that I have most anxiously and concientiously discharged all that Lord Nelson could have expected from me if he were now alive, & I am *most sincerely grieved* that I have failed of success. The point is not absolutely decided, but I should be inexcusable if I were to give you any hope.

I leave London to-morrow, and from Cuffnells I will write to Mr Bolton on the affairs which interest him. I am, etc.

Evidently the "gentleman from the East Indies" decided against the purchase of Merton, for in just over six weeks' time Emma was beseeching the Duke of Queensberry to buy it. Her letter, especially towards the end, has a tone reminiscent of her first letter to Greville. It is almost "what shall I dow?" over again.

Richmond, September 4th 1808.

My dear Lord & friend, may I hope that you will read this, for you are the only hope I have in this world to assist and protect me, in this moment of unhappiness and distress. To you, therefore, I appeal. I do not wish to have more than what I have. I can live on that at Richmond, only that I may live free from fear – that every debt may be paid. I think, and hope, £15,000 will do for everything. For my sake, for Nelson's sake, for the good I have done my country, purchase it (Merton); take it, only giving me the portraits of Sir William, Nelson, and the Queen. All the rest shall go. I shall be free and at liberty. I can live at Richmond on what I have; you will be doing a deed that will make me happy, for lawyers will only involve me every day more and more – debts will increase new debts. You will save me by this act of kindness. The title deeds are all good and ready to deliver up, and I wish not for more than what will pay my debts. I beseech you, my dear Duke, to imagine that I only wish for you to do this, not to lose by it; but I see that I am lost, and most miserable, if *you* do not help me. My mind is made up to live on what I have. If I could but be free from Merton – all paid, and only one hundred pounds in my pocket, you will live to see me blessing you, my mother blessing you, Horatia blessing you. If you would not wish to keep Merton, perhaps it will sell in the spring better – only let me pass my winter without the idea of a prison. 'Tis true my imprudence has brought it on me, and villany and ingratitude has helped to involve me, but the sin be on them. Do not let my enemies trample on me; for God's sake then, dear Duke, good friend, think 'tis Nelson who asks you to befriend, etc.

It was hardly surprising that the Duke did not wish to purchase Merton. It remained on the market until April of the following year, when it was bought by one of the Goldsmid family; not by Abraham, as has often been stated, but by his younger brother, Ascher.

The years of over-eating and heavy drinking were having their effect. Emma had been in poor health before she moved to Richmond, and probably because she contracted jaundice and became quite ill she decided to make her will.

Dated Richmond, October 16th, 1808.

This I declare to be my last Will and Testament, October the 16th, 1808. If I can be buried in St Paul's, I should be very happy to be near the glorious Nelson, whom I loved and admired, and as once Sir William, Nelson and myself had agreed we should all be buried near each other. If the King had (not) granted him a public funeral, this would have been, that three persons who were so much attached to each other from virtue and friendship should have been laid in one grave when they quitted this ill-natured slanderous world. But 'tis past, and in heaven I hope we shall meet. If I am not permitted to be buried in St Paul's, let me be put where I shall be near my dear mother, when she is called from this ungrateful world. But I hope she will live, and be a mother to Nelson's child, Horatia. I beg that Merton may be sold, and all debts paid; and, whatever money shall be left after all debts are paid, I give to my dear mother, and after her death to my dear Horatia Nelson. I also give all that I am possessed of in this world to my dear mother, Mary Doggin, or Cadogan, for her use, and, after her death, to Horatia Nelson. I give them all my ready money, plate, linen, pictures, wearing apparel, household furniture, trinkets, wine, in short, everything I have in this world to my mother during her life, and after her death to my dearest Horatia Nelson. I hope Mr George Rose will be my executor, and take care of my dear mother and Horatia, and if he should not be living, I hope his eldest son will do me this last favour to see justice done to Nelson's daughter, and also I beg His Royal Highness the Prince of Wales, as he dearly loved Nelson, that His Royal Highness will protect his child, and be kind to her; for this I beg of him, for there is no one that

I so highly regard as His Royal Highness. Also my good friend the Duke of Queensbury, I beg of him, as Nelson beseeched him to be kind to me, so I commend my dear mother and Horatia to his kind heart. I have done my King and country some service, but as they were ungrateful enough to neglect the request of the virtuous Nelson in providing for me, I do not expect they will do anything for his child; but if there should be any administration in at my death who have hearts and feelings, I beg they will provide for Horatia Nelson, the child who would have had a father if he had not gone forth to fight his country's battles, therefore she has a claim on them. I declare before God, and as I hope to see Nelson in heaven, that Ann Connor, who goes by the name of Carew and tells many falsehoods that she is my daughter, but from what motive, I know not, I declare that she is the eldest daughter of my mother's sister Sarah Connor, and that I have the mother and six children to keep, all of them, except two, having turned out bad. I therefore beg of my mother to be kind to the two good ones, Sarah and Cecilia. This family having by their extravagance almost ruined me, I have nothing to leave them, and I pray to God to turn Ann Connor, alias Carew's heart. I forgive her, but as there is madness in the Connor family, I hope it is only the effect of this disorder that may have induced this; bad young woman to have persecuted me by her slander and falsehood. I give all my papers, books, lace, and indeed, everything to my dear mother and Horatia Nelson. This I declare to be my last Will and Testament, and to do away with all other wills.

In November Emma wrote to Charles Greville:

Sunday Morning.

Dear Sir,

I was on the point of coming to you when I got your note, but I feel sorry to-day I cannot call on you at your house, for I am to meet some of my trustees and my soliciter, at 2 o'clock, on particular business. As to my dear friend, Mrs Greffer, it was not any favour she wished for herself, for she wou'd not ask one of the King, and I have taken care to give her such letters for the Queen, and beg'd of Her Majesty by the sacred memory of Nelson, by *the charge she has placed in me*, that she will be good to Mrs Greffer, whom she allways marked with the Royal Notice… . I will call soon to see you, and inform you of my present prospect of happiness. At a moment of desperation, when I thought they neglected me, Goldsmid and my Citty friends came forward, and they have rescued rne from distruction. Distraction brought on by *Earl*

Nelson's having thrown on me all the bills for finishing *Merton*. Nelson, who attested in his dying moments that I had well served my Country. All these things, and papers of my services and my illtreatment I have laid before my trustees; they are paying my debts. I live in retirement, and the citty are going to bring forward my claims; in short, I have put myself under their protection, and nothing, *no power on earth shall* make me *deviate* from my present system. On Friday next, I come to finsbury Square to Mrs Goldsmid, and Monday I shall be in Broad Street with Sir John and Lady Perrin for a week, and one of those days I will come to you for a horse, for I have not my horses at present; but I do not want them, friends are so good to me. You will be pleased to hear my mother is well and delighted with my house and small establishment. Horatia is well, and you will, I think, be pleased with her education. Goldsmid has been, and is an angel to me, and his bounty shall never be abused. I hope you will mend as the Spring advances, and if you shou'd ever come to Richmond, pray call and see me, and pray believe me, yours affectionately,

Emma Hamilton.

The nature of her "particular business" is set out in detail in a document dated 25th November 1808:

At a meeting of the friends of Lady Hamilton, held at the house of Sir John Perring, Bart., the 25th Nov[r], 1808.

Present

Sir John Perring	Mr McClure	Mr Nichol
Mr Davison	Mr Goldsmid	Mr Wilson
Mr Moore	Sir Robert Barclay	Mr Lavie
Mr Gooch		

Mr Dawson attending as Sol[r] to Lady Hamilton.

Read A letter from Lady Hamilton addressed to the gentlemen attending the Meeting. *Read* A list of debts delivered in by Mr Dawson as obtained by advertizement, also a list of additional debts delivered in by Lady Hamilton herself, the whole debt estimated at £8,000, exclusive of £10,000 required to pay off annuities.

Upon consideration of the property possessed by Lady Hamilton the same was ascertained as follows:

Books	£1,500
Wine	2,000
Statues, Vases, China, Pictures, and other articles of fancy	1,500
Furniture and Fixtures	1,500
House & 32 Acres	7,500
40 Acres	3,500
Taken at a very low rate	£17,500

The above property being independent of her annuities under the wills of Sir William Hamilton and Lord Nelson, and her claim on Government.

RESOLVED. That an assignment of the whole of Lady Hamilton's property be taken, and that the same be made to:

> Sir John Perring, Bart.
> Alexander Davison, Esq.
> Abraham Goldsmid, Esq.
> Richard Wilson, Esq.
> and
> Germain Lavie, Esq.

as Trustees for Sale, etc.

That in order to afford an immediate relief the following sums be advanced by

Alexr Davison	One thousand pounds
Abm Goldsmid	One thousand pounds
John Gooch	Five hundred pounds
Richd Wilson	Five hundred pounds
Sir Robert Barclay	Five hundred pounds
J ohn Perring	Two hundred pounds

to be secured by the said Trust with interest.

That the money collected by the above advances be applied in payment of all incumbrances absolutely necessary to be immediately discharged.

That all the creditors be applied to to execute the Debt of Trust, and to agree to accept payment out of the Trust Estate.

That pending the Trust Lady Hamilton be allowed to receive her annuities, but in case of deficiency the same shall be applied in liquidating the balance.

That the Trustees be a Committee to follow up the claim on Government, in which all the friends of Lady Hamilton be requested to co-operate.

That the Trustees do go to market in the most advantageous mode possible, so as not to injure the property by a premature sale.

Signed   Robert Barclay   Geo Gooch

            Alex^r Davison   A. McClure

            F. Moore   George Nicol

            Ab^m Goldsmid   Richd Wilson

            Germain Lavie   John Perring.

On 23rd April 1809, the Hon. Charles Greville died at his house at Paddington Green. He had lived barely sixty years. There is no written comment to show how much or how little his demise affected Emma's personal feelings. It did, however, affect the payment of her annuity from Sir William's estate. In this respect, there is a note among the archives of Messrs. Coutts & Co. which reveals the protective, almost fatherly, hand of the Duke of Queensberry. Dated 29th June 1809, it reads:

As Lady Hamilton experiences some inconveniency from the delay in the payment of her Jointure which has taken place in consequence of the death of Mr Greville, to pay her drafts to the extent of £180 for the quarter due at Midsummer last charging them as usual to her account for which he (the Duke of Queensberry) promises to be answerable if we should not receive the Jointure for that period – if we do receive it – it will of course replace the overpayment and he requests that Lady Hamilton may not be informed of his interference upon this occasion.

The £180, due on 24th June, was not credited to her until 10th August, by which time her account was overdrawn by £169.

She was now raising money by any means she could. Her title, no doubt, enabled her to obtain considerable credit from tradesmen and there is evidence that she gave two promissory notes, each for £250, to Sir Charles Cockerill, one payable on 30th June 1810 and the other on 21st October 1810. That she was spending money on clothes and travel is obvious from a letter of Mrs Bolton's, dated 29th September 1809:

Now, my dear Lady, I think your visit to Ashfold must be over, & all your summer excursions must be nearly at an end, & you will now turn your thoughts towards Cranwich, where you will be most cordially received... .

The kindly side of Emma's nature still showed itself through her worries and tribulations and her concern for her own relations, and apparently for their friends as well, is clear from a letter, in two hands, addressed to her from Greenwich. Perhaps she was amused by the unconscious humour.

Thomas Kidd and Jonathan Ingham to Lady Hamilton
Greenwich, November 17th 1809.
I rec^d yours, and should have been happy had it been in my power to have acted according to your directions, which it is not possible for me to do as I would wish. For I declare my small cloaths are scandoulos, and my hat has the crown part nearly off, but Mr and Mrs Ingam has contriv'd it so that what I was in need of they have lent me. I have to inform you that your brother Chas. is in Greenwich College, and has been here since the 6th inst; and when I informed Mr and Mrs Ingam that he was here, they have given him a strong invitation for to pass what few hours he has to spare to abide at their house, and Mr Ingham has got him removed from the Hall where y^r brother was, to an appartment belonging to the Hall where Mr Ingham is. From y^r aff^{te} cous^n, etc.

(Letter from Jonathan Ingham)
Your kind offer to do me a service is more than I could ever expect; but I believe, by what I have been credittly informed, that there will be a vacancy for a porter at the West Gate at Christmas next, as the man who is porter now is very old and infirm that he is not able to do his duty, so that he is to be super-annuated; so I hope that your Ladyship's indisposition will not prevent you from making intercession in my behalf, by letter or in person, to the Lords of the Admiralty, who, I make no doubt, by so doing I shall meet with that encouragement as I desire. But should I be dissuppointed of the situation of porter, there is the resting cook very ill at this time, and, should that place be vacant, will prove acceptable to me.

P.S. As to my character when I was in His Majesty's service, I believe it to be justifiable in every degree, for I have served as a sailor on board the Barfleur and Prince near 10 years, and never had one complaint against me. So J remain, etc.

In 1810 Emma's debts and troubles increased. On 14th January her mother died. The loss affected her very deeply, for Mrs Cadogan had been her staunchest supporter through the years, unwisely uncritical of her daughter as she undoubtedly was. Overcome with grief, Emma arranged for her mother to be buried in a vault in the church, newly built since her happy days there, on Paddington Green.

She had now left Richmond, having removed from Herring House to a very much less pretentious address in Bridge Street, and was again in London, in lodgings in Bond Street.

Determined to muster as many wealthy friends to her aid as possible, it seems that Emma had opened up a correspondence with one of her oldest flames – Sir Harry Fetherstonhaugh. It was not so very strange that she should write to him for, since her return to England, they had met a number of times at social functions. Sir Harry, now well into his fifties, had changed completely from the hard-riding young blood that Emma had known at Up Park. From the general tone of the letter that she received a day or two after her mother's death, it would appear that the lurid past had never been referred to and that they were both in pretence and in fact two very different people. It suited Emma to forget and, without doubt, Sir Harry was immensely relieved to find that she did not wish to remember. He had grown soft with good living, and rather pompous into the bargain. In another twenty years' time he was to marry his dairymaid. He wrote:

Up Park, Thursday, (January 14th 1810.)

It gives me the greatest pleasure to receive a more favourable account from you, and I trust you will soon be relieved from all that load of anxiety you have had so much of lately, & which no one so little deserves. That arising from our own ill-health & the indisposition of others, we are all liable to, but *feeling* minds only surfer much for the latter. As I am alive to all nervous sensations, be assured I understand your language. They are troublesome and *de trop* sometimes, yet I would not wish to be altogether without them, & wrap myself up in cold indifference. Pray take care of yourself. Endeavour to obtain rest which you have been so long without, & make use of all the resources of a strong mind & a happy disposition. I generally stay here till the end of March, and shall hardly be in town before my usual time. Be assured I shall lose no time in seeing you, which I wish much to do, having many things to say to one, who, I am pleased to think, feels an interest for me. Tho' I lament that there should be such a reason for your quitting Richmond, because none such ought to exist had you common justice done you, yet your judgment is good in doing so, and at all events I shall stand a better chance of seeing more of you. I hope you received the first basket of game as well as the last. You shall certainly continue to have a supply from time to time. Receive it as a mark of attention most gratifying to myself to shew. Pray let me hear from you occasionally, & when you get out again you may have some entertaining observations to make. Do you often hear from, and sometimes see (when you get out) the D. of Q.? Tho' Napoleon may not be acting from *passion*, he is playing a most nice political game. I should like to *prié aux noces* [*sic*]

A fortnight later he expressed his sympathy, having heard of Emma's recent loss. It is a kind, if long-winded, letter of no particular interest, except perhaps for the incredible manner in which he refers to their friendship as if there had never ever been a cross word between them. "I wish I had been on the spot," he writes, "to have offered to contribute to the relief of your mind by friendly interviews, which, I am sure, you would have admitted of from *me*, as it is best procured in the conversation of those on similar occasions who are persuaded of the interest which each may feel for the other."

In February he again wrote, making it clear that Emma had changed her address.

Up Park, "Monday 19" (February 1810)

I am very much pleased to find that you are fixed in a situation which has the *agréements* you mention, & be assured the first place I visit after I get to London will be No. 76 Piccadilly; but it will not be so soon as I would otherwise wish, did not business engagements detain me here longer than I expected. I must wait to receive a party *chez moi* the end of next month, then, *chemin faisant*, I must pay a visit for a week or ten days, which will make it the middle of April before I take you by the hand. We have a deep snow at present, of all weathers the most disagreable, and I know of no place worse in it than London, unless you make up your mind not to go out at all. Have you music often? Do you go out, or how do you pass your time? No one better deserves to be happy. You have resources within yourself which no one can deprive you of, & which will better administer comfort and restore you to cheerfulness than all the extraneous gifts of fortune. Have you got your young *élèves* with you again? Napoleon will soon dispose of the Peninsular, which anyone of common sense might have foreseen, yet our wise Government is subsidising a Portuguese army. *Quelle folie étonnante!* Pray continue to write, you may always find something interesting to say, whereas my letters must always partake of the dulness of a country gentleman.

I will order some gibier under the rose to be sent to-morrow, as the time is past the *long tails* must not appear.

Let me know they come safe.

In July the Duke of Queensberry came forward again to help pay Emma's debts. He arranged with his bankers, Messrs. Coutts & Co., to transfer £2,500 to an account in the name of Abraham Goldsmid, instructing him to see that her outstanding bills were duly paid. The old Duke was fully aware of Emma's spendthrift nature, however, for there is a note among his bankers' papers which states: "Lady Hamilton is not to touch *a shilling* of the money on any account whatsoever."

All the same, an inspection of Abraham Goldsmid's account makes one wonder very much whether the good-natured financier did not turn a blind eye to the Duke's very definite instruction. It will be seen below that there are only two payments made in round figures (£500 and £300), both of which are to "L. Hamilton". Surely it is too much to believe that Emma should have two such precise debts to a person with a name so closely resembling her own! Admittedly there was a "Mr Hamilton" to whom she owed £51 5s. 6d.

July	24	By Cash received of Lady Hamilton	£2,500	-	-
July	24	To Cash paid Morgan & Co.	549	-	-
		L. Hamilton	500	-	-
	27	Mr Salter	290	12	6
	28	Mr Bridgman	92	6	-
August	3	Mr Hamilton	51	5	6
	6	Mr Radbury	49	16	9
	10	L. Hamilton	300	-	-
	11	Holford	141	3	-
		Alder & Co.	62	13	2
	13	Mr Robertson	223	12	-
	30	Him (i.e. Abraham Goldsmid)	239	11	1
			2,500	-	-

About this time Emma received a letter from "Emma Carew" which provides the last known facts of her life. She undoubtedly went abroad, as she says she was about to do, and thereafter nothing more is heard of this pathetic little figure. Emma evidently felt that in her present circumstances she could not afford to admit the facts that Miss Carew so obviously suspected. What reply, if any, she made is not known.

"Sunday morning" (1810)

Mrs Denis's mention of your name and the conversation she had with you, have revived ideas in my mind which an absence of four years has not been able to efface. It might have been happy for me to have forgotten the past, and to have began a new life with new ideas; but for my misfortune, my memory traces back circumstances which have taught me too much, yet not quite all I could have wished to have known – with you that resides, and ample reasons, no doubt, you have for not imparting them to me. Had you felt yourself at liberty so to have done, I might have become reconciled to my former situation and have been relieved from the painful employment I now pursue. It was necessary as I then stood, for I had nothing to support me but the affection I bore you; on the other hand, doubts and fears by turns oppressed me, and I determined to rely on my own efforts rather than submit to abject dependance, without a permanent name or acknow-ledged parents. That I should have taken such a step shews, at least, that I have a mind misfortune has not subdued. That I should persevere in it is what I owe to myself and to you, for it shall never be said that I avail myself of your partiality or my own inclination, unless I learn my claim on you is greater than you have hitherto acknowledged. But the time may come when the same reasons may cease to operate, and then, with a heart filled with tenderness and affection, will I shew you both my duty and attachment. In the meantime, should Mrs Denis's zeal and kindness not have over-rated your expressions respecting me, and that you should really wish to see me, I may be believed in saying that such a meeting would be one of the happiest moments of my life, but for the reflection that it may also be the last, as I leave England in a few days, and may, perhaps, never return to it again. I remain, etc.

Almost at the same time, a letter came from Sarah Connor who was bravely doing her best for Emma under trying circumstances. The Mrs "Daumier" whom she mentions (as Domier) was Emma's landlady in Dover Street.

Monday, September 17th (1810)

Your two last letters I got, and thank you for them. I found the codicils and took them to Lord Herdly (Lord Eardley) but did not see him. I am almost ashamed to write the old story to you again. It is now 3 o'clock and no Mr Goldsmid is come, nor do I look for him now to-day, so when I shall get to you God knows. Their's one excuse for him

240

– the clerk told me the other day that it was feared he should lose a large sum of money. It would not ruin him has he was so rich, but that the amount was large. I hope it may turn out better than he expects. He is a good man; it's a pity he should suffer. The enclosed is, has you will find, from Mrs Domier. It's true she is cunning, and you are right in keeping staunch to your plans but, I think, has you do, she must gaine from you. She wants the weeks that we are all away to be paid the same, and that, she says, will make up for the pound a-day not being enough when all is at home. What do you mean to do about coals? Has the weather is getting cold you will want fires when you come home. They are sixty pounds 1 shilling now, and will soon get to seventy. The worst of it is that their is not a cellar for us, but she talks of giving up the wine-cellar; that you, I daresay, whould not like that she should. Still, when she does offer, for convenience take it; you pay for all, it's no favor. Mr Dillon found out that you was from home, wrote me a letter dated from Sloane Square to come and dine with her has yesterday, but I did not go, for that would be renewing the aquaintance againe. The Captain has got a ship and has sailed – that, I am glad of, and you will be glad to hear of it. Still, I think he might have called upon you before he went, has you was very kind to him. I suppose he was led astray by his wife's lies. Love to Horatia, and tell her I am obliged to her for writing to me, and I will answer herself.

In September the ruin foreshadowed in Sarah Connor's letter caught up with Abraham Goldsmid. He committed suicide. He never really recovered from the shock when his brother, Benjamin, took his own life in 1808, and for the last few months he had been very worried by heavy financial losses. In May 1810, he and Baring Brothers had sponsored two loans which amounted together to £13,400,000. By September the stock was at a 3½ per cent. discount, and Abraham was holding, probably as a speculation, £800,000 in his own name. On the 11th of the month, the sudden death of Sir Francis Baring caused alarm in the City and Goldsmid's holding was now at a discount of 6½ per cent. As if this was not enough, the East India Company panicked and demanded payment for £350,000 worth of Exchequer Bills, which he was negotiating for them by 28th September. He had already tried to retrench by dismissing all the outside labour employed at Morden Hall, but he was now at his wits' end. On the fatal 28th, as was reported in the Annual Register, "about half-past seven o'clock in the morning, Mr Goldsmid was seen to pass over the bridge that leads to the wilderness, or rookery, in the grounds at Morden-House: shortly after the coachman, as was usual, inquired what horses were to go to town; upon which he was referred to Mr Goldsmid, being told at the time which way his master had walked. The coachman went in search of him, and was the first that found him weltering in his blood, with the pistol grasped in his right hand. Life was not quite extinct, but before any aid could be procured, Mr Goldsmid expired."

A further death was to follow very soon, for just before Christmas the old Duke of Queensberry died – and Mrs Bolton immediately wrote, in the worst of bad taste:

Xmas Day 1810.

Shall I say I congratulate you or condole with you on the death of the poor Duke; I hope you will be a great *gainer*; a loss I am sure he was to you, but we, alas, well know what the loss of friends are, but a rich sorrow better than a poor *one*. We long to hear what he has left you; God bless you with *it*. You would smile to hear us talk of you; Mr Bolton wishes to have a bet on the sum; Anne dances; Tom says he is as nervous as my Lady to hear the contents; Susanna says she is low for fear it should not be so much as we all wish; as to Lady Bolton and myself, we are full of hopes that both you and Horatia will have a good legacy.

We shall be truly happy to see you as soon as you can conveniently leave town, which I hope will be as soon after the funeral as you can; it will change the scene at any rate & we will endeavour to make Cranwich as cheerful as we can. Bring the Miss Conners with you, dear Horatia of course. I cannot write upon any other occasion. We all unite in kind regards, & believe me, etc.

Considering the money that the Duke had already disbursed on Emma's behalf, the legacy that he left her – £500 a year – was a generous one, though Emma had hoped for much more. He also remembered Sarah Connor, Horatia's governess, in his will, although, in fact, Sarah's duties had now been taken over by her sister Cecilia, who was, according to Walter Sichel, "musical but far less literate". Owing to the Queensberry will being disputed, however, Emma never benefited from her legacy, as by the time it was settled, she herself had died.

When she informed Sir Harry Fetherstonhaugh, who had also known the Duke, of her bequest, she received the following in return:

Up Park, December 30th 1810.

Many thanks for your kind communication about the old Duke's will as far as you are concerned; if you had been remembered more largely, I should have been still better pleased, but we both know him to have been a little capricious throughout. Thomas made me acquainted with his mite out of such a mass of wealth, which I trust, however, will make him comfortable, for he deserves to be. *My* intelligence announces the K- is not likely to *live* long; in *his* state it seems hardly desirable that he should, & a regency, especially with restrictions, is never a *strong* government. We so often are told of our perilous situation, that I am not much alarmed. No change for the better in point of *climate* would induce me to change my native abode, for I have seen enough of other countries to feel the value of this. The utmost extent of my wishes is to re-visit Paris, but that liberty seems at a most frightful distance. Notwithstanding the bad weather lately, we had two ladies who attended us through all the battues here & made an excellent fight of it through all the extremities of wet & deep ground. I don't think this would exactly suit you, but I shall have great pleasure in your taking a view of old Up Park *dans la belle saison*, when even here it may be passable. Be assured, if the *envois* of *gibier* are acceptable, & you receive them as they are *meant, je suis enchanté.* You never told me whether you got any venison last *summer.* Pray do in your next, as sometimes things never reach their destination, & when I know it, I take measures accordingly. *Portez-vous toujours bien,* & believe me at all times, etc.

The Hon. Robert Fulke Greville was not as efficient an executor as his late brother had been, and there were inconvenient delays in the payments under Sir William's will. Early in 1811, Lord Mansfield wrote a word of warning to Emma, concerning her finances:

Great Cumberland Street, Monday. (Early in 1811)
    I hope there is this time no delay, & that the steward has paid in the quarter for your jointure, for which Mr Greville gave him the most *positive directions*; if so, there is no doubt of Mr Coutts letting you have it without my writing, and if it is not paid in you must write to the steward, as we have done everything towards making him pay regularly. Allow me to add, that I hope you never anticipate the quarter you *expect to* become due, so as to occasion any pressing demand, as I am afraid Mr Coutts might think it impertinent in me to trouble him *again* on the same subject; besides that, I am sure Mr Coutts would tell you that, in fact, it could do you no good. Excuse my saying thus much, & adding a word of advice – that you should be *cautious* not to increase your expenditure till your affairs *are settled,* or your creditors will become very troublesome from the apprehension that you will spend

the legacy bequeathed to you, without their reaping the advantage they expect of being *first paid*. I am, etc.

This sensible advice fell on deaf ears, for Emma was borrowing money from anyone who would lend it to her. Her rashness can be realised from the fact that she even got Carlo Rovedino, the singer who had enjoyed her hospitality at Merton, to accept two bills for £150 from her, at two months' date. The unwisdom of this action is revealed by a warrant of attorney, dated 14th May 1811, to Messrs. Dixon and Leach to secure the payment of these two bills.

A month before this, Mr Matcham had written:

April 15th 1811.

It is very fortunate that you applied to me at this instant; had you applied five days ago, I had not a hundred to lend, but having received seven hundred pounds three days ago since to be invested in the funds for Mrs M. & the children, Mrs M. has consented to withold one hundred pounds of that sum for you. I know you will repay it as soon as you can, but do not mention my having lent you any money. I wish not the trustees to be acquainted with it. The Earl & Lady Nelson, Lady Charlotte, and Mr Hood are with us. Do let us see you, and Horatia, and your cousin soon. God bless you. Inclosed is the order on my banker. Pray write us a line on the receipt of this letter, that we may be satisfied of its safe arrival.

Major Pryse Lockhart Gordon who had last seen Emma at a ball on board the *Vanguard* in Palermo, was walking through Greenwich Park on Friday, 26th April (1811), when he met two women and some half-dozen young children. He scarcely recognised the elder woman, wrapped in a shawl and wearing a shabby cap on her head, as the same Emma. She was with Cecilia Conner, and they were going to the Ship Inn to celebrate her birthday by giving a little party for Horatia and her school friends. From this recorded meeting it would appear that she had begun to lose interest in her personal appearance.

Two more letters emphasise her increasingly hopeless position. First, it was Cecilia Connor who wrote:

Manley Place, Kensington Common, July 26th (1811).

I take the liberty once more to address your Ladyship concerning the sum of thirty guineas for teaching Miss Horatia Nelson, for which I had a voucher signed by your Ladyship.

I merely mention this latter circumstance as a proof of your Lady-ship's acknowledgements – by no means upon the ground of dispute, but as my qualification of appeal to your Ladyship in the present instance. My future wellfare constrains me to renew the solicitation, having a situation of advantage submitted to me which I must be compelled, with grief, to resign unless your Ladyship supports my views by affording me, on account, the sum of ten pounds between this & next Monday – the time limited to consider the proposal.

This is the last resource I have. Being denied a character from your Ladyship, obliges me to give up the thought of applying any longer for a preparatory governess, which I had the honor of attending on dear Horatia. Excuse, dear Lady Hamilton, this familiar term, but it is what I most sincerely feel for you both. Could I forget for a moment the many obligations me and my family owe to your Ladyship, I hope God will forget me, and He is now the only friend I have.

Time will bring forth everything, & then I think your Ladyship will find you have been misinformed in many circumstances concerning me. Let me, dear Lady Hamilton, intreat a favourable answer, as it will release my mind greatly. Would that it could relieve my heart from the sorrow that I feel at being deprived of a friend & guardian like you!

And later from Mrs Bolton:

Cranwich, September 18th 1811.

I am requested by Mr Bolton to inform you that he has seen Bob Nelson & has seen an account of his debts. He has advanced him one hundred p^{ds}, & as you kindly promised to do something for him, if you could do the same it would raise a deserving man from distress & enable him to get forward in the world. You, I hope, would one day get repaid in money as well as thanks. It is needless to *urge* you, who are always willing to assist the distressed, as to recollect this man, had my dear brother been living, would never have wanted a friend. To add more is unnecessary *to you*. Mrs Pierson has told you of all the invalids of this family. Hope all will be well to receive you at Xmas. Believe me, etc.

Emma moved again to an address in Bond Street possibly because the lodgings were cheaper, but also for the more pressing reason of dodging her creditors. She was becoming frantic and, in view of the ill-health that was soon to overtake her, drinking to excess.

Rather a silly letter from Sir R. Puleston shows that she still tried to keep up a façade of prosperity:

... Many thousand thanks for your kind invitation to your *fairy palace* in Bond Street, where I shall be most happy to pay my earliest respects when I get to town, but that, I grieve to think, will scarcely be before the spring. How soon do you return there? I presume to ask this question in case any unforseen event should take me up sooner than I intend at present.

How delighted I shall be next year to escort you & ramble with you over your almost native mountains, & to tell you, which is true, *that we have met before*, but it is many years since, & the impression you then made, tho' I had not the happiness of your acquaintance much as I then wished for it. I most truly & sincerely wish you a speedy & decisive victory over your present disagreement & that your enemies, such you have, may turn their hearts; in short, that all the world may as sensibly feel your merits as I do, & as sincerely wish you well... .

In December, Emma heard again from Sir Harry. His bland assumption that she was living quietly but comfortably in London was quite possibly tact on his part, as it would seem by his generous and frequent presents of game that he really knew of her straitened circumstances. He wrote:

Sunday (December 1811)

I hope you received my last *envoi* in due time for the purpose, & that you will also find half-a-doz. I have directed to be sent not much amiss. This more substantial form of correspondence is better than any stupid letters I could send you from hence, where my life is so uniform, & can afford but little of interest to others; but you will be glad to hear that I am *bien portant*, enjoying the amusements & resources of a place to which I have always been so partial, without one wish to see more of the *grand monde* than *comes to me*. I have had a pretty good taste of it in my time, & I flatter myself not without fully appreciating its value. You have been a long while silent, which I regret, as I am always happy to hear what is doing & where you are. Notwithstanding all your partiality for a warm climate, Sicily would hardly be a pleasant *séjour* just now. What are you going to do, and what is the real state of facts, for I conclude you still have high correspondence there? After the finest weather I ever remember at this season of the year for three weeks, we are now in a constant hurricane, which will last till some hard frost sets in. I conclude you are now fixed in London for what is called the season, and enjoying the society of a few you like, which is more to the purpose than all the *grand* & heterogeneous compositions which many are condemned to. I had promised a visit to Paget at Beaudesert this time, but when it comes to the point I cannot leave the comforts of home for so long a winter journey, so have sent my excuses, & shall be stationary here, at 57 *il n'y a pas grand mal de se tenir tranquille*. I suppose you see a good deal of the Duchess of Devonshire. The young Duke has a pretty good game before him if he plays it well. What do you think of him? If you feel so disposed, you can not fail to write something interesting or amusing at least from London, so I shall expect the pleasure of a billet now and then.

During 1812 Emma lay very low. She was now quite hopelessly in debt and realised that to show herself in public was courting disaster. In a vain attempt to escape her creditors, she spent the last few weeks of the year in Fulham, in the house of the singer, Mrs Billington, but somehow her whereabouts became known and during the last week of December she was arrested for debt. Her creditors who had put up for so long with promises and evasions, had now taken action.

The result of the arrest was that Emma, and Horatia with her, were taken to what was known as a "spunging house" within the "rules" of the King's Bench Prison.

A paragraph in the "Report from the Committee appointed to Enquire into the Practice and Effects of Imprisonment for Debt" (1792) throws some light on the particular process of the law to which she was subjected:

If a Defendant under Arrest do not either pay the Plaintiff his Demand, or find Bail to the Satisfaction of the Sheriff, he must remain in the Custody of the Officer for Twenty-four Hours at least (32 Geo. II Cap. 28); and may then, or sooner if, in the case provided for by the Statute, it becomes necessary, be carried to Gaol. But though the Officer *may* then carry him to Gaol, he is not bound so to do, but may keep him in Custody in what is commonly called a *Lock-up* or *Spunging House*.

Most of the debtors' prisons had their "Rules". This meant a prescribed area round the particular prison in which the prisoners were allowed on payment of a fee of 4s. 6d. per day, to wander at their will. In this area were situated the spunging houses, and, in the case of the King's Bench Prison, the extent of the "Rules" was as follows:

From Great Cumber Court, in the Parish of Saint George the Martyr, in the County of Surrey, along the North Side of Dirty Lane and

Melancholy Walk, to Blackfriars Road, and along the Western Side of the said Road to the Obelisk, and from thence along the South West Side of the London Road, round the Direction Post in the Centre of the roads near the Public House known by the Sign of the Elephant and Castle; from thence along the Eastern Side of Newington Causeway to Great Cumber Court aforesaid. And it is also ordered, that the New Gaol, Southwark, and the Highway, exclusive of the Houses on each Side of it, leading from the King's Bench Prison to the said New Gaol, shall be within and Part of the said Rules: And it is lastly ordered, that all Taverns, Victualling Houses, Alehouses, all Wines Vaults, and Houses or Places licensed to sell Gin or other Spirituous Liquors, shall be excluded and deemed no Part of the said Rules.

The spunging house to which Emma was taken was No. 12 Temple Place. It was one of a terrace of some twenty houses on the east side of Blackfriars Road where it joins what is now called St George's Circus, where the "Obelisk" then stood.

Some of the answers given by an official of Newgate Prison to the Parliamentary Committee, already mentioned, are enlightening on the subject of spunging houses in general:

Q. When you state the Number who actually go to Goal, is it exclusive of those who go to Lock-up or Spunging Houses?
A. Most certainly, because they must amount to some Thousands who go to Lock-up Houses. Q. Is not this attended with great Expence?
A. I have never made any Inquiry in my Official Situation, having never had any Complaint made to me; but I have an Opportunity of knowing, in Point of Fact, that it is attended with very considerable Expence.
Q. May every Prisoner in a Lock-up House call for what expensive Provisions and Liquors he pleases?
A. I know of no objection.
Q. Are the Articles used by Prisoners in Spunging or Lock-up Houses charged to them by the Persons keeping such Houses at an exorbitant Rate?
A. I have understood so, but I cannot state it as a Fact within my own Knowledge.

Apart from the extortionate charges made by the keepers of these grim houses, the Marshal of the King's Bench Prison claimed a discretionary fee for giving the benefit of the Rules. This seems to have been about 7½ guineas if the debt was up to £50 and 10 guineas if £100.

The reason why Emma and the many other prisoners similarly situated were willing to pay these extortions, was that while they were within the Rules for one debt, they could not be dunned by their other creditors. A further comment from the Parliamentary Report covers this aspect by admitting that "Some of the Prisoners within the Rules live in separate Houses, and from the Manner of their living seem to be in a Situation capable of paying their debts".

On the first Sunday of her enforced residence in the lock-up house, Emma wrote to James Perry, who, it will be remembered, was her neighbour at Merton. He was a journalist and eventually became the editor and proprietor of the *Morning Chronicle*. Even in the dire trouble that she now found herself, Emma had a thought for her faithful old servant:

12 Temple Place, January 3rd 1813.

Will you have the goodness to see my old Dame Francis, as you was so good to say to me once at any time for the present existing and unhappy circumstances you wou'd befriend me, &, if you cou'd, at your conveneance, call on me to aid me by your advice as before? My friends come to town to-morrow for the season, when I must see what can be done, so that I shall not remain here, for I am so truly unhappy & wretched, & have been ill ever since I had the pleasure of seeing you on dear Horatia's birthday, that I have not had either spirits or energy to write to you. You that loved Sir William & Nelson, & feel that I have deoerved from my country 3ome tribute of remuneration, will aid by your counsel your ever affectionate and gratefull, etc.

Later she wrote to the Abbé Campbell. The letter has little of interest in it, but it does show that Emma was putting on as bold a face as she could under the most distressing circumstances.

"Ten o'clock."

Perhaps, my dear friend, you have done right in going away without saying good-bye; but my heart feils much more than you think it does. You was beloved and honor'd by my husband, Nelson, & myself; knew me in all my former splendours; you I look on as a dear, dear friend and relation. You are going amongst friends who love you; but rest assured none reveres you nor loves you more than your ever, etc.

P.S. Poor Horatia was so broken-hearted at not seeing you. Tell dear Mr Tegart to call on me, for I do indeed feil truly folorn and friendless. God bless you, as glorious Nelson said. Amen, amen, amen.

James Perry did all he could on Emma's behalf and Alderman Joshua Smith, another Merton neighbour, gave her £400 for the contents of the house she had had at Richmond (which incidentally included Nelson's blood-stained uniform). As a result of these actions Emma was freed from her imprisonment within a few weeks; she had been keeping up her spirits by drafting out further petitions to be sent to members of the Government, the Prince of Wales and even the King himself. She corresponded with the Boltons and the Matchams, the latter pressing her to let Horatia go to them at Ashfold Lodge, Slaugham, near Brighton, saying that they would meet the child at Reigate, if Emma "could not manage to come".

After her release, Emma, who had kept Horatia with her in spite of the Matchams' offer, found her way back to Bond Street and lodged at No. 150.

It would almost seem that the strain of the past few years and the hardships caused by her arrest were having an effect on her mental health. On Easter Sunday she addressed a strange, almost demented, note to Horatia:

April 18th 1813.

Listen to a kind, good mother, who has ever been to you affectionate, truly kind, and who has neither spared pains nor expense to make you the most amiable and most accomplish'd of your sex. Ah, Horatia! if you had grown up as I wish'd you, what a joy, what a comfort might you have been to me! for I have been constant to you, and willingly pleased for every manifestation you shew'd to learn and profitt of my lessons, and I have ever been most willing to overlook injuries. But now 'tis for myself I speak & write. Look into yourself well, correct yourself of your errors, your caprices, your nonsensical follies, for by your inattention you have forfeited all claims to my future kindness. I have weathered many a storm for your sake, but these frequent blows have kill'd me. Listen, then, from a mother who speaks from the dead! Reform your conduct, or you will be detested by all the world, & when you shall no longer have my fostering arm to sheild you, whoe betide you! you will sink to nothing Be good, be honourable, tell not false-hoods, be not capricious, follow the advice of the mother whom I shall place you in at school, for a governess must act as mother. I grieve & lament to see the increasing strength of your turbulent passions; I weep & pray you may not be totally lost; my fervent prayers are offered up to God for you; I hope you will yet become sensible of your eternal wellfare. I shall go join your father & my blessed mother & may you on your death-bed have as little to reproach yourself as your once affectionate mother has, for I can glorify, & say I was a good child. *Can Horatia Nelson say* so? *I am unhappy to say you CANNOT.* No answer to this? I shall to-morrow look out for a school, for your sake & to *save you,* that you may bless the memory of an injured mother.

P.S. Look on me now as gone from this world.

It seems likely that Emma's creditors waited to see if her latest memorials, those addressed to the Prince of Wales and to the King, were going to have any effect. By June, they evidently decided to hold back no longer, for in the Judgment Book of the King's Bench, there are three entries relating to persons suing her for debts. On 12th June and 30th June the litigants are "William Gillman & another" (the amount of the claims not being mentioned), and on 22nd June "Mr Francis McGowran" is recorded as proceeding against Emma Hamilton for £1,000.

The unfortunate and inevitable result of this was that by July, Emma was back again at No. 12 Temple Place. Depressed as she must have been at finding herself once more a prisoner, she was to learn, scarcely a month later, that her intimate friend, Mrs Bolton, had died. Her own health, which had not been good for some time, now took a turn for the worse; so much so that she was permitted to take drives in a carriage, though whether the vehicle was allowed to go beyond the Rules is not known. Evidence of these outings is found in a letter from one of the Matcham daughters who wrote to Emma on 21st November 1813, saying:

Mama only received your letter, dated 23rd October, yesterday, which I hope will account to you for my not writing before. We have sent Horatia two or three letters since the date of your's, which must have made it appear still more extraordinary, but we were most happy to find you are better and can take an airing in the carriage... .

Mr Matcham also wrote on the same day, with kind offers and a derogatory remark about his brother-in-law the Earl

November 21st 1813.
Pray let us know the carrier's name of the waggon which passes your house. We will supply you with potatoes all the winter, and send you a turkey by the first opportunity. If you find it impossible to pay us a visit, Mrs M. and I shall be tempted to go to Temple Place before the close of

the winter and pass a day with you. We have been always sensible of the ingratitude you have met with, but is it not better to be wholly freed from any attention of that man, who is insensible to everything but what immediately appertains to his own interest? Write as soon as ever you can, and give directions for anything our farm can supply… .

Some weeks before she received this letter and at a time when she was particularly low in health, Emma struck out at Horatia again with a second unmotherly and extraordinary letter:

October 31st 1813.

Horatia, – Your conduct is so bad, your falsehoods so dreadfull, your cruel treatment to me such that I cannot live under these afflicting circumstances; my poor heart is broken. If my poor mother was living to take my part, broken as I am with greif and ill-health, I should be happy to breathe my last in her arms. I thank you for what you have done to-day. You have helped me on nearer to God, and may God forgive you. In two days all will be arranged for your future establish-ment, and on Tuesday at 12, Col & Mrs Smith, Trickey, Mr and Mrs Denis, Dr Norton will be here to hear all. Every servant shall be put on their oath, as I shall send for Nany at Richmond – Mr Slop, Mrs Sice, Anne Deane – and get letters from the Boltons and Matchams to confront you, & tell the truth if I have used you ill; but the all-seeing eye of God knows my innocence. It is therefore my command that you do not speak to me till Tuesday, & if to-day you do speak to me, I will that moment let Col & Mrs Clive into all your barbarous scenes on my person life and honnor.

A glimpse of No. 12 Temple Place at this time is given by Sir William Dillon who wrote, in December 1813:

I found a letter from Lady Hamilton inviting me to dine with her. Three years had elapsed since I had seen her… . When the hour approached, the rain was pouring down in torrents. I engaged a post-chaise for the remainder of the evening, then started for the residence indicated.
    Upon my arrival her Ladyship greeted me most sincerely. "How did you know I was in Town?" I demanded. She acquainted me that a friend who had seen me at the Admiralty had told her, and that she was highly delighted to shake me again by the hand. I noticed a splendid display of plate on the table, and covers laid for four, but made no enquiries who the guests were … .

While we were thus occupied, I was surprised by the entrance into the room of H.R.H. the Duke of Sussex. Soon afterwards Mrs B. made her appearance (this was the Duke's lady-of-the-moment, Mrs Bugge). The Prince was all kindness, and wondered I had not been to see him ...

The dinner being served, the conversation turned in another direction. I had to do the honours – carve, etc. The first course went off on complete order, and I could not help thinking that rather too much luxury had been produced. H.R.H. did not expect such an entertainment from the lady who received him. However, there was a sad falling off in the second course, and a great deficiency in attendance, as also of knives and forks. I had to carve a good-sized bird, but had not been supplied with the necessary impliments. Time passed on, but no servant made his appearance. At last Lady H. said: "Why don't you cut up that bird?" I told her I was in want of a knife and fork. "Oh!" she said, "you must not be particular here." "Very well my lady," I rejoined. "I did not like to commit myself in the presence of H.R.H. but since you desire it, I will soon divide the object before me. Besides, you are aware that, as a Midshipman, I learnt how to use my fingers!" Then, looking round, I found what I wanted, and soon had the bird in pieces. My reply produced some hearty laughter, and the repast terminated very merrily. After a sociable and agreeable entertainment, I took my leave of the company.

It was a bad winter to be confined to uncomfortable quarters, for the Annual Register recorded on 1st February: "The Thames, between Blackfriars and London Bridges, continued to present the novel scene of persons moving on the ice in all directions, and in greatly increased numbers. The ice, however, from its roughness and inequality is totally unfit for amusement, though we observed several booths erected upon it for the sale of small wares; but the publicans and spirit dealers were most in the receipt of custom!" A week later, however, high tides had broken up the ice.

The foolishness of keeping incriminating letters and her disobedience to Nelson's wise counsel that she should burn his to her, produced, in the spring of 1814, a most upsetting situation for Emma. She became aware of the publication, in two slim volumes, of *The Letters of Lord Nelson to Lady Hamilton, with a Supplement of Interesting Letters by Distinguished Characters*. The book was printed by Macdonald & Son, Smithfield, for Thomas Lovewell & Co., Staines House, Barbican ("and sold by all the booksellers"), but no mention was made as to who was responsible for bringing the letters to light. It has been deduced from a letter written by Horatia in later life (and published in the *Cornhill*

Magazine) that James Harrison, the bookseller of Paternoster Row, was guilty of creating the scandal. He had frequented Emma's house while writing a life of Nelson and it is thought that he had taken advantage of this opportunity to steal some of her letters. The public was now left in no doubt whatever of the relationship between Emma and Nelson, and furthermore there were certain remarks in Nelson's letters which could not be expected to please the Prince of Wales. If it was unlikely that Emma's petitions would receive favourable attention before, it was now impossible.

In desperation, Emma wrote to James Perry:

12 Temple Place, April 22nd 1814.

To my great surprise I saw yesterday in the *Herald* that Lord Nelson's letters to me were published. I have not seen the book, but I give you my honour that I know nothing of these letters. I have been now nine months in Temple Place, & allmost all the time I have been very ill with a bilious complaint, brought on by fretting & anxiety, & lately I have kept my bed for near twelve weeks, nor have I seen any person except Dr Watson & Mr Tegart, who have attended me with kindness & attention, & to whoes care I owe my life. About four years ago my house in Dover Street was on fire, & I was going into Sussex for 3 months, & I left part of my papers in a case with a person to whom I thought I cou'd depend on. Weather this person has made use of any of these papers, or weather they are the invention of a vile, mercenary wretch, I know not, but you will oblige me much by contradicting these falsehoods, and you will much gratify your gratefull, etc.

P.S. If I had not been so ill, I shou'd have answer'd the Poet Laureate's [Southey's *Life of Nelson* was published in 1813] falsehoods, which they tell me he has publish'd in an abridgment of the life of the good & glorious Lord Nelson; but this I will do & prove, that all he has said relating to the affair of Carraciola is false. But Nelson, Sir William, & myself did too much for the good cause not to make enimys amongst those who wish'd to abolish royalty & level every one who thought and acted right. I am now suffering for having been too generous, for I might have been rich if I had only thought of myself & not of my country. I have now given all up to pay my debts, not having ever received one farthing from Government, neither as the widow of a minister who served 37 years, and for the last ten years my indefatigable pains and the procuring of the letters for the supplying of the fleet before the glorious Battle of the Nile, which was the first deathblow to the French and again revived dear old England at a moment of dispondency. Yet all this has hitherto been neglected, nor have my great and glorious friend's wishes in the moment of death & victory been listened to. God bless you, my dear sir, my heart is too full to say more.

Once again James Perry and Joshua Smith strove to obtain her release. Smith bought the few remaining valuables that Emma still had in her possession and a small sum was collected from her well-wishers in the City. By July, after a whole year spent in detention, Emma was allowed to leave Temple Place. Her position, however, was so perilous, in view of the further writs which might at any moment be served upon her, that she was advised to leave the country without delay. Emma needed no persuasion. The very idea of a further sojourn in the Rules was more than she could bear, and so, during the first week of July 1814, Emma, with less than £50 in her purse, and with Horatia at her side, boarded *The Little Tom* at Tower Wharf. The vessel was sailing to Calais, travellers being free to land in France now that Napoleon was in exile in Elba.

Owing to bad weather, and possibly to putting in at other places in the Thames Estuary, it was three days before Emma and Horatia were ashore in Calais. Here, with Emma's non-existent ideas of economy, they went to Dessein's Hotel, which was famous, comfortable – and expensive. However, it very soon became evident that some cheaper establishment must be found and a move was made to a smaller hotel – Quillac's. At this address, mother and daughter waited the arrival of their faithful old Dame Francis, whose travelling expenses had been found by one of Emma's friends, probably James Perry. With Dame Francis to keep house, the three of them settled into quarters in a farm bordering a common in the village of St Pierre, two miles from Calais.

After Temple Place, the description of her new life, which Emma wrote to George Rose, sounds simple, healthy and restful. The letter was written the day after her arrival in France and it may well be that the visit to the *fête champêtre* mentioned in it led to the finding of the later accommodation in St Pierre.

Hotel Dessin, Calais. July 4.

We arrived here safe, dear Sir, after three days' sickness at sea, as for precaution we embarked at the Tower. Mr Smith got me the discharge from Lord Ellenborough. I then begged Mr Smith to withdraw his bail, for I would have died in prison sooner than that good man should have suffered for me, and I managed so well with Horatia alone that I was at Calais before any new writs could be issued out against me. I feel so much better, from change of climate, food, air, large rooms and *liberty*, that there is a chance I may live to see Horatia brought up. I am looking out for a lodging. I have an excellent Frenchwoman who is good at everything; for Horatia and myself, and my old dame who is coming, will be my establishment. Near me is an English lady, who has resided here for twenty-five years, who has a day school, but not for eating and sleeping. At eight in the morning, I take Horatia; fetch her at one; at three we dine, and then in the evening we walk. She learns every thing – piano, harp, languages grammatically. She knows French and Italian well, but she will improve. Not any girls but those of the first families go there. Last evening we walked two miles to a fête champêtre pour les bourgeois. Everybody is pleased with Horatia. The General and his good old wife are very good to us, but our little world of happiness is in ourselves. If, my dear Sir, Lord Sidmouth would do something for dear Horatia, so that I can be enabled to give her an education, and also for her dress, it would ease me, and make me very happy. Surely he owes this to Nelson. For God's sake, do try for me, for you do not know how limited. I have left everything to be sold for the creditors, who do not deserve anything, for I have been the victim of artful mercenary wretches, and my too great liberality and open heart has been the dupe of villians. To you, Sir, I trust, for my dearest Horatia, to exert yourself for me, etc.

A letter that she wrote to the Hon. R.F. Greville in September shows that Emma was quite incapable of understanding her financial difficulties. Her references to "annuitants" seem to show that she had been pledging portions of her income against loans of ready money, which she had spent. Since the days of Charles Greville's protection, she had never had to worry her head over money matters and now it did not seem possible to her that sufficient funds could not be raised on demand.

Common of St Pierre, 2 miles from Calais.
Direct for me chez Desin, September 21st (1814)

You know that my jointure of eight hundred pounds a year has been now for a long time accumulating. If I was to die, I should have left that money away, for the annuitants have no right to have it, nor can they claim it, for I was most dreadfully imposed upon for my good nature, in being bail for a person whom I thought honorable. When I came away I came with honor, as Mr Alderman Smith can inform you, but mine own innocence keeps me up, and I despise all false accusations and aspersions. I have given up everything to pay just debts, but annuitants never will. Now, sir, let me entreat you to send me a hundred pounds, for I understand you have the money. I live very quiet in a farm house, and my health is now quite established. Let me, sir, beg this favour to your, etc.

P.S. Sir Wm Scott writes me there is some hopes of my irresistible claims – such are his words.

The best meat here five pence a pound, 2 quarts of new milk 2 pence, fowls 13 pence, a couple of ducks the same. We bought 2 fine turkeys for four shillings, an excellent turbot for half-a-crown, fresh from the sea, partridges five pence the couple, good Bordeaux wine, white & red for fiveteen pence the bottle, but there are some for ten sous, halfpence.

Ld Cathcart past 3 days ago. Horatia improving in person & education every day. She speaks French like a French girl, Italian, German, English, etc.

In his position of trust as the executor of Sir William's will, the Hon. R.F. Greville was placed in an unenviable position, and his reply, frustrating as it seemed to the desperate Emma, was the only one he could possibly make under the circumstances:

Gt Cumberland St, Sept. 27th 1814.
Oxford St,

Madam,

Your letter of Sept. 21 I received only by yesterday's post. It is now some time since the regular payments from me of your annuity of eight hundred pounds a-year were very unexpectedly interrupted by a notice addressed to me by professional persons, and on the ground that you had made over the greater part of the same for *pucuniary considerations received by you*, and in consequence warning me not to continue the payment of your annuity otherwise than to them to the extent of their claims.

Not hearing from you in the long intermediate time which followed respecting your not receiving your payments as usual, I could scarce doubt the unpleasant statements I had received. Still I have demurred making any payments when called on, and under existing circumstances I must not venture to make payments in *any direction*, until this mysterious business is made known to me, and whereby my acts by legal authority may be rendered perfectly secure to me. This done, of course I shall pay arrears, and continue all Future payments *whenever they shall be due* with the same precision and *punctuality* as has hitherto *always* been maintained by me, and which were attended to *to*

257

the Day, until thus interrupted. But now, *my own Security* requires that I should clearly *know how this mysterious business actually* stands, e'er I shall deem it prudent or safe for me to take a step in a case where I am resolved not to act on doubtful reports.
I remain, Madam,
Your obedient humble servant,
Robert F. Greville

By the end of the summer, Emma was forced to leave St Pierre and to find cheap lodgings in the town of Calais itself; and it was to a house in the Rue Française that the last move was made. The quarters were uncomfortable and sunless, but Emma was now too ill to be much concerned. The grimness of her last days has been described by Horatia:

… She was in great distress, and had I not, unknown to her, written to Lord Nelson to ask the loan of £10, and to another kind friend of hers, who immediately sent her £20, she would not literally have had one shilling till her next allowance became due. Latterly she was scarcely sensible. I imagine that her illness originally began by being bled whilst labouring under an attack of jaundice whilst she lived at Richmond. From that time she was never well, and added to this, the baneful habit she had of taking spirits and wine to a fearful degree, brought on water on the chest. She died in January 1815, and was buried in the burying ground attached to the town. That was a sad miserable time to me.
    The service was read over the body by a Roman Catholic priest who attended her at her request during her illness. Lady H. had, ever since she had been in Calais, professed herself a Catholic.
    Latterly her mind became so irritable by drinking that I had written to Mr Matcham, and he had desired that I would lose no time in getting some respectable person to take me over and that I was to come to them, where I should always find a home. After her death, as soon as he heard of it, he came to Dover to fetch me.
    With all Lady H's faults – and she had *many* – she had many fine qualities, which, had she been placed early in better hands, would have made her a very superior woman. It is but justice on my part to say that through *all her* difficulties she *invariably* till the last few months, expended on my education etc., the whole of the *interest* of the sum left me by Lord Nelson, and which was left entirely in her control.

Emma's death was recorded by the Calais authorities in the following words:

"A.D. 1815, Janvier 15, Dame Emma Lyons, agée de 51 ans, née à Lancashire, à Angleterre, domicilée à Calais, fille de Henri Lyons, et de Marie Kidd, Veuve de William Hamilton, est decédé le 15 Janvier, 1815, à une heure après midi au domecile du Sieur Damy, Rue Française."

Whether it was Earl Nelson who fetched Horatia back from Calais, as Walter Sichel has it, or whether it was "some respectable person" who accompanied her as far as Dover where she was met by George Matcham, the Earl did nothing that reflects to his credit. He did not even pay the funeral expenses. Brought back to the Matcham home – George, junior, recording in his diary that his father "arrived with Horatia from Dover" – Horatia lived with them until 1822 when, at the age of twenty-two, she married the Rev. Philip Ward. It is pleasant to record that the rest of her life was happy. She lived to the age of eighty and had a large family.

The funeral expenses in Calais were initially defrayed by the British Consul in that town, whose name, by a strange coincidence, was Henry Cadogan. Subsequently he was reimbursed by one of the very genuine friends who had already done much to help Emma in her last years of trouble – Alderman Joshua Smith – as two small documents show:

Funeral expenses of the late Lady Emma Hamilton, as paid by me, Henry Cadogan, at Calais in France, Jan^ry 1815:-
An oak coffin, casked, church expenses, priests, candles, burial ground, men sitting up, dressing the body, spirits, etc, etc. £28. 10. -.
Henry Cadogan.

Rec^d, Feb^ry 4th, 1815, of J.J. Smith Esq. the sum of twenty-eight pounds ten shillings, being the amount of funeral expences for the late Lady Emma Hamilton, at Calais, in France, as paid by me.
£28. 10. -.
(Signed) Henry Cadogan.

At the end of the First World War the following letter appeared in *The Times:*

Sir,
Some of your readers will be interested to learn that a plaque has been placed on No. 27 Rue Française, Calais, to the following effect:
Emma Lady Hamilton, the Friend of
Admiral Lord Nelson died in this
house January 15
1815

This tablet is erected by British officers
serving in Calais during the Great War
in memory of Lord Nelson's last request.
1918.
Your obedient servant
Dillon

As Mr Oliver Warner states, this plaque was lost during the rebuilding of Calais, but another has been put up to mark the site.

Appendices

Appendix I

Accounts of Emma Hart at Edgware Row

Dated Between October 27th, 1784, And February 21st, 1785 (17 Pages Quarto)

Emma Hart. The Day Account Book. October 27th, 1784

Oct.		£	s.	d.			£	s.	d.
						Butter Bill	0	5	0
27th	Baker's Bill,					Milk	0	2	3
	one week	0	4	11		Gardener	0	2	0
	Butter Bill,				2nd	Butcher	0	2	6
	one week	0	5	1		1 Sack of Coals	0	3	6
	Butcher	0	7	8 ½		Oysters	0	0	8
	Wood	0	1	0		Porter	0	0	2
28th	Pidgeons	0	2	0		Eggs	0	0	4
29th	Mold Candles	0	2	3		Handkerchirfs	1	10	0
	Gloves	0	1	6		Stockings	2	10	0
	Letters	0	0	4	3rd	Mrs Hackwood	4	12	6
	Coach	0	1	0		Widgeings	0	2	6
	Apples	0	0	2 ½.		Coals	0	3	6
	Poor Man	0	0	0 ½.	4th	Mutton	0	2	0
	Mangle	0	0	5		Fowl	0	2	4
30th	Tea	0	12	0	6th	Coals	0	3	6
	Sugar	0	9	9	7th	Oysters	0	0	6
	Butcher	0	5	4		Mutton	0	3	0
	Scotch Gaize	0	0	6		Candles	0	2	9
31st	Porter	0	0	2		Mold Candles	0	1	6 ½
	Eggs	0	0	4		Starch	0	1	0
						Blue	0	0	6
Nov.						Soap	0	2	0
1st	Magazines	0	1	0	8th	A Pint of Porter	0	0	2
	Cotton & Needles	0	0	9		2 Rabbits	0	1	3
	Coach	0	1	0		Beef Stakes	0	0	8
	Baker's Bill	0	4	11		Coals	0	3	6

		£	s	d
	Butter Bill	0	4	9
9th	Baker's Bill	0	4	11
	Milk	0	2	3
	Gardener	0	2	0
10th	Writing Paper, Wax, &c.	0	2	6
	Coach	0	2	0
	A Fowl	0	2	0
	Black Lead	0	0	2
	Pins & Thread	0	0	8 ½
	Porter	0	0	2
11th	Eggs	0	0	6
	A Fowl	0	2	4
	Chees	0	0	6
12th	Coals	0	3	6
13th	Tea	0	6	0
	Coals	0	3	6
	Wood	0	1	0
	Porter	0	0	2
	Brick Dust	0	0	0 1½
	Nurse	0	2	6
	Coach	0	1	0
14th	Porter	0	0	2
	Dimity Handerchifs, &c, &c.	8	8	0
	Baker	0	4	0
15th	Butter	0	4	11
	Fish, &c.	0	4	0
16th	Fowls	0	4	8
	Coals	0	3	6
17th	Porter	0	0	2
	Cheese	0	0	11
	Fowls	0	4	0
18th	Meat	0	2	0
	Beef & Mutton	0	5	11 ½
	Coach	0	1	0
19th	Coals	0	3	6
	Wood	0	1	0
20th	Vinegar	0	0	7
	Rabbit	0	0	10
	Coals	0	3	6
	Fowls	0	4	8
21st	Porter	0	0	2
22nd	Tea	0	6	0
	Baker's Bill	0	4	9
24th	Butter Bill	0	5	0
	Meat	0	5	0
26th	Oil	0	1	6

		£	s	d
	Coach	0	1	0
27th	Fowls	0	4	8
	Scowering paper	0	0	2
	Letters	0	0	8
	Brickdust	0	0	2
28th	Brush	0	2	0
	Segers	0	2	6
29th	Meat	0	3	0
	Coach	0	1	0
	Baker's Bill	0	4	9
30th	Butter Bill	0	4	5
31st	Milk	0	4	3
Dec.				
1st	Gardener	0	2	4
2nd	Candles	0	1	11
	Coach	0	1	0
	Fowls	0	4	8
3rd	Soap	0	2	0
	Blue	0	1	1
4th	Coach	0	1	0
	Lamb	0	4	0
	Powder, Pomatum, &c.	0	1	9
5th	Orranges	0	0	6 ½
	Tea	0	6	0
	Mrs Jones	3	3	0
	Butcher	0	5	0 ½
	Coach	0	1	0
6th	Baker	0	4	4 ½
	Butter Man	0	4	9 ½
7th	Gardener	0	2	0 ½
	Milk	0	2	6
	Vinegar	0	0	9
	Saycepan	0	0	6
	Wood	0	1	0
	Kitchen Candles	0	0	8 ½
	Pork	0	1	0
8th	Needles	0	0	1
	Eggs	0	0	4
9th	Muffins, &c.	0	0	3
	Meat	0	2	11
10th	A Fowl	0	0	1
	Barly	0	0	6
	Bird	0	8	0
11th	Beef	0	3	7 ½
	Flanel	0	0	10
	Scrubbing Brush	0	0	7

		£	s	d
12th	Fowls	0	5	0
	Veal	0	2	0
13th	Blacklead	0	0	4
	Mustard	0	1	3
	Scowering Paper	0	0	1
	Paid Nelly	1	19	10
	Paid Molly	2	13	11
	Baker's Bill	0	4	2 ½
	Butter Bill	0	4	1 ½
	Milk	0	2	3
14th	Gardener	0	1	9
	Pins	0	0	2
	Muffins	0	0	3
15th	Table Cloaths, Dusters. &c.	3	9	0
	Meat	0	2	11
16th	Fowls	0	4	0
	Lamb	0	3	6 ½
17th	Apples	0	0	2
	Porter	0	0	3 ½
	Oysters	0	1	0
	Fish	0	2	6
18th	Tea	0	12	0
19th	Scowering Papper	0	0	1 ½
	Milkman	0	2	6
	Baker's Bill	0	3	11 ½
	Butter Bill, Pork, &c.	0	4	10 ½
20th	Gardener	0	2	0 ½
	A leg of Mutton	0	3	7
	Oatmail	0	0	3
21st	Muffins	0	0	3
	Oil	0	1	6
22nd	Soap, Starch, &c, &c.	0	2	0 ½
	Meat	0	2	7 ½
23rd	Mr Fry	0	0	3
	Fowls	0	4	6
	Orranges	0	0	2
25th	Letters	0	0	4
	Beef	0	7	11
	Pork	0	2	9
	Coach	0	2	0
26th	Wood	0	1	0
	Meat	0	2	4
27th	Thread, &c.	0	0	2
	Suggar	0	9	0
28th	Fowls	0	7	3
	Padrole	0	5	0
	Mangle	0	1	4
	Musling	0	2	6
29th	Edgeing	0	1	4
	Brewer	0	2	0
	Mutton	0	3	3
	Oil	0	3	0
	Baker	0	4	9
	Butter, &c, &c.	0	5	4
	Milk	0	2	9
30th	Orranges	0	0	2 ½
	Candles	0	2	7 ½
	Wood	0	1	0
	Paper	0	1	0
	Birch Broom	0	0	2 ½
31st	Muffins	0	0	3
	Bell Man	0	0	2
1785 Jan.				
1st	Butcher's Boy	0	1	0
	Candles	0	1	3
	Milk	0	2	5
	Lace	0	1	6
2nd	Vinegar	0	0	10
	Soult	0	1	0
	Muffins	0	0	3
	Bacon	0	2	0
3rd	Apples	0	0	4
	Wrighting Paper	0	1	0
	Magazines	0	1	0
4th	Fowls	0	7	6
	Muffins	0	0	3
	Snuf	0	0	2 ½
5th	Bell Man	0	0	4
	Mangle	0	0	3
	Paper	0	0	6
6th	Wood	0	1	0
	Suggar	0	1	0
	Meat	0	4	0
	Baker's Bill	0	4	10 ½
	Butter Bill, Pork, &c.	0	6	0
7th	Candles	0	1	9 ½
	Starch, &c.	0	0	10
	Milk	0	2	0 ½
8th	Coach	0	1	0

		£	s	d
	Blue	0	1	0 ½
	Meat	0	6	0
9th	Fowls	0	4	0
	Wood	0	1	0
	Mr Birks	0	15	10
	Coach	0	1	0
10th	Matches	0	0	1
	Muffins	0	0	3
11th	Paid N. for			
	Muffins	0	0	9
	Bell Man	0	0	4
12th	Post Man	0	0	7
	Meat	0	4	0
	Lamp Oil	0	1	0
13th	Muffins	0	0	3
14th	Candles	0	1	9
	Fowls	0	4	8
15th	A Leg of Mutton	0	3	2
	A Quarter of Tea	0	3	0
	The Brown			
	Sugger	0	1	6
16th	Coach	0	1	0
	Baker's Bill	0	4	9
	Butter, &c	0	5	0
17th	Gardener	0	2	3
	Milk	0	2	4
	Muffins	0	0	6
18th	Beef	0	3	10
	Fowls	0	4	6
	Muffins	0	0	3
19th	Chimmey			
	Sweeper	0	0	6
	Coach	0	1	0
20th	Wood	0	1	0
21st	Muffins	0	0	3
	Meat	0	4	0
22nd	A Leg of Mutton			
	& Stakes	0	7	0
	Fowls	-	-	-
	Grots, Oatmail,			
	Pins, &c	0	0	10
	Muffins	0	0	3
	Half a Pound of Tea	0	6	0
23rd	Trencher Dish, &c	0	0	11
	Nutmeg, spice, &c	0	0	1
	Muffins	0	0	3
	Candles	0	3	0
24th	Baker	0	4	5 ½
	Butter Man	0	5	6
	Gardener	0	3	0
	Milk	0	2	11
25th	Soap, Starch, &c	0	2	0
	Paid the Brewer	2	9	0
	Coach	0	2	0
	Meat	0	4	0
26th	Scowering Paper,			
	&c	0	0	2
	Black Lead	0	0	3
	Wood	0	1	0
	Coals	0	1	0
	Muffins	0	0	3
	Brick Dust	0	0	1
27th	Eggs	0	0	4
	2 Orranges	0	0	3
	Coach	0	1	0
28th	Lamp Oil	0	2	0
	Gown	2	12	6
	Baker's Bill	0	4	9
	Butter Bill	0	5	3
	Gardener	0	2	5
	Milk	0	2	6 ½
	Coach	0	2	0
29th	Wood	0	1	0
	Candles	0	2	0
	Meat	0	5	0
	Muffins	0	0	6
	Fowles	0	4	10
30th	Lamp Oil	0	3	0
	Apples, 2	0	0	3
31st	Mutton, a Leg	0	4	0
Feb.				
1st	Parsley	0	0	1
2nd	Coach	0	1	0
3rd	Birch Broom	0	0	2
4th	2 Fowls	0	5	6
	Miss Harkwood,			
	Coach, &c	0	8	0
	Orranges, Muffins	0	0	6
	Baker's Bill	0	5	0
5th	Butter	0	4	9
	Candles	0	2	6
	Coach	0	1	0
6th	Gardener	0	2	0
	Milk	0	2	3
	Black Lead	0	0	2

7th	Meat	0	6	0		Meat	0	3	11 ½
	Fowls	0	2	10	21st	Coach	0	2	0
	Pin, Thread, &c	0	0	4		Baker's Bill	0	3	11
8th	Beer	0	3	6		Gauze	0	1	9
	Lamp Oil	0	2	0		Butter Bill	0	4	9
	Soap, Starch, &c	0	2	11					
9th	Wood	0	1	0					

Money received from October 27, 1784.

							£	s	d
	A Leg of Mutton	0	2	6	Oct.				
	Sugger	0	6	1 ½	27th received			5	5	0
10th	Baker's Bill, for				received			8	8	0
	Bread	0	4	0	29th received			1	1	0
	Coach	0	1	0					
11th	Butter	0	4	9 ½	Nov.				
	Muffins, Paid to				11th received			1	1	0
	Nancy	0	1	0	received			1	1	0
12th	Mopp	0	1	0	13th received			8	8	0
	Orranges	0	0	2	16th received			2	2	0
13th	Milk	0	2	1 ½	20th received			1	10	6
14th	Fowls	0	4	0	29th received			5	5	0
	Coach	0	1	0					
	Paper	0	0	6	Dec.				
	Magazines	0	2	0	3rd received			1	1	0
15th	Eggs	0	0	6	received			1	1	0
	Wood	0	1	0	8th received			5	5	0
	Brick Dust	0	0	2	11th received			2	2	0
16th	Apples	0	0	6	13th received			3	3	0
17th	Beef Stakes,				16th received			2	2	0
	Mutton, &c	0	4	0	20th received			5	5	0
	Beer	0	3	6					
	Porter at different								
	times	0	1	2	Jan.				
18th	Oil & Mustard	0	0	9	9th received			5	5	0
	Pepper	0	0	3	20th received			5	5	0
	Cotton for				29th received			5	5	0
	Mending Stockings	0	0	2	7th received			1	1	0
19th	Apples	0	0	6	received			5	5	0
	Kitchings' Candles	0	1	2					
	Brown Sugger	0	0	6	Paid Molly Dring			2	3	11
	A Nutmeg	0	0	1 ½	Paid Nelly Gray			1	19	10

Molly Lunn came here the 13th of December 1784.
Ann Murphy came here the 13th of December 1784.

Appendix II

Extracts from the Day Book of George Romney

1782

Friday March 12th	Mrs Luitridge at 1
	Capt. Dalton
	Miss Ht at 11
	Mrs Rooke at ½ pt 2
	A Gent at ½ pt 3
Saturday March 20th	Mrs Ht at 12
	Mr Willet at ½ pt 10
	Mrs Rooke at 2
Sunday June 9th	Mrs Ht at 1
	Miss Clavering at ½ pt 2
	Mr Lushington at 11
	Capt. Dalton at 9
Monday June 17th	A Gent at 2
	A Gent at ½ pt 10
	Mrs Ht at ½ pt 1
Monday July 8th	Mr Townshend at 11
	Mrs Hart at 1
Thursday July 11th	Mrs Hart at 1
	Lady G. Cavendish at ½ pt 3
Monday July 15th	Mrs Hart at 1
Thursday July 18th	Mrs H. at 1
	Cap. Forbes at 9
	Dine with Mr Long
Monday July 22nd	Mrs H. at 1
Wednesday July 24th	Mrs H. at 1
Saturday July 27th	Mrs H. at 12
Monday July 29th	Mrs H. at 12
Wednesday July 31st	Mr Hartley at 9
	Mrs H. at 12
	Mr Robinson at 2
Saturday August 3rd	Mrs H. at 12

1783

Friday December 19th	Mrs Hart at ½ pt 10
Monday December 22nd	Mrs Hart at 10
	Mr Shadwell
Friday December 26th	Mrs Hart at 10
Monday December 29th	Mrs Hart at 10

(There were appointments in this year for: Sir William Hamilton, 24th, 28th November, 2nd 5th, 7th, 10th, 15th, 31st December. Mrs Siddons, 2nd, 7th, 8th, 11th February, 9th April, 11th May.)

1784

Tuesday January 6th	Mrs Hart at 10
	A Lady at 12
Tuesday January 13th	Mrs Hart at 10
Wedesnady January 21st	Mrs Ht at 11
Tuesday January 27th	Mr Shadwell at 1
	Mrs H. at ½ pt 10
Friday January 30th	Mrs H. at ½ pt 10
Tuesday February 3rd	Mrs Bracebridge at 12
	Mrs H. at 10
Saturday February 7th	Mr Bearcroft at 10
	Mrs H. at 12
	Mr Oliver at 2
Wednesday February 11th	Mrs H. at 10
Wednesday February 18th	Mrs H. at 10
	Lord Falmouth at 2
	Mr Gray at 12
Monday February 23rd	Mrs Willson at 11
	Mr Brown at ½ pt 9
	Mrs H. at 1
Thursday March 4th	Mrs H. at 10
	Mr Gray at 12
Tuesday March 9th	Mrs Wilson at 2
	Mrs Hart at 10
Tuesday March 16th	Mrs H. at 10
	Mrs Willson at 2
	Cap. Kingsmill at 12
Tuesday March 23rd	Mrs H. at 10
	Mrs Willson at 2
	Lord Falmouth at 12
Friday March 26th	Girl at 9
	Mrs H. at 10
Tuesday March 30th	Mrs Willson at 2
	Mr Stephenson at ¼ to 10
	Mrs H. at 12

Monday April 5th	Lord Donegall at 12
	Mrs H. at 10
	Lady Townsend at 2
Monday April 12th	Mrs H. at 10
	Mrs Wilson at 12
	Lady Townshend at 2
Thursday April 15th	Col. Camach at 12
	Mrs H. 10
Wednesday April 21st	Miss Brunker ½ pt 12
	Mrs Hart at 10 Edgware Road
	Mrs Sullivan at ½ pt 11
Monday May 17th	Mr Shadwell at 2
	A Lady at 2 (Miss Lockwood)
	Mrs H. 10
Tuesday May 25th	Mrs H. at 10
	Mr St John at 12
	Lady Eglington at 2
Tuesday June 1st	Mrs H. at 10
	Lady Eglington at 1
Wednesday June 2nd	Mrs H. at 10
	Miss Rodbord at ½ pt 12
	Engaged at 2
Thursday June 3rd	Mrs H. 10
	Bishop of Salisbury at 12
	Engaged at 2
Tuesday July 27th	Mrs H. at 10
	Mr Trevelyan at 12
	Mrs Robinson at 2
Monday August 2nd	Mrs H. at 10
	Mrs Thornhill at 2
Thursday August 5th	Mrs H. at 10
	Mrs Robinson at 1
Monday August 9th	Mrs H. at ½ pt 9
	Mrs Holmes at 6
	Col. Cathcart at 2
	Mr Legg at 12
Saturday August 14th	Mrs. H. at 10
	Mr Legg at ½ pt 12
	Lord Mornington at 2
Wednesday August 18th	Mrs H. at 12
Monday August 23rd	Mr Legg at 12
	Mrs H. at 10
	Moddel at 1
Friday October 22nd	Mrs H. at 10
Monday October 25th	Mrs H. at 10
Thursday October 28th	Mrs H. at 10
	Mr C. Raikes at 3
Monday November 1st	Mrs H. at 10

	Moddell at 1
Friday November 5th	Mrs H. at 10
Monday November 8th	Mrs H. at 10
Thursday November 11th	Mr Raikes at ¼ to 3
	Mrs H. 10
Saturday November 13th	Mrs Hoare at 12
	Mrs H. at 10
Tuesday November 16th	Mrs H- at 10
Friday November 19th	Mrs H. at 10
	Dr Farmer at 2
Tuesday November 23rd	Mrs H. at 10
Friday November 26th	Mrs Hart at 10
Monday November 29th	Mr Raikes at 2
	Mrs Hart at 10
Wednesday December 1st	Mrs H. at 10
Friday December 3rd	Mrs H. at 10
Saturday December 4th	Mrs H. at 2
Monday December 6th	Mrs H. at 10
Thursday December 9th	Mrs H. at 10
Saturday December 11th	Mrs Hart at 10
Sunday December 12th	Mrs H. at 11
Friday December 24th	Mrs H. at 10

1785

Day Book lost for this year.

1786

Thursday January 5th	Mr Serjt. Adair at 12
	Mrs Hart at 10
	Mrs Smith at 2
	Monday January 9th
	Mr Wilbraham (Bootle) at ½ pt 12
	Mrs Hart at 10
Saturday January 14th	Mr Grose at 12
	Hon. Mrs Hart (no time given)
	Mr Raikes at 1
Monday January 16th	Mrs Smith at 1
	Miss Lushington at ½ pt 2
	Mrs Hart at 10
Friday January 20th	Mrs Mangles at 12
	Mrs Hart at 10
	Mrs Smith at ½ pt 1
Wednesday January 25th	Mrs H. at 10
	Mr Mangles at ½ pt 12 till 2
	Miss Boore at 2
Tuesday February 7th	Mrs H. at 10

271

	Cap. Beauchamp at 1
	A Gent at ½ pt 2
Wednesday February 8th	Mrs H. at 10
	Mrs Smith at ½ pt 1
Monday February 13th	Mrs H. at 10
	Lady Robimson at 3
	Miss Lushington at 1
	Mr Glynn at 9
Saturday February 18th	Cap. Beauchamp at 10
	Mrs H. at 12
	Mr Wilbraham (Bootle) at 2
Monday February 20th	Mrs H. at 11
	Miss Lushington at 1
	Mr Stevenson at ½ pt 12
Friday February 24th	Mrs H. at 11
	Mrs Raikes at 2
	Cap. Beauchamp a ¼ pt 12
Wednesday March 1st	Mrs H.
	Mr Camden at 3
	Mr Mangles at ½ pt 12 till 3
Wednesday March 8th	Mrs H. at 10
	Mr Beauchamp at ½ pt 3
	Mr & Mrs Mangles at ½ pt 12 till 3
	Mr Camden at ¼ pt 2

1791

Thursday June 2nd	Mrs H. at ½ pt 9
	Lady Townshend at 1
	Mr Miles at 3
Saturday June 4th	Mrs H. at 10
	Mrs Acton at ½ pt 11
	Mr Legh at 3
	Mrs Shore at 1
Wednesday June 8th	Lord Petre at ½ pt 4
	Mrs Hart at ½ pt 9
	Mrs Oliver at 1
	Mrs Milles at ½ pt 2
	Lady Ann Belloses at 3
Saturday June 11th	Mrs H- at 9
	Mrs Shore at 1
	Lady Belgoney at ½ pt 2
Tuesday June 14th	Mrs H. at 9
	Lady Ann Bellyoses at 1
Friday June 17th	Mrs H- at 9
	Sir R. Harland at ½ pt 1
	Mr Legh at 3
Sunday June 19th	Mrs H- at 9

Monday June 20th	Mrs H. at 9
	Miss Hannah (i.e. "Hannay") at I
	Lady Holt at ½ pt 2
Wednesday June 22nd	Mrs H. at 9
	Mrs Robinson at 1
	Mrs Bonor at ½ pt 11
Thursday June 23rd	Mrs H. at 9
	Miss Drummond at 1
Saturday June 25th	Mrs H. at 9
	Sir R. H. at ½ pt 12
Monday June 27th	Mrs H. at 9
Tuesday June 28th	Miss Hannay at 1
	To go into the country
Wednesday June 29th	Mrs H. at 9
	Sir R. Harland at ½ pt 2
	Lady- at ½ pt 1
Friday July 1st	Mrs H. at 9
	Sir R. Harland at ½ pt 1
Saturday July 2nd	Mrs H. at 9
	Miss Drummond at 1
	Mr Elliot at ½ pt 2
Sunday July 3rd	Mrs H. at 9
	Mr Milnes at 1
Monday July 4th	Mrs H. at 9
	Dine at Mr Pain at ½ pt 4
	Sir R. H. at 1
Wednesday July 6th	Mrs H. at 9
	The Hon. Mr Elliot at ½ pt 2
Thursday July 7th	Mrs H. at 9
	Miss H- at 1
	Mrs A- at 3
Saturday July 9th	Mrs H. at 9
	Mr Grosvenor at ½ pt 2
	The Hon. Mr Eliot at 1
	Mr F. H- at 3
Sunday July 10th	Mrs H. at 9
Monday July 11th	Mrs H. at 11
	Mr F. H- at 9
	Mr Grosvenor at ¼ to 2
Tuesday July 12th	Mrs H. at 9
	Dine at Greenwich
	Mr Wallop at 1
Thursday July 14th	Mrs H. at 9
	Lady Ann Bellsses at 2
Saturday July 16th	Mrs H. at 9
	Mr Grosvenor at 1
Monday July 18th	Mrs H. at 9
	Mr Wyndham at 3

Tuesday July 19th	Mrs H. at 9
	Sir R. Arden at 12
	Dine at Greenwich at 4
Wednesday July 20th	Mrs H. at 9
	Mrs Bonor at ½ pt 11
	Mr P. A. at ½ pt 2
Monday July 25th	Mr Trivealand (Trevelyan) at ½ pt 10
	Lady Warren at ½ pt 1
	Mrs H. at 3
Monday August 22nd	Mr Oliver at 10
	Mrs H. at 1
	Mrs Milles at 3
Tuesday August 23rd	Mrs H. at ½ pt 9
	Mrs Milnes at 2
Friday August 26th	Mr Hoare at 1
	Mrs H. at ½ pt 10
Sunday September 4th	Mrs H. at 10
Monday September 5th	Mrs Hart at 9
Tuesday September 6th	Lady Hamilton at 11.

Appendix III

Lord Nelson's Accounts Concerning the Journey to England

£	s	d	
1094	2	4	Half the expence of the journey to England.
255	0	0	Lent on the road.
927	14	0	At Palermo.
2276	16	4	Owing to Ld N.
957	19	3	
1218	17	1 [29]	Due Ld N.
62	8	1	Owing Sir Wm Hamilton.
1156	9	0	Due Ld Nelson.
52	10	0	
1103	19	0	

Merton, Sept. 21st 1802.

Money drawn by Lord Nelson

	£	s	d
Mr Tyson, Leghorn, brought away	258	0	0
Ancona, by bill	100	0	0
Trieste do	150	0	0
Myrolf	6	0	0
Vienna, Aug. 19th	100	0	0
21st	100	0	0
22nd	300	0	0
Sept. 13th	200	0	0
21st	300	0	0
23rd	100	0	0

		£	s	d
Prague	29th	100	0	0
Dresden Oct.	6th	100	0	0
Hamburg	28th	400	0	0
	29th	150	0	0
	30th	656	0	0
Yarmouth		287	0	0
Colchester		50	0	0
Money borrow'd		<u>40</u>	<u>0</u>	<u>0</u>
		3397	6	0
Mr Oliver		<u>34</u>	<u>10</u>	<u>0</u>
Drawn for & paid out by Ld N.				
between July 13th & Nov. 18th		<u>3431</u>	<u>16</u>	<u>0</u>

Spent by Lord Nelson

		£	s	d
To	Sept 13th	110	10	0
	21st	100	0	0
Wine for Mr Greffer		12	0	0
Hambg.	Oct. 28th	100	0	0
	30th	506	13	3
Yarmth. Nov.		<u>58</u>	<u>10</u>	<u>0</u>
Total by Ld N.		<u>988</u>	<u>13</u>	<u>3</u>

Sir Wm. Hamilton

		£	s	d
To	Sept 13th	205	0	0
Hambg.	Oct. 28th	<u>50</u>	<u>0</u>	<u>0</u>
		<u>255</u>	<u>0</u>	<u>0</u>

	£	s	d
To be deducted from the bills drawn	1243	13	3
	<u>3431</u>	<u>16</u>	<u>0</u>
To be divided	<u>2188</u>	<u>4</u>	<u>9</u>
Sir Wm H. proportion	1094	2	4
	<u>255</u>	<u>0</u>	<u>0</u>
Due Lord Nelson	<u>1349</u>	<u>2</u>	<u>4</u>

Appendix V

Accounts for the Journey to Milford Haven

(In Lord Nelson's handwriting)

Dated between 20th July and 21st September, 1802

Subscribed Sir Wm. Hamilton & myself at Merton, July 20th 1802 £100 each, being £200.

	£	s	d
8 Horses, Merton to Hounslow, not paid Mr Woodman			
Horses from Hounslow to Maidenhead	3	9	4
From M. to Henly	2	2	0
Benson	2	11	4
Oxford	2	16	0
Bill at the "Star" Oxford & Servants	27	0	10
Dorton, Dresses	23	2	0
University Servts	1	1	0
Horses to Woodstock	2	0	0
Bill to do. & Servts.	15	2	2
Same at Blenheim	2	2	0
Francatello	1	7	0
Horses to Troymill from Burford	3	14	0
To Gloster	3	5	4
Eating at	0	5	0
Bill at Gloster	6	15	9
Same at the	2	2	0
To Ross	3	14	8
Monmouth	2	8	0
Do. by Water	3	6	0
Bill at Ross	0	19	0
Francatello	0	16	8
Bill at Monmouth	8	11	10

To Abergavenny	3	14	8
Brecon	4	13	4
Bill at Brecon	7	13	9
To Myrter Tydder	8	8	0
Francatello	0	8	2
Bill at Myrter Tidder	6	1	0
Servts. at do.	1	5	0
From Brecon to Trecastles	2	11	0
Trecastles & Landovery	2	2	0
Bill at do.	2	10	2
Servts	0	17	6
To Carmarthen 27m	6	6	0
Drivers, turnpikes, gearing, etc.	2	4	0
Playhouse	3	3	0
Ventriloquist	1	1	0
Bill at Carmarthen & servts	4	3	4
St Clairs for breakft	0	18	0
From Carn. to Narbeth 2 pair	2	19	0
From Carn. to Har. Wt. 2 pr.	3	4	0
Drivers	0	16	0
Ringers at Narbeth	1	1	0
From Nbth to Milford 2 pr	2	17	2
Haverfd Wt. to Milford 2 pr	1	3	4
Drivers, except two posts from Merton to Milford	_11_	_0_	_6_
Journey to Milford	189	12	10

Sir Wm Hamilton & myself subscribed 30 guineas each on August 5th, being £63.

	£	s	d
Bill at Milford, Breakfast & Servts	56	1	5
Dinner & Horses to Picton	5	5	0
Oyster Man	0	2	6
Boats to Picton	2	2	0
Drivers to Picton	0	5	0
Coachman	1	1	0
Rider	0	7	0
Servt Maids	1	1	0
Drivers to Ridgeway	0	6	6
Letters	0	1	6
Drivers to Stackpole	1	4	0
Feed for Horses and Men at Pembroke	0	14	0
Return Turnpikes	0	1	6
Coachman at Ld C.	1	1	0
Francatello	0	15	4
Bill at Tenby	8	7	6
Servts	0	7	6
Horses as by bill from Narbeth to Stackpole, Pembroke, Tenby & St Clairs	14	4	4

Drivers	1	8	0
Turnpikes paid by Drivers	0	1	6
Bill at St Clairs	3	12	10
Servts	0	7	0
Ostler	0	2	0
Horses to Cartha^N	2	2	0
Drivers	0	10	6
From Carthe^N to Lennon	2	16	0
Drivers	0	12	6
To Clairmont	3	0	0
Drivers	0	12	0
Drivers to Swansey	0	11	0
Ringers	2	2	0
Greasing the Carriages	0	3	0
Bill for Horses to Swansey; yesterday to Pyll	7	0	0
Drivers	0	16	0
Gardner at Margorn	0	3	0
From Pyll to Yewbridge, & servts, & eating	3	8	8
Drivers	0	12	0
To Cardiff	3	0	0
Drivers & Turnpikes	0	16	0
Francatello	1	3	0
Bill at Cardiff, including Horses to Newport	7	15	9
Drivers	0	12	0
From Newport to Chepstow	4	0	0
Drivers	0	14	0
Bill at Chepstow	2	10	0
Servt	0	7	0
Rep^g Carriage	0	2	6
Horoco to Monmouth	4	15	0
Drivers	0	16	0
Francatello	0	18	0
Bill at Monmouth, incldg Servt	4	15	6
Horses to the Kymin & to Reedhall	3	11	0
Drivers	0	16	0
Ross, bill for Horses to Hereford, & 2 pr to Leominster & Drivers	6	15	10
Horses, 2 pr from Hereford to Leominster	2	6	6
Horses from Leominster to Ludlow	2	10	0
Drivers & Turnpikes, and Drivers from Hereford	1	1	0
Eating at Leominster	<u>1</u>	<u>1</u>	<u>0</u>
	170	14	2

Bill at Ludlow for going to Downton, returning to Tenbury & Repairg the Coach	5	19	8
Drivers to Downton &	0	16	0
Do. to Tenbury	0	10	6
Turnpikes	0	6	0
Horses to Hundred House	2	16	0

Drivers	0	12	0
Turnpikes	0	2	0
To Worcester	2	11	4
Drivers	0	12	0
Bill at Worcester	4	7	8
Servants	1	5	6
Francatello	1	12	6
Cyder & Perry	12	16	10
From Worcester to Broomsgrove	3	0	8
Drivers	0	12	0
Ostler	0	2	0
Horses to Birmingham	3	0	10
Drivers	0	12	0
Bill at Birmingham	8	16	0
Men servts	1	11	6
Female do.	1	10	0
Bootcleaner	0	2	6
Francatello's Bill for Washing	5	0	0
Horses to Hockley – paid wrong	2	18	0
Drivers	0	12	0
Ostler	0	4	0
To Warwick	2	6	8
Drivers	0	12	0
Turnpikes	0	6	0
Bill at Warwick	9	15	0
Male Servts	1	1	0
Female Do.	0	10	6
Bootcleaner	0	2	0
Ostler	0	4	0
Horses to Coventry	2	6	8
Drivers	0	10	8
Turnpikes	0	2	0
Bill at Coventry	1	1	0
Horses to Danchurch	2	11	4
Drivers	0	12	0
Turnpikes	0	3	0
To Daintree	1	17	4
Drivers	0	10	6
To Towcester	2	16	0
Drivers	0	12	0
Ostlers	0	2	0
Bill at Towcester	1	6	0
Servts	0	5	0
Horses to Sy Stratford	1	17	4
Drivers	0	10	6
Ostlers	0	2	0
To Brisley	2	2	0
Drivers	0	10	6

APPENDIX V

Ostler	0	1	0
To Dunstable	2	6	8
Drivers	0	11	4
Francatello's Bill	1	7	0
Bill at Dunstable	2	14	8
Male Servts	0	15	0
Female Do.	0	7	0
Ostler	0	4	0
Bootcleaner	0	2	0
Horses to St Albans	3	5	1
Drivers	0	12	0
Ostlers	0	2	0
	109	11	2

Horses to Watford	2	0	0
Drivers	0	10	6
Ostler	0	1	0
To Brentford	4	0	0
Drivers	0	14	0
To Merton (11 miles)	2	15	0
Drivers	0	12	0
Bridge	0	1	6
Francatello	0	11	8
	11	5	8

11	15	8
189	12	10
170	14	2
109	11	2
481	3	10

Received	406	0	0	
	481	3	10	
	75	3	0	Pd by Ld N.
	37	11	11	Sr Wm half
	100	0	0	Received from Sr Wm
	62	8	1	Due Sir Wm from Ld N.

Bibliography

Manuscripts
Morrison MS. British Museum.
Additional MS. – Nelson Papers. British Museum.
Egerton MS. British Museum.
Llangattock MS. Monmouth Museum.
National Maritime Museum MS.

Books
The collection of autograph letters and historical documents formed by Alfred Morrison. The Hamilton and Nelson Papers.
Emma Lady Hamilton. Walter Sichel.
Emma Lady Hamilton. Hilda Gamlin.
Emma Hamilton and Sir William. Oliver Warner.
Lady Hamilton and Lord Nelson. J.C. Jeaffreson.
Emma Hamilton. O.A. Sherrard.
Memoirs of Emma Lady Hamilton. Anon. (edited W.H. Long).
Emma Lady Hamilton. J.T.H. Baily.
Lady Hamilton. A. Fauchier-Magnan.
Patriotic Lady. Marjorie Bowen.
A Great Adventuress. Joseph Turquan and Jules D'Auriac.
Nelson's Legacy. Frank Danby.
The Story of Lady Hamilton. E. Hallam Moorhouse.
Miledi. Bradda Field.
Emma in Blue. G. Hamilton and D. Stewart.
The Letters and Despatches of Vice-Admiral Lord Viscount Nelson. Sir Harris Nicolas.
Nelson's Letters to His Wife. (edited) G.P.B. Naish.
Nelson. Carola Oman.
A Portrait of Lord Nelson. Oliver Warner.
Nelson's Wife. E.M. Keate, M.B.E.
Life of Nelson. Robert Southey.
Memoirs of the Life of Vice-Admiral Lord Viscount Nelson, K.B. T.J. Pettigrew, F.R.S., F.S.A.
Nelson's Band of Brothers. Ludovic Kennedy.
Lord Nelson's Home and Life at Merton. Rev. J.E. Jagger, M.A.
Poseidon. Renalt Capes.
The Nelsons of Burnham Thorpe. M. Eyre Matcham.
The Letters of Lord Nelson to Lady Hamilton. Anon.

BIBLIOGRAPHY

The Bourbons of Naples. Harold Acton.
Nelson and the Neapolitan Jacobins. H.C. Gutteridge (Navy Records Society 1903).
The French in Italy. Angus Heriot.
Memoirs of the Comtesse de Boigne, 1781-1814.
The Remains of the Late Mrs Richard Trench.
The Autobiography of Miss Cornelia Knight.
The Letters of Horace Walpole, Fourth Earl of Orford.
The Farington Diary.
Old Q's Daughter. Bernard Falk.
Britain against Napoleon. Carola Oman.
The Letters of King George IV, 1812-1830.
Romney. Humphry Ward and W. Roberts.
Romney. Catalogue Raisonée. H. Ward and W. Roberts.
George Romney. Lord Ronald Sutherland Gower.
The Great Dr Burney. Percy A. Scholes, M.A., D.Mus., F.S.A.
Greater London. Edward Walford, M.A.
London in the 18th Century. Sir Walter Besant.
Sketches in London. James Grant.
Invitation to Ranelagh. Mollie Sands.
Richmond. Kathleen Courlander.
A History of Merton and Morden. Evelyn M. Jowett, M.A., F.L.A.
Dearest Bess. Dorothy Margaret Stuart.
Jews of Britain. Paul H. Emden.
The State of the Prisons in England, Scotland & Wales. James Neild.
Freshly Remembered. C. Aspinall-Oglander.
The Journeys of Celia Fiennes.
A History of Wimbledon. Rev. W.G. Bartlett.

Articles

"The Brothers Goldsmid and the Financing of the Napoleonic Wars." Paul H. Emden.
"At the Three Crowns." R. Brooke-Caws.
"Paper against Gold." William Cobbett.
"Nelson's Home at Merton." Prof. J.K. Laughton, M.A.
"Reminiscences of Old Merton." W.H. Chamberlain.
"Lord Nelson's Visits to Monmouth." Horatia Durant.
"Nelson and the Hamiltons in Wales and Monmouthshire." E.C. Freeman and Edward Gill.
"Il Convito Amoroso." James Graham.
"A Lecture on the Generation, Increase and Improvement of the Human Species." James Graham.

Parliamentary Papers

Report from the Committee of the King's Bench, Fleet and Marshalsea Prisons, 1815.
Report from the Committee appointed to Enquire into the Practice and Effects of Imprisonment for Debt, 1792.

BIBLIOGRAPHY

References in:

The Victoria History of the County of Surrey
The Gentleman's Magazine
The Lady's Magazine
The Annual Register
The European Magazine

Notes

1   Louisa was Lady Stormont, wife of Charles Greville's brother, Robert, after the death of Lord Stormont. Both she and "the Duchess" (of Atholl) were also Sir William Hamilton's nieces, born Cathcart. "Granby Ly", afterwards Duchess of Rutland, born Lady Mary Somerset and declared the most beautiful woman in England, was much in the Hamilton-Cathcart circle and appears often in Cathcart MSS. Lady B. C. does not appear to have been a Cathcart.

2   This picture is of Emma Hart as a Bacchante, by Romney. Several versions exist. One has a goat.

3   Sir Harry Harpur, husband of Charles Greville's sister, Lady Frances Greville.

4   "Lady C." was the widow (but divorced) of Lord Craven. She afterwards married the Margrave of Anspach. "Mrs D." was the Hon. Anne Seymour, only child of General Conway. She was a renowned sculptress and also a widow: Mr Damer had shot himself.

5   The two daughters of Lord Middleton married, Dorothea becoming Mrs Richard Langley; Henrietta, Countess of Scarbrough.

6   Gavin Hamilton, artist and antiquarian (1730-97).

7   Proprietor of the diligence which Sir William's major-domo Coffier met at Geneva.

8   Henry Benedict de Saussure, 174?-99, the famous Swiss geologist.

9   Partner of Sir William's bankers, Ross and Ogilvie.

10 Lady Bolingbroke was born Lady Diana Spencer and, after divorcing Lord Bolingbroke, married the Hon. Topham Beauclerc, who died in 1780. She was another of the widows whom Sir William had considered.

11 Sir Thomas Rumbold had been aide-de-camp to Clive at Plassey. His first wife, mother of his son who died 1786, had been Frances Berriman; his second was Joanna, daughter of Bishop Law of Carlisle.

12 The early picture of Emma in the black dress is reproduced in *Emma, Lady Hamilton* by H. Baily (1905). The one by Angelica Kauffmann has been frequently reproduced since it was first engraved by Say in 1806. It does not resemble other portraits, but has Vesuvius in the background and is evidently genuine.

13 George Robert Fitzgerald, known as "Fighting Fitzgerald", was executed at Castlebar on 12th June 1786 for the murder of Patrick McDonald, whom he ordered a party of armed men to kill.

14 George, Lord Brooke (1772-86), only son of the Earl of Warwick and his first wife, Georgiana Peachey.

15 The famous naturalist after whom was named the Banksia rose.

16 Graeffer, landscape gardener and protégé of Banks, designed the royal gardens at Caserta and was Nelson's agent at Brontë.

17 Married Mr John King after the death of her earl in 1779.

18 William Henry, Duke of Gloucester, married (1766) Maria, Countess Dowager Waldegrave.

19 The Cavaliere Gatti was court physician to Leopold, Grand Duke of Tuscany.

20 Rehberg's book of Lady Hamilton's "Attitudes" can be easily seen. The portrait in a gypsy hat, with oranges, is reproduced by Sichel, who attributes it to Opie.

21 Rehberg's book of Lady Hamilton's "Attitudes" can be easily seen. The portrait in a gypsy hat, with oranges, is reproduced by Sichel, who attributes it to Opie.

22 The Duchess of Argyll, born Elizabeth Gunning, had first been married to Sir William's cousin, the Duke of Hamilton.

23 The picture known as *The Ambassadress*, the last by Romney, is reproduced by Baily and was engraved by Appleton in 1905. It was painted on her wedding day.

24 This picture, bought by the Prince of Wales, is reproduced by Baily. There are several versions, and even poses.

25 John Udney, British Consul at Leghorn.

26 Lord Minto had known Nelson intimately in Corsica and had always shown jealousy of Lady Hamilton's influence. His brother, Hugh Elliot, was touchy on the subject of matrimonial triangles as he had divorced a first wife.

27 This superb picture is in the Wallace Collection, London.

28 Horatia's date of birth had been put back three months. Nelson had been at sea in the previous February.

29 Nelson has made a mistake of £100 to his disadvantage.